The Couch and the Silver

The Couch and the Silver Screen is a collection of original contributions which explore European cinema from psychoanalytic perspectives. Both classic and contemporary films are presented and analysed by a variety of authors, including leading cinema historians and theorists, psychoanalysts with a specific expertise in the interpretation of films, as well as the filmmakers themselves. This composite approach offers a fascinating insight into the world of cinema.

The Couch and the Silver Screen is illustrated with stills throughout and Andrea Sabbadini's introduction provides a theoretical and historical context for the current state of psychoanalytic studies of films. The book is organized into four clear sections – Set and Stage, Working Through Trauma, Horror Perspectives and Documenting Internal Worlds – which form the basis for engaging chapters including:

- Easily readable and jargon-free film reviews.
- Essays on specific subjects such as perspectives on the horror film genre and adolescent development.
- Transcripts of live debates among film directors, actors, critics and psychoanalysts.

The cultural richness of the material presented, combined with the originality of multidisciplinary dialogues on European cinema, makes this book appealing not only to film buffs, but also to professionals, academics and students interested in the application of psychoanalytic ideas to the arts.

Andrea Sabbadini is a psychoanalyst in private practice in London and a lecturer at UCL. He is founding editor of *Psychoanalysis and History* and book review editor of *The International Journal of Psychoanalysis*. He chairs the European Psychoanalytic Film Festival and a series of film events at the ICA.

THE NEW LIBRARY OF PSYCHOANALYSIS

General Editor   Dana Birksted-Breen

Advisory Board   Catalina Bronstein, Sara Flanders, John Keene
and Mary Target

The New Library of Psychoanalysis was launched in 1987 in association with the Institute of Psycho-Analysis, London. It took over from the International Psychoanalytical Library, which published many of the early translations of the works of Freud and the writings of most of the leading British and Continental psychoanalysts.

The purpose of the New Library of Psychoanalysis is to facilitate a greater and more widespread appreciation of psychoanalysis and to provide a forum for increasing mutual understanding between psychoanalysts and those working in other disciplines such as history, linguistics, literature, medicine, philosophy and the social sciences. It aims to represent different trends both in British psycho-analysis and in psychoanalysis generally. The New Library of Psychoanalysis is well placed to make available to the English-speaking world psychoanalytic writings from other European countries and to increase the interchange of ideas between British and American psychoanalysts.

The Institute, together with the British Psycho-Analytical Society, runs a low-fee psychoanalytic clinic, organizes lectures and scientific events concerned with psychoanalysis and publishes *The International Journal of Psychoanalysis*. It also runs the only UK training course in psychoanalysis which leads to membership of the International Psychoanalytical Association – the body which preserves internationally agreed standards of training, of professional entry, and of professional ethics and practice for psychoanalysis as initiated and developed by Sigmund Freud. Distinguished members of the Institute have included Michael Balint, Wilfred Bion, Ronald Fairbairn, Anna Freud, Ernest Jones, Melanie Klein, John Rickman and Donald Winnicott.

Previous General Editors include David Tuckett, Elizabeth Spillius and Susan Budd. Previous Associate Editors include Ronald Britton, Christopher Bollas, Juliet Mitchell, Eglé Laufer, Donald Campbell, Michael Parsons, Rosine Jozef Perelberg, David Taylor and Stephen Grosz.

ALSO IN THIS SERIES

THE NEW LIBRARY OF PSYCHOANALYSIS
—— 44 ——

General Editor: Dana Birksted–Breen

The Couch and the Silver Screen

Psychoanalytic Reflections on European Cinema

Edited by Andrea Sabbadini

 Brunner-Routledge
Taylor & Francis Group

HOVE AND NEW YORK

First published 2003
by Brunner-Routledge
27 Church Road, Hove, East Sussex BN3 2FA

Simultaneously published in the USA and Canada
by Brunner-Routledge
29 West 35th Street, New York, NY 10001

Brunner-Routledge is an imprint of the Taylor and Francis Group

Typeset in Bembo by Keystroke, Jacaranda Lodge, Wolverhampton
Printed and bound in Great Britain by TJ International Ltd, Padstow, Cornwall
Paperback cover design by Sandra Heath

British Library Cataloguing in Publication Data
A catalogue record for this book is available from the British Library

Library of Congress Cataloguing-in-Publication Data
The couch and the silver screen : psychoanalytic reflections on European
cinema / edited by Andrea Sabbadini.–1st ed.
p. cm. – (The new library of psychoanalysis)
Includes bibliographical references and index.
1. Motion pictures–Europe–Psychological aspects. 2. Psychoanaylsis
and motion pictures. I. Sabbadini, Andrea. II. Series.

PN1993.5.E8C68 2003
791.43′75′019–dc21
2003004236

ISBN 1–58391–951–1 (hbk)
ISBN 1–58391–952–X (pbk)

Contents

Contents

Contributors

Michael Apted studied history and law at Cambridge University before beginning his career in film and television. His twenty major feature films include *Triple Echo*, *The Coal Miner's Daughter*, *Gorky Park*, *Gorillas in the Mist*, *Moving the Mountain*, *The World is not Enough* and *Enigma*. His acclaimed *Seven Up* documentary is being followed up every seven years since it first appeared in 1963. In 1999 he received the Career Achievement award from the International Documentary Association.

Candy Aubry, MD, is a candidate of the Swiss Psychoanalytical Society. Trained as a child psychiatrist and psychotherapist, she works in private practice in Geneva and is involved in teaching medical students. Her recent publications include 'Comments on Judy Gammelgaard's paper metaphors of listening' (*Scandinavian Psychoanalytic Review*, 2002) and 'Mutisme sélectif: étude de 30 cas' (*La Psychiatrie de l'enfant*, 2003).

Michal Aviad is a documentary filmmaker, in charge of the Museum of Fine Arts Film Program at Tel Aviv University. Her films include *Acting Our Age* (1987) on women and ageing, *The Women Next Door* (1992) on Palestinian and Israeli women in the conflict, *Ever Shot Anyone?* (1995) on Israeli male culture from a woman's perspective, *Jenny and Jenny* (1997) on two working-class teenagers, *Ramleh* (2001) on the lives of women from marginalized communities, *For My Children* (2002) asking whether the filmmaker should raise children in war-stricken Israel. Aviad's films have participated in many festivals, received awards and have been aired on television stations around the world.

Emanuel Berman is a training analyst at the Israel Psychoanalytic Institute, and a professor of psychology at the University of Haifa and at New York University. He edited *Essential Papers on Literature and Psychoanalysis* (1993). His papers on film include 'The film viewer: from dreamer to dream interpreter' (1998), and discussions in the *International Journal of Psycho-Analysis* of *Vertigo* (1997), *Night Moves* (1998) and *Exotica* (2000).

Bernardo Bertolucci, the leading Italian film director and the Honorary President of the *European Psychoanalytic Film Festival*, was born in Parma in 1941. His films include *Before the Revolution, The Spider's Strategem, The Conformist, Last Tango in Paris, 1900, La Luna, The Last Emperor, The Sheltering Sky, Little Buddha, Stealing Beauty* and *Besieged*.

Stefano Bolognini, training and supervising analyst of the Società Psicoanalitica Italiana, has been its Scientific Secretary from 1997 to 2001. He is a member of the Theoretical Working Party of the European Psychoanalytic Federation and a member of the European Editorial Board of the *International Journal of Psycho-Analysis*. He has published in all the main Italian and international journals. He is the editor of *The Dream 100 Years After* (2000) and the author of *Like Wind, Like Wave*, a collection of short stories that won the Gradiva Prize 2000, and of *Psychoanalytic Empathy* (2002).

Michael Brearley is a member of the British Psycho-Analytical Society, and full-time practitioner in private practice. Previously he was a professional cricketer and lecturer in philosophy. He writes, teaches and lectures on psychoanalytical matters, and occasionally on sport and the links with leadership and team building. He is a member of the organizing committee of the *European Psychoanalytic Film Festival*.

Hugh Brody is both an anthropologist and a filmmaker. As well as *Nineteen Nineteen*, his work includes documentary films for British and Canadian television and the books *Maps and Dreams, Means of Escape* and *The Other Side of Eden*. He is an Honorary Associate of the Scott Polar Research Institute (University of Cambridge) and of the School of Comparative Literature (University of Toronto).

Donald Campbell, a child, adolescent and adult psychoanalyst, works in the UK National Health Service and in private practice. He has written on violence, suicide, child sexual abuse and adolescence. He served as Chairman of the Portman Clinic and as President of the British Psycho-Analytical Society.

Ian Christie is Anniversary Professor of Film and Media History at Birkbeck College, University of London. From 1997 to 1999 he was Professor of Film Studies, University of Kent. He was the co-founder with Michael Grant of the journal *Film Studies*. Vice-President of 'Europa Cinemas', he is also a regular broadcaster on film. Recent publications include *A Matter of Life and Death* (2000) and *Medea in Performance 1500–2000* (2000).

Elizabeth Cowie is Reader in Film Studies at the University of Kent at Canterbury. She published *Representing the Woman: Cinema and Psychoanalysis* (1997); more recently her work has focused on documentary film, in 'The spectacle of actuality' (1999), as well as on trauma in relation to *Hiroshima* *mon amour* in 'Traumatic memories of remembering and forgetting' (2000), and the horror film, in 'The lived nightmare: trauma, anxiety, and the ethical aesthetics of horror' (2003).

Diana Diamond, Associate Professor in Clinical Psychology and Adjunct Assistant Professor of Psychiatry, has co-authored *Affect and Attachment in the Family* (1998) and *Borderline Patients: Extending the Limits of Treatability* (2000). She has published on attachment theory, borderline personality disorders, trauma studies and film and psychoanalysis and coedited a volume of *Psychoanalytic Inquiry* on *Projections of Psychic Reality: A Centennial of Film and Psychoanalysis* (1998). She is a candidate at the New York University Post-doctoral Program in Psychoanalysis and is in private practice in New York.

Ljiljana Filipović is the author of the books *Nesvjesno u filozofiji* [The Unconscious in Philosophy], *Filozofija i antipsihijatrija Ronalda D. Lainga* [Philosophy and Anti-Psychiatry of Ronald D. Laing], *Sokol u susteraju* [The Hawk in the Shoe-maker's Shop] and *Nevidljivi pas* [The Invisible Dog]. She teaches the psychoanalysis of drama at the Academy of Dramatic Arts in Zagreb and is currently working on a manuscript on Theatre of the Unconscious.

Paola Golinelli, Italian consultant for the *European Psychoanalytic Film Festival*, has a degree in foreign literature and psychology and is a member of the Società Psicoanalitica Italiana. Between 1994 and 2001 she led seminars and supervisions in Zagreb, Croatia, as part of that country's programme towards the achievement of IPA Study Group status and for the development of psychoanalysis in Eastern European countries. She has published articles on the application of psychoanalysis to cinema, theatre, literature and painting.

Michael Grant is Senior Lecturer in Film Studies at the University of Kent at Canterbury. His publications include studies of contemporary poets, essays on philosophy and on the horror film, a monograph on *Dead Ringers* (1998) and a collection entitled *The Modern Fantastic: The Cinema of David Cronenberg* (1999). He has also edited *The Raymond Tallis Reader* (2000).

Annegret Mahler-Bungers studied literature, philosophy and history of arts. She is a psychoanalyst and training analyst of the International Psychoanalytical Association and a member and teacher at the Alexander Mitscherlich-Institut in Kassel (Germany). She has published on psychoanalysis and group analysis, psychoanalysis of culture and literature, literature of the Holocaust and anti-Semitism.

Chris Mawson is a member of the British Psycho-Analytical Society and of the organizing committee of the *European Psychoanalytic Film Festival*. He first trained as a clinical psychologist and worked with adolescents and children at the Tavistock Clinic and in the Child Psychiatry department of the

Paddington Green Children's Hospital. He now works in private practice and is particularly interested in the study of groups and organizations from a psychoanalytic perspective.

Nanni Moretti, film director, actor, producer and distributor, was born in 1953. Among the films he has directed are *Io sono un autarchico* (1976), *Ecce Bombo* (1978), *Bianca* (1984), *La messa è finita* (1985), *Caro Diario* (1994, Best Direction, Cannes Festival) and *La stanza del figlio* (2001, Palme d'Or, Cannes Festival). In 1986 he founded with Angelo Barbagallo 'Sacher Film'. Since 1996 he has chaired the Sacher Festival of short films.

Laura Mulvey is Professor of Film and Media Studies at Birkbeck College, University of London, and Director of the Arts and Humanities Research Board (AHRB) Centre for British Film and Television Studies. Her essays have been published in *Visual and Other Pleasures* (Macmillan 1989) and *Fetishism and Curiosity* (British Film Institute 1996). She also wrote *Citizen Kane* (BFI Film Classic 1993). She has co-directed six films with Peter Wollen as well as *Disgraced Monuments* with Mark Lewis (Channel Four 1994).

Liliana Pedrón de Martín, Argentine psychologist and member of the International Psychoanalytical Association, is the Culture Commission Coordinator (Argentine Psychoanalytical Association), a member of the Family and Couple Psychoanalysis Department and Co-professor of the Seminar on Freud's Social Writings Today. She has published on Virginia Woolf and Marguerite Yourcenar and organized the *First Congress of Film and Psychoanalysis* (1996) and the *Congress of Image and Sound* (1998).

Timna Rosenheimer is a documentary film director, writer and artistic editor of *Helicon*, an anthological series of contemporary poetry. Her film *Fortuna*, a 53-minute documentary, a family saga about six sisters, won numerous awards, was broadcast on Israeli television, shown in film festivals in Europe and bought by broadcasters abroad. Her book *Home – Spaces, Objects, People* was published in 2001.

Andrea Sabbadini is a member of the British Psycho-Analytical Society, Honorary Senior Lecturer at University College London, and Chairman of the *Life Cycle* series of films and of the *European Psychoanalytic Film Festival*. He is also founding editor of *Psychoanalysis and History* and book review editor of *The International Journal of Psychoanalysis*. He has published extensively in psychoanalytic journals and edited *Time in Psychoanalysis* (1979) and *Even Paranoids Have Enemies* (1998).

Steven Jay Schneider is completing PhDs in Philosophy at Harvard University and in Cinema Studies at New York University's Tisch School of the Arts. He has published widely on the horror genre in various journals and edited collections. Forthcoming books as author and editor include *Freud's Worst*

Nightmares: Psychoanalysis and the Horror Film (Cambridge University Press), *Understanding Film Genres* (McGraw-Hill) and *Dark Thoughts: Philosophic Reflections on Cinematic Horror* (Scarecrow Press).

Jed Sekoff is a psychoanalyst practising in Berkeley, California. His writing focuses on the intersection of psychoanalysis, memory and culture (including the films *Frankenstein, Nineteen Nineteen* and *Blue Velvet*). Currently, he is clinical consultant to Survivors International, an organization offering psychotherapeutic evaluation and treatment to survivors of repression and torture.

Fiona Shaw, one of Britain's leading stage actors, has a growing collection of film credits, playing the pretentious anglophile in *The Butcher Boy*, the headmistress in *Three Men and a Little Lady* and having credits for films as diverse as *My Left Foot* and *Super Mario Brothers*. She has received three Laurence Olivier Best Actress Awards, two London Critics Awards and the New York Critics Award for her performance in T. S. Eliot's *The Wasteland*.

Juliet Stevenson, Laurence Olivier Best Actress Award winner, starred in Anthony Minghella's screening for Channel Four of Samuel Beckett's *Play* (with Kristin Scott-Thomas and Alan Rickman) which was shown at the Barbican Theatre in September 2001 with all the other eighteen screenplays of Beckett's work.

Helen Taylor Robinson is a member of the British Psycho-Analytical Society and Honorary Senior Lecturer in InterDisciplinary Studies (Literature and Psychoanalysis) at University College London. Her public lectures include: '"As it would seem": approaches to the unconscious through the work of Samuel Beckett and Sigmund Freud', 'Beckett and Bion/the emergence of meaning' and 'The bespoke universe: Shakespeare, Freud and Beckett, Tailors and Outfitters' (*British Journal of Psychotherapy*, 2000).

Foreword

Laura Mulvey

It is fascinating to see the way in which the innovative and exciting *First European Psychoanalytic Film Festival* has evolved into a volume that not only maintains the diversity of the original event but also coheres into thematic sections that create, once again, their own internal dialogues. While the contributors are united by their collective interest in psychoanalysis, the volume brings together a wide range of approaches and professional perspectives. The driving concept behind both the event and the book was to provide a forum for interaction between practising psychoanalysts, film directors and actors, film critics, academics and theorists. These differing professional perspectives also embrace differing schools of psychoanalytic practice and film theory. Ideas and concerns are approached from different directions and then work in unexpected ways to create lines of thought and thematic threads from contribution to contribution. But the book has another kind of diversity built into it. The opening part leads the reader in, as though through a fascinating threshold, with a series of discussions between directors, analysts and critics which include contributions from members of the audience. A sense of lively debate, of disagreements and sudden insights gives the book a texture that is very much its own.

From my personal point of view, the decision to concentrate on European cinema is of special interest. My own critical background was influenced by the intense relationship forged by Seventies feminist film theory with psychoanalytic theory and Hollywood cinema. Feminist interest in Hollywood emerged in response to certain characteristics, or even defining obsessions, that marked the collective culture of its cinema. Gender definition, sexual iconography, the emblematic representation of femininity refracted through the star system, as well as Oedipal drama, the melodrama and motherhood, and so on, all preoccupied feminist psychoanalytic film theory. However, the focus on European cinema produces motifs and themes that lead to a very different psychic world.

The key points are summarized by Andrea Sabbadini in his Introduction in the following terms: 'the impact of traumata on our lives, the presence of "horror" scenarios in our unconscious minds, the constant preoccupation, in filmmakers and psychoanalysts alike, with documenting reality, be that the objective one of the external environment or the more subjective one of our internal worlds' (p. 8). The last of these three themes, the recurring question of the relation between film and reality, has always been a key issue for film theory in general. However, when approached from a psychoanalytic perspective, the question of reality cannot be separated from the two preceding points: the reality of trauma and the role of the unconscious in mediating that reality into symptom. The inexpressible finds its expression in displaced forms. Trauma, as many contributors to the book repeatedly point out, may be experienced in two ways. It may be personal, private and marked only on the individual unconscious, returning as symptom of the repressed within the history of a single psyche. This is the terrain that has always been the primary concern of psychoanalytic theory and practice. On the other hand, trauma may be collective, social and marked as the repressed or unspeakable within history, returning within culture and its symptoms. The chapters in this book suggest that cinema can play an important part in mediating between ideas that have grown out of specific analytic practices and the wider, elusive questions raised by trauma experienced collectively. The possibility of 'documenting' these phenomena, between a reality that eludes consciousness and its displaced, skewed, expression within a culture, is a constant preoccupation for those for whom psychoanalysis is a therapeutic practice, a creative inspiration or a theoretical resource. The contributions collected in this volume bear eloquent witness to 'documentation of reality' as a point of fascination and frustration, despair and aspiration. It is perhaps the equivalent for artists and intellectuals of the 'interminable' in Freud's assessment of analytic practice.

A constant presence within the European tradition of cinema, to which this book refers, is the representation and understanding of history. History, however, takes on multiple forms so that the idea of a unified intellectual concept is fragmented through and on film: the traces of the past preserved in landscapes, places and faces, the re-enactment of events that hold collective memory, the politics of the return of the repressed. These problems of representation necessarily push their creative protagonists beyond the intractable issues of reality towards fiction and those realities of the unconscious that show complete disregard for rationality, as, for instance, in the nightmare or horror film. But these are primarily issues of content, important in their own right and translated to the screen with their own cinematic aesthetics.

The book also raises questions about form and the cinema as mechanism that are of interest to both psychoanalytic and film theory, leading to a consideration of cinema as 'philosophical toy' or 'allegory' of human consciousness. To my mind, one interesting aspect of this line of thought is cinema's relation to uncertainty. This may, of course, be a matter of ambivalence in the face of the cinema's credibility effect. Christian Metz compared this, when it worked, to the psychoanalytic concept of denial and to the fetishist's relation to a fetish object, *believing* in its preciousness while 'really' knowing it to be valueless. But the pleasure may also be derived from the fragility of the cinema's credibility. In a *trompe-l'œil* effect, a fiction can collapse to reveal the reality behind its production and a documentary, in its turn, can reveal its artifice and the cinema's own mechanism can erupt into consciousness within either. At moments like these, the cinema exists on a razor's edge between reality and illusion so that it ultimately throws doubt on both. In this way, cinema has an allegorical interest for psychoanalysis, mapping a terrain that goes beyond a simple 'either/or' towards an aesthetics and ethics of uncertainty. The human mind's interest is not, that is, only in being 'fooled' by the spectacle and then realizing its own foolishness, but in recognizing the delusion of certainty as such and speculating about other ways of understanding the world. That is, for the human mind, uncertainty offers a better position from which to understand reality, as certainty must, of necessity, be illusory.

I would like to end with Freud himself and his relation, or rather non-relation, to the cinema. For many years it mystified me, and even annoyed me, that Freud would have shown no interest at all in the cinema, as the editor points out in his Introduction. It was only recently that I began to have some sense of why, for Freud, an interest in cinema would have been incompatible with a psychoanalytic interest in the structure of the mind. Reading Stephen Heath's comments on the subject, I noticed that Freud dismissed the cinema in terms of flapper fashion: the *Bubikopf*, or the bobbed hair-cut, that was all the rage in the mid-Twenties. The cinema seemed to him to stand for novelty and the new-fangled and also, by a process of condensation, the newness of the young modern woman. There is an echo, here, of Freud's earlier rejection of Wilhelm Jentsch's psychoanalytic reflections on phenomena of the uncanny in his famous article of 1919 'The "uncanny"'. There, Freud firmly rejects the idea that 'life-sized automata' and 'the new and unfamiliar' could arouse an uncanny effect and emphasizes that only 'that class of frightening that leads back to the old and familiar' can be of interest to psychoanalysis. To put it another way, for an emotional effect to have a relation to the unconscious mind, it must have undergone a process of repression from which it may return. Thus, from Freud's perspective, the very modernity of the cinema rendered it uninteresting, celebrating, as it did, with the newest technology, the novelty, speed and glamour of urban life and, indeed, the robotic, androgynous body of the young modern woman.

Now, of course, the cinema seems to be very different. Overtaken by the novelty of the latest technologies, the electronic and the digital which create their own dimensions of time and space, the cinema belongs as much, or even more, to the past as to the present. In Freudian terms, perhaps, it has moved closer to the archaic, uncanny, body of the mother leaving behind the sheen of youth.

Furthermore, with the actual passing of time, it has fulfilled an aspect of its aesthetic specificity. The cinema always transformed the living human body into its inorganic replica, animated only by the movement of celluloid through the projector. As a number of the contributors to *The Couch and the Silver Screen* point out, the cinema has had an affinity with the ghostly. Across the whole history of cinema we see more of the dead on the screen than the living, and the mechanism that started out as a means of creating an illusion of movement has now become a means of creating an illusion of the living dead. Although it might be difficult to claim that the cinema approximates to the cultures of antiquity that fascinated Freud, it has certainly acquired a past. Perhaps, from this viewpoint, Freud might accept the cinema as able to reflect on those aspects of the human mind with which he was concerned. Given the way that the contributions and debates presented here bring psychoanalysis and the cinema into mutual illumination, I would expect him to be convinced.

Acknowledgements

Not unlike films themselves, books are always the products of the collective efforts of many people. I would like then to thank at least some of these, and first of all the authors and those who participated in the presentations and discussions reported here as transcripts from audiotapes – including those anonymous members of the audience simply referred to as A1, A2, etc. (Chapters 1, 2, 3, 12 and 15).

It was the *First European Psychoanalytic Film Festival*, held in London in November 2001, which also produced as a most welcome side-effect the material contained in this volume. My gratitude goes to my friends and colleagues from the British Psycho-Analytical Society whose work was invaluable in transforming our wish for a festival into a reality: Michael Brearley, Chris Mawson and, especially, Helen Taylor Robinson, who offered an additional important contribution to the book with her ideas, time and labour.

My thanks also go to Laura Mulvey for agreeing so enthusiastically to write her Foreword; to Dana Birksted-Breen, General Editor of the New Library of Psychoanalysis, for her continuous support to this project, as well as for offering much appreciated comments on various drafts of my Introduction; and to my daughter Marta J. Sabbadini, technical coordinator at the festival, for transcribing and editing from the audiotapes with the impeccable competence and efficiency which characterize her.

Photographs appear by courtesy of the following individuals and organizations: Michal Aviad (*Ever Shot Anyone?*); Bernardo Bertolucci (*Novecento*); Nanni Moretti and Sacher Film (*The Son's Room*); Vinko Brešan and Interfilm (*Marsal*); Lindy Heymann, Marilyn Milgrom and First Take Films/APT Films (*Kissing Buba*); Timna Rosenheimer and Sheleg Productions (*Fortuna*); Miguel Sapochnik and Ivor Powell (*The Dreamer*); X Filme Creative Pool GmbH (*Run, Lola, Run*); Blue Light (*Festen*); Opera Film S.r.l (*Phenomena*); Diaphana Production and Artificial Eye (*Harry, He Is Here to Help*); Deutsches Filmmuseum

(*Vampyr*); Hugh Brody and British Film Institute (*Film, Nineteen Nineteen*); Michael Grant (*The Beyond*); Michael Apted and MGM (*The World Is Not Enough*); Svensk Filmindustri (*Wild Strawberries*).

A. S.

INTRODUCTION

Andrea Sabbadini

> The uniqueness of cinematography in visibly portraying psychological events calls our attention, with exaggerated clarity, to the fact that the interesting and meaningful problems of man's relation to himself – and the fateful disturbance of this relation – finds here an imaginative representation.
>
> (Otto Rank 1914, p. 7)

This book could be considered as a metaphorical meeting place not only where readers can 'encounter' their authors, but also where different voices, coming from different cultural and geographical lands and using different languages, can comment upon the world from their own perspectives – and, let us hope, be listened to by others and have an impact on them. Here practising psychoanalysts and film scholars have come together to participate in lively discussion with European filmmakers about their creative products and the complex network of factors involved in them: psychological, interpersonal, political and technical (to name only a few!).

Another such meeting ground, only marginally less metaphorical than the printed one just referred to, was the *First European Psychoanalytic Film Festival* (London, 1–4 November 2001) from which the material collected in this volume originated. There, in interaction with an interested general public attending the event, film critics and scholars offered their theories and cultural or historical frames of reference; psychoanalysts, their reflections and interpretations; filmmakers, their labours of love; while the movies themselves spoke the language of images and sounds, providing sensations and emotions to all who came to watch and hear.

★★★

1

Originally intended by Freud as a form of therapy for the neuroses, psychoanalysis soon became a more ambitious project: a general psychology for the investigation of mental functioning. This opened up a number of areas for the 'application' of psychoanalysis outside its original scope: the extra-clinical utilization of psychoanalytic knowledge, or indeed aspects of the psychoanalytic approach, in relation to cultural products or events, or to 'explanatory, methodological, or technological problems arising in disciplines or human endeavours other than psychoanalysis' (Edelson 1988, p. 157), such as the arts, education, history and sociology.

Of course, any extension of the original psychoanalytic enterprise creates methodological problems, the awareness of which is a precondition for applying analytic tools outside the clinical setting. To start with, as there are obvious differences between work with live patients (who free associate and respond to interpretations) and applied analysis of texts (which do not), speculations on the psychopathology of artists or historical or fictional characters who have never gone near a psychoanalytic couch are of dubious value. Another risk concerns the narrow-minded attempts to utilize analytic concepts at the exclusion of other interpretative approaches rather than in combination with them, thus placing psychoanalysis itself in a position vulnerable to justified attacks of reductionism by scholars from other disciplines or with different critical orientations.

In spite of such dangers, however, the application of psychoanalysis to other fields has often been fruitful. A special case concerns the cinema if it is true, as I believe it is, that it has a privileged tie to our mental activities and emotional experiences, that

> it is a type of mime of both mind and world. . . . Breaking from the confines of photography and theatre, it is unique in its representation of an abundant world in motion. . . . There is a persistent sense that cinema imitates the movement of the mind, that there is a correspondence (however elusive) to be discovered between psyche and cinema.
>
> (Lebeau 2001, p. 3)

The oft-mentioned historical twinship between cinema and psychoanalysis can be construed as both having developed from the same ambivalent attitude to the positivistic culture dominating the end of the nineteenth century.[1] An important aspect of this elusive 'correspondence' concerns some remarkable analogies between filmic language and the analytic idiom used to describe unconscious processes. As Claude Chabrol stated in an interview explaining why he collaborated with a psychoanalyst in the writing of his film *La Cérémonie* (1995), 'it's very hard, when you deal with characters, not to use the Freudian grid, because the Freudian grid is composed of signs that also apply to the cinema' (Feinstein 1996, quoted in Gabbard 2000, p. 1). Or, in Gabbard's own words, 'to a large extent, film speaks the language of the unconscious' (1997, p. 429).

2

For instance, the psychoanalytic notion of *screen memories* might also be a suitable definition of films; the concept of *projection* is crucial to both cinema and psychoanalysis; *free associations*, mostly visual in the former and verbal in the latter, have in both idioms the purpose of encouraging the exploration of deep emotional meanings and of the often uncertain boundaries between reality and fantasy.

A special place concerns *dreams*, the interpretation of which constitutes a royal road to the unconscious, in so far as they use, for the purpose of circumventing repression, mechanisms comparable to those of many works of art and, more specifically, of movies – especially at the editing stage. These mechanisms include condensation, displacement, symbolic expression and distortions of time and space.[2] It may not be a coincidence that already in 1931 Hollywood was being described as a *Traumfabrik*, a 'dream factory' (Ehrenburg 1931).[3]

★★★

In a more general sense, cinema and psychoanalysis share an area that we can refer to by the term *insight*, meaning 'inner sight' or a kind of 'within-the-mind' seeing. Film analysis,[4] especially when it emphasizes a psychoanalytic under-standing of unconscious dynamics, requires such an in-depth insight. Cinema itself gives us these insights through the filmmakers' combined 'inner sight' or imagination, then transformed inside a camera – that magic box which we can also think of as 'the mind' – into a product to be enjoyed by the public in a dark theatre, where sounds and words can be heard from loudspeakers and visions are projected on a silver screen. Pure illusion maybe, yet also more than that, as can be said of other contents and products of our minds.

Psychoanalysis too, of course, offers 'insights': by means of the analysand, the analyst and their separate, yet con-flowing, ambivalent desires to see and yet not-see what is unconscious, unknowable, unseeable, in the consulting room's 'set', or on its 'screen', where new views may appear. Filmmaking, film analysis and psychoanalytic work, then, operate in this area of insight and of the gradual releasing of awareness from unawareness, the sightings and findings on which the cinematic imagination and the psychoanalytic process continuously throw new light. It is this interconnected or shared ground, as well as the distinctness of difference, which shapes each discipline to create a challenging form in the writings that follow.

★★★

Given this common ground, it is not surprising that screenwriters and filmmakers should in their works adopt, and as it happens also frequently abuse, psychoanalytic ideas about the human mind and interpersonal relationships. The earliest example of something approaching the presence of psychoanalysis in a

3

film can be found in *Le Mystère des roches de Kador* [*The Mystery of the Rocks of Kador*], directed in 1912 by Léonce Perret, where a 'celebrated foreign alienist physician' saves our heroine Suzanne from madness by utilizing the 'luminous vibrations of cinematographic images' in order to induce in her an hypnotic state lending to psychotherapeutic suggestion (see Bergstrom 1999, pp. 15–20).[5]

At times films have attempted – and to a large extent failed – to represent, with an either fictional or documentary approach, the psychoanalytic profession itself. One of the problems concerning many of these misrepresentations is a certain confusion, especially in the minds of Hollywood filmmakers and their audiences, between psychoanalysis and psychiatry,[6] an oversimplification which can partly be attributed to the American ban, in force until recently, on the practice of 'lay' (that is, non-medical) analysis. Furthermore, psychoanalysis has often been portrayed in the inaccurate yet dramatically effective version of the therapist being merely engaged in the cathartic recovery of repressed traumata for the explanation of current events, with much use of flashbacks as the filmic device equivalent to memory, and symbolic decoding of dream sequences; famous is the one designed by Salvador Dalí for Alfred Hitchcock's *Spellbound* (1945). Freud himself, the subject in 1962 of John Huston's biopic *Freud: The Secret Passion* based on the original script by Jean-Paul Sartre (1984), was sceptical. Having been asked – only a few months after having declined Samuel Goldwyn's substantial offer of 100,000 dollars for a script on famous love stories – to co-operate on the first major film about psychoanalysis (Georg Wilhelm Pabst's *Geheimnisse einer Seele* [*Secrets of a Soul*] [1926]), Freud wrote in a letter to Karl Abraham: 'I do not believe that satisfactory plastic representation of our abstractions is at all possible' (Letter of 9 June 1925, in Abraham and Freud 1965). And he added: 'I would much prefer if my name did not have anything to do with it at all'. He must have known that this would be impossible; on 26 July 1926 the *New York Times* claimed that Freud himself was going to direct the film![7]

★★★

Psychoanalytically oriented critics often focus their attention on textual analysis, that is on the description and interpretation of the content of a film – its subject, its themes, the treatment of its characters – as if it corresponded to the material brought by analysands to their sessions. Articles of textual psychoanalytic criticism are sometimes concerned with movies (e.g. those by François Truffaut) which display a special sensitivity to the psychological factors contributing to their characters' behaviour, or which deal with powerful feelings, for instance the fear often associated with a realistic or paranoid sense of being persecuted (e.g. those by Alfred Hitchcock); or more generally with films, such as those by Luis Buñuel, which use a cinematic language deliberately reminiscent of unconscious functioning and even conveying a disturbing sense of what Freud

(1919) described as 'the uncanny',[8] especially in relation to the phenomenon of the *Doppelgänger*.[9]

Many films, either within the comic or, more often, the dramatic tradition, are of special interest to analysts primarily because they deal with themes also familiar to psychoanalytic enquiries: different forms of mental pathology, such as neurotic or narcissistic disturbances (Woody Allen), psychotic disintegration (Roman Polanski) or sexual perversions and gender confusion (Pedro Almodóvar); crises in subjectivity related to developmental stages or acute existential and moral dilemmas (Ingmar Bergman, Michelangelo Antonioni, Akiri Kurosawa, Krzysztof Kieslowski); incestuous or other conflictual family constellations, often with an emphasis on Oedipal themes (Luchino Visconti, Bernardo Bertolucci).

★★★

Psychoanalytic theories – especially those originating from the ideas of Jacques Lacan on the distinction between real, imaginary and symbolic orders,[10] on the 'mirror stage' of development,[11] on 'suture',[12] on the dynamics of desire, on the perversions of fetishism and voyeurism – tend to concentrate on the deep structures underlying the production of meaning in films. Such theories have been influential since the late 1960s in academic film criticism, for instance on the pages of the prestigious journals *Cahiers du Cinéma* in France, *Screen* in Great Britain and *Camera Obscura* in the United States, and through the work of such authors as Christian Metz. In his seminal essay, 'The imaginary signifier', Metz observed that what unfolds on the screen 'is real (the cinema is not a phantasy), but the perceived is not really the object, it is its shade, its phantom, its double, its *replica* in a new kind of mirror' (1974, p. 45). What is peculiar about the cinema, he says, is not only that it allows us to perceive our object from a distance (through the senses of sight and hearing), but also that 'what remains in that distance is now no longer the object itself, it is a delegate' (ibid., p. 61). This 'delegate' is a prime instance of the Lacanian *manque* ('lack'): like any other form of desire, its essence depends on being fulfilled, while its existence comes to an end the moment it is. Film is suspended, for Metz, in the imaginary space of this paradox.[13]

Under the influence of Lacanian-coloured semiotics, feminist theories and postmodern deconstructionism, psychoanalysis has also given a contribution to our understanding of film 'spectatorship'. This term refers to the complex of psychological, socio-economic and more generally cultural phenomena which affect filmmakers in their construction, and audiences in their reception, of cinematic products, as well as the mythologies associated with them: for instance exploring the relationship between spectators and Hollywood 'stars'. Psycho-analytically influenced film scholars with a feminist orientation, prominent among them Laura Mulvey (1975, 1989), Teresa de Lauretis (1984) and Mary Ann Doane (1987), have provided original perspectives on issues of sexuality in

5

films, such as gender stereotyping and the role of women as fetishes or as the objects of male voyeuristic gaze.[14]

It may be useful here to refer to Francis Baudry's discussion of the psychoanalytic interpretation of literary texts, as what he says about them clearly also applies to the film texts analysed by psychoanalysts. Baudry outlines four different approaches:

> In the first approach, the analytic writer treats a novel, play, or poem as a case history, ignoring the as-if nature of the literary text and performing a type of character analysis. The second approach relates the text to the mental life (both normal and abnormal) of the author. The text is viewed as a modified form of free association. The third approach considers the text in its own right and carries out a thematic analysis identifying traces or derivatives of mental contents. The fourth approach concerns itself with the reaction of the reader and the production of poetic and aesthetic effect.
>
> (Baudry 1984, p. 552)

With this in mind, it can be noticed that in recent years – and complementarily with, if not in opposition to, the Lacanian approaches to film criticism which emphasize, often at the expense of everything else, the semiotics of the film language and its implications on spectatorship[15] – film reviews have begun to appear on a regular basis also in non-Lacanian psychoanalytic literature. Mostly written by practising clinicians, in contrast with the academic scholars of Lacanian orientation, these reviews, which can now be found in many psychoanalytic journals,[16] tend to explore the film texts,[17] using a variety of relevant psycho-analytic theoretical parameters. These have included interpretations of films in the light of unconscious defensive mechanisms, internal objects[18] and their relationships, developmental stages and positions,[19] modalities of attachment and separation-individuation,[20] transitional phenomena,[21] Oedipal predicaments, psychodynamic understandings of mental pathology.[22] Of special importance in this context are issues of transference and countertransference: these concepts – which refer to the ways in which aspects of our childhood scenarios cause distortions to our current experiences of others, in particular in the here-and-now of the psychoanalytic encounter for both analysand (transference) and analyst (countertransference) – can be useful also to our interpretation of films: not just in so far as they can help us understand some of the underlying meanings of the relationships among characters on the screen, but also because they can throw a significant light on the emotionally charged interrelationships between filmmakers, their artistic products and their audiences.

In complement to the film studies with a Lacanian matrix, these approaches, rooted in classical Freudian theories and in the ideas developed by later psychoanalytic authors, attest to a new pluralistic orientation also reflected in the pages of this book. It is in recognition of this shift that Glen Gabbard states in his introduction to a collection of such reviews that 'over time a variety

6

of methodologies have attained some degree of legitimacy as psychoanalytic approaches to film' (Gabbard 2000, p. 5).

As a result of such cultural ferment, psychoanalysts with an interest in cinema as well as film scholars from an analytic orientation have in recent years published several important works exploring the interface, and therefore also the boundaries, between cinema, psychoanalysis and other related fields of inquiry.[23] It is then within this more open attitude of mutual exchange and constant cross-referencing that I would like to locate this book of 'reflections' (in more senses than one). This should provide a measured access to the representation of ideas and approaches derived from the separate areas or disciplines to which the authors belong, as well as an opportunity for some rewarding exploration of their points of contact.

★★★

Having briefly reviewed here ways in which psychoanalysis as a method of inquiry can be applied to cinema studies, I would like now to move beyond this and endorse a view of 'interdisciplinary exchange' between these cultural fields. This was also the dominating feature and underlying ideological purpose of the *First European Psychoanalytic Film Festival*, where it was clear throughout that filmmakers were as keen to listen to psychoanalytically informed observations about their movies, as the analysts were genuinely interested in learning from the filmmakers themselves about the complex processes involved in creating their works. Both psychoanalysts and filmmakers had the chance to explore what the imaginative form (the film) could do in the way of enlarging and deepening perspectives of the mind and challenging psychoanalytic thinking, at the same time enjoying the more theoretical, historical and sociological contributions provided by the film academics. The potential for cross-fertilization among these disciplines is a substantial one.

★★★

As in all collections of articles from many contributors, there are in this book some inevitable discrepancies of language and style. However, through my selection and sequencing of the material, I have attempted to create an organic text – as well as to re-create with it something of the stimulating atmosphere of the event where much of the book was originated – which should amount to more than the sum of its component parts, and thus provide its readers with a consistent, if varied, tool for psychoanalytical reflections on European cinema. The decision to limit the scope of this book, and of the festival before it, to European cinema was only in part intended to offer a more precise geographical focus to our analytic inquiries. Faced with the overwhelming commercial domination of Hollywood's products – technically sophisticated, but often ideologically and artistically poor – it was a deliberate choice to concentrate all our attention instead on the quality films produced and directed on this side of the Atlantic.

My intention in the selection and assembly of the material for the book was then to build a landscape of perspectives on important European films, organized around themes with considerable psychoanalytic significance: the impact of traumata on our lives, the presence of 'horror' scenarios in our unconscious minds, the constant preoccupation, in filmmakers and psychoanalysts alike, with documenting reality, be that the objective one of the external environment or the more subjective one of our internal worlds, while at the same time finding that the two cannot be clearly separated.

The first part of the book, a sort of platform called 'Set and stage', includes the transcripts from two encounters between psychoanalysts, filmmakers, actors and academics. In Chapter 1, film director Bernardo Bertolucci, the Honorary President of the festival, discusses with actor Fiona Shaw and psychoanalyst Chris Mawson the group dynamics that develop among the filmmaker and his or her 'colony', comprising all those artists and technicians who come together to create a film. What occurs in the director's mind and what happens on and around the film set, the vicissitudes of fictional and material reality, are explored and uncovered with intelligence and humour by this workshop's participants and by the audience whose comments and questions are also reported here.

In Chapter 2, film historian Ian Christie and stage actor Juliet Stevenson interact with each other and with psychoanalyst Helen Taylor Robinson in discussing playwright Samuel Beckett's only creation for cinema, the remarkable 21-minute *Film* starring Buster Keaton. This movie attempts to use the medium of the camera as the 'eye' that is configured as our organ to perceive the external world, while also being the 'I' of self-perception. The academic's contextualization of this work within the history of cinema, the actor's perspective on 'what it is like to be' a Beckett character and the psychoanalyst's considerations on the difference between imagination and the unconscious, together with the comments from a moved audience, address the contribution of the Beckettian imagination and the impact of his blow to our conventions of what it is to receive reality.

The next part 'Working through trauma' comprises five chapters on films centred on traumatic events, their impact on the characters and on the viewers, and the means of working through them – or more often of failing to do so. It could be argued that creating an artistic product on the theme of trauma, or perhaps even creating any artistic product, could have as one of its functions to resolve conflict and to overcome the depression following real or imagined losses. Psychoanalysts influenced by the theories of Melanie Klein, in particular, have argued that the deep psychological roots of creativity can be found in the unconscious need to repair objects unconsciously damaged by the child's envious and destructive attacks on the mother – a view many consider fascinating, but also perhaps reductionist. Chapter 3 is the transcript of the encounter of psychoanalysts Paola Golinelli, Stefano Bolognini and Andrea Sabbadini with the Italian actor-director Nanni Moretti to discuss his film *The Son's Room* in which a psychoanalyst, portrayed here by Moretti himself with a sensitivity uncommon in most other movies, is trying to come to terms in his personal and professional life with the tragedy of the death of his adolescent son in a diving accident.

American psychoanalyst Jed Sekoff, in Chapter 4, finds in the concept of 'torn mourning' a link between two British short films: *The Dreamer* by Miguel Sapochnik, a high-tech experimental work 'enabling a deep journey through a range of identifications with victims and victimizers', and *Kissing Buba* by Lindy Heymann where a young girl (and we viewers with her) is confronted with her grandmother's incapacity to face her past of persecution and is taken by her through a different journey, a textured one 'through fear, trembling, and incomprehension toward the possibilities of forgiveness, remembrance, and love'.

Annegret Mahler-Bungers, in Chapter 5, draws on the uses of language, literature, cinematic form, psychoanalytic dream theory and views of adolescence, and yields a *tour de force* on that fast-moving piece of postmodern cinematography entitled *Run, Lola, Run*. With her mind engaged at thinking-speed, she evokes in her writing the very object that film director Tom Tykwer sets himself to aim for in his movie: 'how to film the pace of thoughts'.

In Chapter 6, Argentine psychoanalyst Liliana Pedrón de Martín examines the film *Festen* by looking at the issues of denial and disavowal as human processes, presented here in opposition to the attempt to disclose incest within a family. She addresses the syntax of the film and the construction of meaning achieved by a number of technical devices which Thomas Vinterberg, a representative of the 'Dogma 95' group of Danish filmmakers, uses to spell out confrontation, revelation and denunciation. As Pedrón de Martín puts it, 'the hand-held camera compromises the spectator and forces him to see and hear without avoiding the facts'.

Diana Diamond's exploration of the film *Sunshine* in Chapter 7 also approaches the theme of incest, unspeakable (but filmable) violence and transgenerational Holocaust trauma, and the ways in which cinema can realize in sight and sound the nature of horrors while still remaining a work of fiction. Narrative form, imagery and the creation of signifiers, as well as the depiction of primal scene fantasies that combine the erotic and the aggressive, are explored in this portrait of horror ironically termed 'sunshine'.

This chapter provides a bridge to the next part of the book which collects four chapters on 'Horror perspectives'. The conventional classification of film in genres – of which 'horror' is an increasingly important one in our hyper-technological culture – is of little concern to us here. More important, instead, are the psychoanalytic considerations on the profound, often unconscious, nature of the fascination that so many filmmakers and viewers have for such products, as well as on the specific language shared by them.

Steven Jay Schneider introduces this part with a concise historical analysis of the development of what he calls the 'Euro-horror' tradition. This refers specifically to French, Spanish, Italian and German post-1970 films characterized by a sexualized violence with a degree of explicitness not found in most Hollywood products. Euro-horror, however, is a term with ambiguous, even contradictory meanings and therefore, argues Schneider, it requires a new 'comprehensive theoretical (including psychoanalytical) inquiry into its narratives, conventions and imagery'.

In Chapter 9, Donald Campbell, a psychoanalyst with experience of clinical work with disturbed adolescents, weaves his film texts with insights on the function of those horror movies which focus on deformed or distorted bodies. Such films, like Dario Argento's *Phenomena*, which he analyses in detail, resonate in young people's own anxieties about the 'monstrous' changes to their physical appearance and sensations.

In Chapter 10, Kleinian author Candy Aubry finds a manifestation of the unconscious processes of projection, splitting and re-introjection, in the almost surreal world of Dominik Moll's *Harry, He's Here to Help*. The ever-so-helpful persecutor Harry is interpreted by Aubry as the 'dark side' of his victim, unable until the last therapeutic moment of his horrific journey to disentangle himself from his double.

This part is concluded by Chapter 11 on the aesthetics of horror movies, illustrated here by an analysis of Carl-Theodor Dreyer's *Vampyr* and Lucio Fulci's *The Beyond*. Film scholar Michael Grant, with reference to the work of R. G. Collingwood, presents art as the unique means by which the constituents of emotions may be represented in a given setting. Obsessed with fantasies of living death, the horror genre allows an approach, Grant suggests, to the postmodern phenomenon of the problematic and the ambiguous: that 'essential abyss of non-meaning, of the empty nothingness that is organic life'.

The book's final part, 'Documenting internal worlds', consists of four chapters where authors from different disciplines and with different perspectives on European cinema examine the complex interrelationship between reality and fiction or, more specifically, their cinematic representations as documentaries or features. This is a theme of direct interest to psychoanalysts as well, constantly struggling to redefine the often confused boundaries between internal worlds and external realities, constructions and reconstructions, objective facts (for instance of childhood abuse) and the subjective experience of them in their patients' lives.

Chapter 12 is the transcript of a presentation by Michael Apted of his work both as a director of major features and as a documentarist. In the latter role he is much respected for his television series *Seven Up* on a group of British children who were filmed and interviewed on what they thought and felt about all kinds of issues, a process still being followed up every seven years – an original film form which has spawned many offspring. The implicit parallels between Apted's cinematic eye documenting external reality and the psychoanalytic ear on our inner existence constitute a theme of relevance to both artistic and therapeutic work.

In Chapter 13, film scholar Elizabeth Cowie looks at the nature of the epistemic uncertainties for the spectator. From the perspective of Freudian theory on dream-work, Cowie examines cinema as a dreaming-machine by concentrating on oneiric sequences within films, a useful exercise which she applies here with great attention to detail to Ingmar Bergman's masterpiece *Wild Strawberries*.

Chapter 14 focuses on Brešan's *Marshal Tito's Spirit*, a film which ridicules the cultural dominance of the former Yugoslavian communist regime. Here the tension between individual needs and social concerns, expressed in the film language itself through the use of irony and the abundance of metaphors, adds another dimension to the one, outlined above, between internal and external realities, and means of representing it. Ljiljana Filipović undertakes a reading of this witty psychodrama about the 'return' of the dead, dishonoured but once also revered, dictator, back to life – with all the ideological and socio-political issues that this brings in tow for a small community of Croatian islanders. Filipović finds here useful frames of reference in Freud's early theories of catharsis and abreaction, the 'return of the repressed' and the relation of jokes to the unconscious.

Chapter 15 is the transcript of another live debate. Psychoanalyst Emanuel Berman introduces and discusses here with the audience and two Israeli directors, Timna Rosenheimer and Michal Aviad, their documentaries *Fortuna* and *Ever Shot Anyone?* Their protagonists are real flesh-and-blood individuals (as different from, though not opposed to, actors performing a scripted part) who draw the directors into complex interactions. This mirrors, it is argued, the complexity of the analyst/analysand transferential and countertransferential dynamics, with difficult and yet imaginative outcomes. Not surprisingly, what is at the start consciously or unconsciously aimed for in the mind of the director, or of the analyst, has to be reconsidered in the light of what emerges as a result of the protagonists', or of the analysands', needs.

The book is concluded by two complementary contributions from anthropologist and filmmaker Hugh Brody (director of *Nineteen Nineteen*, one of the most important features on psychoanalysis) and from psychoanalyst Michael Brearley, on the theme of filming psychoanalysis itself: indeed, on whether this is at all possible. Can the camera have access inside the intimacy of the psychoanalytic encounter without becoming an instrument of voyeuristic gratification? If the answer is in the negative, are there other means of cinematically documenting, re-creating and representing psychoanalysis without distorting its meaning or interfering with its process?

★★★

This introduction is intended to emphasize that *The Couch and the Silver Screen* consists of individual readings of cinema from a variety of traditions. Such readings rely on an awareness of the structural and functional differences between cinema and psychoanalysis, as well as of some of their complementarities and continuities. Different methodologies are reflected in the ways the chosen topics for each individual chapter have been conceived and developed. Cinematic issues of form; gender, cultural and social considerations; psychoanalytic models of the mind and of interpersonal relationships; literary critical, historical and film studies approaches, all are used in varying combinations by each author to explore the themes which interest him or her.

As I have already indicated, readers will also come across, alongside more 'conventional' chapters, the transcripts of workshops on the cinematic creative process. These more discursive and spontaneous debates are concerned with such issues as directorial authority and the impact of group dynamics on the cinematic product; the complementary roles of imagination and technique in the artistic process; the boundaries between documentary and feature filmmaking; problematic relationships between documentary directors and the subjects of their inquiries. Longer articles and critical discourse can then be found here alongside informal presentations, snatches of film texts and question-and-answer discussions with the audience, moving free-associatively rather than in narrative sequence in a lively, often humorous process, always coloured by the conscious and unconscious dynamics among those engaged in it.

These texts required a different kind of writing which involved going behind the camera, the final cut, the projector, the screen; and their dialogic nature allows for a different kind of response from the readers than those to the more structured chapters. What might have been said in passing or improvised could also have a weighting, as it does in the psychoanalytic model of the mind, that may take us into deeper layers of the process, be it filmmaking or psychoanalysis.

Notes

1 The screening of the Lumière brothers' first films in Paris in 1895 coincided with the publication in Vienna of the first psychoanalytic book, Breuer and Freud's *Studies on Hysteria*.
2 Already in 1914 Otto Rank had noticed that 'cinematography . . . in numerous ways reminds us of the dream-work' (p. 4).
3

   Cultural commentators have explored the primacy of 'wish-fulfilment' in the narrative structures of films, and as equivalent to its function in dreams and day-dreams. . . . For film makers themselves, dreams and dream-states seemed from the outset to be an essential part of film's ontology: while 'dream sequences' within films may seem to be bounded, they are never fully sealed off from the film-space which contains them.

   (Marcus 2001, p. 52)

4 Let me notice here that 'film analysis' is only one of several discourses on cinema; others include the study of films from the point of view of, say, technical achievement or commercial marketability.

5 The first book, by now a classic, on the psychology of cinema – Hugo Münsterberg's *The Film: A Psychological Study* – was to be published only four years later, in 1916.

6 See, for instance, the title of the important book on American cinema *Psychiatry and the Cinema* (Gabbard and Gabbard 1999). In their 'Preface to the Second Edition', the authors write:

> Since the appearance of our first edition in 1987, psychiatry has continued to distance itself from psychoanalysis and psychotherapy. Nevertheless, in the cinematic world, the emphasis remains on the talking cure . . . Hence, we continue to use the term *psychiatry* in the broadest possible sense to encompass all mental health professionals, especially those who practice psychotherapy.
> (Gabbard and Gabbard 1999, pp. xix–xx)

7 For a historical reconstruction of the 'good deal of consternation' (Jones 1957, p. 121) and hostile attitude of the psychoanalytic establishment towards Pabst's film, see Ries (1995).

8 According to Freud, 'an uncanny effect is often and easily produced when the distinction between imagination and reality is effaced' (1919, p. 244), or, more precisely, 'when infantile complexes which have been repressed are once more revived by some impression, or when primitive beliefs which have been surmounted seem once more to be confirmed' (ibid., p. 249).

9 Otto Rank (1914), in the opening chapter of his psychoanalytic study on 'the double', gives us the first psychoanalytic interpretation of a film, the German *Der Student von Prag* [*The Student of Prague*] (1913) by the Danish director Stellan Rye, written by Hanns Heinz Ewers (a follower of E. T. A. Hoffmann's, 'the unrivalled master of the uncanny in literature' [Freud 1919, p. 233]) and interpreted by the famous actor Paul Wegener. Freud himself mentions this early film by quoting Rank in a footnote to his text on the uncanny (1919, p. 236, note 1). See also Ian Christie's comments in Chapter 2, p. 41.

10 The 'imaginary order' refers to phenomena in the psychological arena controlled by the Ego, while the 'symbolic order' is for Lacan a mostly unconscious universal structure, concerned with words, language and their function as signifiers. The 'real order' is considered to be an intrinsically impossible dimension, the existence of which can only be conceived in relation to the other two orders.

11 This refers to the time, between 6 and 18 months, when a child first excitedly recognizes his or her own body image in the mirror, a fundamental step towards the establishment of a sense of identity.

12 This term, originally proposed by Jacques-Alain Miller (1966) to describe the imaginary process whereby the subject is 'stitched into' the signifying chain, 'found immediate favour amongst film theorists in order to describe the mechanism by which the spectator is positioned as a cinematic subject . . . takes her or his place in the cinematic discourse' (Cowie 1997, p. 115; see also Heath 1981).

13 In recent years film analysts influenced by Lacanian theories include such authors as Joan Copjec (1994), Stephen Heath (1981), Ann Kaplan (1990) and Slavoj Žižek (1992).

14 Reference is often made in this context to Joan Riviere's (1929) concept of 'womanliness as masquerade', whereby a woman's public success could signify 'an exhibition of herself in possession of the father's penis, having castrated him' (p. 305). Riviere

explains: 'She identifies herself with the father; and then she uses the masculinity she thus obtains by putting it at the service of the mother. She becomes the father, and takes his place; so she can "restore" him to the mother' (ibid., p. 310). The importance of this for cinema rests on the fact that such a 'masquerade' of female identity and sexuality, it is argued, is also mirrored in the (male) representations of women characters on the screen.

15 This corresponds to Baudry's (1984) 'fourth' approach.

16 The main psychoanalytic journals publishing film reviews are the *Psychoanalytic Review* (in the USA), *International Journal of Psycho-Analysis* (in Great Britain) and *Psyche* (in Germany). Among the numerous specialized periodicals I should mention at least *Projections*, the publication of the Forum for the Psychoanalytic Study of Film, an organization founded by American psychoanalyst Bruce Sklarew.

17 This corresponds to Baudry's (1984) 'first' and 'third' approaches. As to his 'second' approach, while it can be useful to consider how the filmmaker's own subjectivity may lead to recurrent themes in his or her works, earlier psychoanalytic 'pathographical' studies of artists are now rare and tend to be discredited.

18 The term 'internal objects' refers to the unconscious mental representation of emotionally significant others.

19 Freud, for instance, distinguishes the 'oral' from the 'anal' and the 'genital' phase in the psychosexual development of the child, while Melanie Klein differentiates the 'paranoid schizoid' from the 'depressive' position.

20 The concept of 'separation–individuation', used by Margaret Mahler *et al.* (1975), refers to a sub-phase during the second year of child development when toddlers begin to move away both physically and psychologically from their parents, needing to come back to them only from time to time for 'emotional refuelling'.

21 These are those psychological experiences located in the 'third' space between the internal and the external worlds and symbolically related to the 'transitional objects', as described by Donald W. Winnicott (1971).

22 One of the major features in Freudian metapsychology, the 'dynamic' dimension refers to the unconscious mind being the seat of conflicts among the different forces actively present in it.

23 See, in particular, Bergstrom (1999), Cowie (1997), Gabbard (2000), Hauke and Alister (2001), Kaplan (1990) and Lebeau (2001).

References

Abraham, H. and Freud, E. (eds) (1965) *A Psycho-Analytical Dialogue: The Letters of Sigmund Freud and Karl Abraham, 1907–1926*. London: Hogarth Press.

Baudry, F. (1984) 'An essay on method in applied psychoanalysis', *Psychoanalytic Quarterly*, 53: 551–581.

Bergstrom, J. (ed.) (1999) *Endless Night: Cinema and Psychoanalysis, Parallel Histories*. Los Angeles and London: University of California Press.

Copjec, J. (1994) *Read My Desire: Lacan Against the Historicists*. Cambridge, MA: MIT Press.

Cowie, E. (1997) *Representing the Woman: Cinema and Psychoanalysis*. London: Macmillan.

de Lauretis, T. (1984) *Alice Doesn't: Feminism, Semiotics, Cinema*. London: Macmillan.

Doane, M. A. (1987) *The Desire to Desire: The Woman's Film of the 1940s*. London: Macmillan.

Edelson, M. (1988) *Psychoanalysis: A Theory in Crisis*. Chicago: University of Chicago Press.

Ehrenburg, I. (1931) *Die Traumfabriki Chronik des Films*. Berlin: Malik.

Feinstein, H. (1996) 'Killer instincts: director Claude Chabrol finds madness in his method', *Village Voice*, 24 December, p. 86.

Freud, S. (1919) 'The "uncanny"', in *Standard Edition 17*. London: Hogarth Press, 1955.

Gabbard, G. O. (1997) 'Guest editorial: the psychoanalyst at the movies', *International Journal of Psycho-Analysis*, 78(3): 429–434.

Gabbard, G. O. (ed.) (2000) *Psychoanalysis and Film*. London and New York: Karnac.

Gabbard, G. O. and Gabbard, K. (1999) *Psychiatry and the Cinema*, 2nd edn. Washington, DC and London: American Psychiatric Press.

Hauke, C. and Alister, I. (eds) (2001) *Jung and Film: Post-Jungian Takes on the Moving Image*. Hove: Brunner-Routledge.

Heath, S. (1981) *Questions of Cinema*. London: Macmillan.

Jones, E. (1957) *Sigmund Freud: Life and Work, Vol. 3*. London: Hogarth Press.

Kaplan, E. A. (ed.) (1990) *Psychoanalysis and Cinema*. London and New York: Routledge.

Lebeau, V. (2001) *Psychoanalysis and Cinema: The Play of Shadows*. London and New York: Wallflower.

Mahler, M., Pine, F. and Bergman, A. (1975) *The Psychological Birth of the Human Infant: Symbiosis and Individuation*. London: Hutchinson.

Marcus, L. (2001) 'Dreaming and cinematographic consciousness', *Psychoanalysis and History*, 3(1): 51–68.

Metz, C. (1974) *The Imaginary Signifier: Psychoanalysis and the Cinema*. Bloomington, IN: Indiana University Press, 1982.

Miller, J-A. (1966) 'Suture (elements of the logic of the signifier)', *Screen*, 18(4): 1977–1978.

Mulvey, L. (1975) 'Visual pleasure and narrative cinema', *Screen*, 16(3): 6–18.

Mulvey, L. (1989) *Visual and Other Pleasures*. London: Macmillan.

Münsterberg, H. (1916) *The Film: A Psychological Study*. New York: Dover, 1970.

Rank, O. (1914) *The Double: A Psychoanalytic Study*. Chapel Hill, NC: University of North Carolina Press, 1971.

Ries, P. (1995) 'Popularise and/or be damned: psychoanalysis and film at the crossroads in 1925', *International Journal of Psycho-Analysis*, 76: 759–791.

Riviere, J. (1929) 'Womanliness as masquerade', *International Journal of Psycho-Analysis*, 10: 303–313.

Sartre, J-P. (1984) *The Freud Scenario*, ed. J-B. Pontalis. London: Verso, 1985.

Winnicott, D. W. (1971) *Playing and Reality*. London: Tavistock.

Žižek, S. (1992) *Enjoy Your Symptom! Jacques Lacan in Hollywood and Out*. London and New York: Routledge.

Set and stage

1

THE INNER AND OUTER WORLDS OF THE FILMMAKER'S TEMPORARY SOCIAL STRUCTURE

Bernardo Bertolucci, Fiona Shaw and Chris Mawson

Chris Mawson (CM)   There is a focus to this panel which is as follows. The filmmaking enterprise involves the creation of a large group, or 'colony', with its own particular anxieties, about which only filmmakers would know. A psychoanalyst could not know these experiences, could, perhaps, guess what the anxieties are likely to be and, indeed, could form guesses about what else might be involved. So, as filmmakers, you have the pleasures and the pains, presumably, of getting together with other people, some of whom you get on with, some of whom perhaps not, but you have to get together and make a film. So that is the focus of this panel: the significance of the working relationships formed when you make a film.

Our guests on this panel alongside yourselves, the audience, are film director Bernardo Bertolucci, and actor on stage and screen, Fiona Shaw.

In an interview with Andrea Sabbadini in 1997, Bernardo Bertolucci said that psychoanalysis was, for him, 'like an additional lens'. Psychoanalysis itself, if one thinks about all of its different applications, involves using different lenses, or different perspectives, on the same phenomena. There is a tradition in modern thought which says that there are no phenomena that may be said to exist 'out there', that they arise, by a process of construction, from the interpretation of a 'text'.

In contrast to this postmodern assumption, I will be paying attention to what I hear today from the approach which says that the social and psychological phenomena are there, all the time, but that we have to try and find ways to observe them.

In this same interview with Andrea Sabbadini, Bernardo Bertolucci said that it is very rare to have a collective dream together, that is: 'We are dreaming with

19

open eyes the same dream which is the movie which we receive in different ways. And it is not the real time of a wristwatch. And characters are not what they seem.'

In my view, what Bernardo was also getting at in that interview was that, as in analysis, things represent other things: there is a slippage.

Fiona Shaw is one of the finest classical actors. She may be less known to some of you because a lot of her work has been on the stage, but that was one of the important reasons why we wanted her here today, because it may be that she can bring her experience of the stage, as well as of the set, to bear on this discussion.

What I have asked both Fiona Shaw and Bernardo Bertolucci to do is to bring to the discussion some of their experience of working with other people in making films. They have got great freedom, as well as a great amount of choice, as to what they pick from. And if there are any links that can be made with the world of psychoanalysis and other organizations, these too will be considered.

Bernardo Bertolucci (BB)   For a long time I thought that a movie was the expression of one person. That's why I started making movies when I was very, very young, and I was coming straight from the experience of being a poet. Poets like to work alone; even if they write their poems on a bus ticket, sitting on a crowded bus, they are alone.

Also, it was the beginning of the Sixties when I started, and the idea of the '*auteur*', the author, was very imposing. So, I was writing my films and I was directing my films, and I thought that I was alone on the set. I loved the confusion on the set because it made me feel even more alone. Later, in the years between 1971 and 1974, I had no choice but to change my mind.

I could pinpoint exactly when I changed my mind and had to capitulate: it was during the shoot of *1900* (1976). I had to accept that the film was also the expression and the result of a collective creation. Everybody in the crew, everybody on the set, participates in my movies. Maybe they don't know it, some of them, but I know that they are part of my creation. For a moment, while doing *1900*, I even thought that the film was much more sensitive than what was written on the box: 400 ASA, 500 ASA, 1000 ASA, for in fact the film can really absorb the feelings of the people around the camera, not only of the people in front and of the director behind. I think that that occasion on the shoot of *1900* when I changed my mind about who makes a film, who is the author of a film, is central to the theme of our discussion here.

The shoot of *1900* was, I think, the longest shooting of an Italian movie. It went on for forty-seven, forty-eight weeks, almost a year, and that is because the story of the film was following the life of two characters – the son of the landowner and the son of the farmer – walking in to the new century. I wanted to give the rhythm of this life to the seasons of the year: the adolescence and the birth of adolescence was during the summer, then they were growing up, and

Plate 1 1900 (Bernardo Bertolucci 1976)

then it was the Fall, and this is when Fascism starts, and then the winter is where Fascism finds its resistance, and then, in the spring, we have the war and the liberation. In fact, the whole movie is contained in one day, April 25th 1945, which is Liberation Day.

It was a film that was supposed to be long, a kind of 'epic'. I wanted to remind Italy that our past, our very close past, was a culture of agriculture, that our grandparents had worked on the land. We shot the whole of *1900* in the places where I was born, and for a few years grew up, in a triangle called the Po Valley in between Parma, Mantova and Cremona. We needed a lot of people to work on the film, so I took with me, from Rome, about 120 people, including electricians, costume-people, design-people, assistants, actors, and so on. I began to view that group of people like a peaceful occupational army, in a way. We were going into these factories with all our trucks, our generators, our walkie-talkies (the first walkie-talkies around!) and I was looking at them and at us, asking myself the following question: what is this strange creature, what is the body of this strange creature which is the 'togetherness' of all these people? Is it a family? Is it a classroom? Is it the team following a rock-star, preparing the stage for a concert?

At the end I realized that it was a kind of utopian, little independent republic. But it could also very well have appeared like a family. I have problems in saying that it was a family, because if it was a family, it would mean my accepting that

Plate 2 1900 (Bernardo Bertolucci 1976)

at that time I was a father, which I was never able to accept, because my own father – as some of you know, through my movies and interviews, perhaps – has been very, very present all of my life, so there has been a refusal on my part to actually be 'the father'! Suddenly, I saw that everybody was looking at me, like the father figure of the group. But I like the idea, because it was close to the film, that we were an independent little republic, born in utopia.

A lot of the crew used to drive back to Rome on Saturdays, which takes five hours by motorway, and then come back on the Sunday night. And what happened, I discovered, during the rest of the week, when they were working in Parma, was that they created for themselves what were, in fact, second families. Many of them had girlfriends or boyfriends, some of them were already married with children, and so for them it was quite fascinating: the fact of being very far from Rome, where they were from, the fact that Parma has some of the best food that you can eat in Italy (!) and, added to this, the fact that I had accepted the co-responsibility of the crew as authors of the film – I was trying to stimulate them and really to involve them in what we were shooting – and also because we were living through the seasons of a year . . . I think that all these factors meant that they got very attached to their second lives. It really was a case of 'a second life'.

One day, however, after nearly one year of shooting, the producer called me and said, 'Listen, what do you want to do? Do you want to go on forever?' I said,

22

'If only! It is a perfect utopian situation, why do you want to ruin it?' He said, 'Because we've run out of money, and so we have to get ourselves together and close up shop.'

So, one Monday morning I collected all the crew and I said, 'Today is Monday. By next Saturday, the movie will be finished.' That created a lot of real big problems. There were people who stopped saying 'hello' to me! They had got so used to their life there that there was even an attempt to create a union, to see if, in terms of the values of the union, this horrible idea that the film had to finish could be in some way avoided. It is not always like that, I know! But I wanted to talk about this experience.

With Fiona we were saying last night, 'My god, we haven't written anything!', and she said, 'Let's hope we don't end up telling anecdotes!' I don't know if this is an anecdote, but in any case it is the reality of what is the construction and the deconstruction of a particular 'film colony'.

Every time is different of course. Apart from the paradoxical and unique case of *1900*, in all my other movies, including *The Last Emperor* (1987), which was long, but not as long to shoot as *1900*, we really did all become very close to one another. There is even the feeling, sometimes, that the stories which happen on the set desire, in a way, to be in competition with the story of the film. That, for me, is very stimulating and enriching because I really give a lot of importance to the opportunity for improvisation. Jean Renoir, who is for me the number one director, and saint, and poet of cinema, once told me, 'Leave the door open on the set, because somebody unexpected can enter anytime and that will be the moment of real cinema'. So I always really try to give a lot of room to improvisation.

We could call it a 'family', if I accepted to be the father. Or we could also see it as a prison, because they (the film members) are in a prison, in a sense. They have to be there at a fixed time in the morning, until a certain time in the evening – of course they can have their second family after eight o'clock in the evening. And yet it is a beautiful, wonderful golden trap. And if it were a prison, then I would be the governor! A classroom? Maybe.

Now a little parenthesis. In this movie group, the film colony, there is an interior element, which is that of the actors. They are very special because they are the ones we see; they are what goes in front of the camera. At the beginning I am always terrified by the idea of having actors and not real people. I say, 'Why do we have real people behind the camera and actors in front of the camera?!' But then, at the same time, I am so in love with cinema, classical cinema, that for a moment I have to swallow that doubt, and then I get the greatest joy from actors.

I had an experience, here, which is not so different from the experience that I had from my thirty years as an honourable patient of psychoanalysis. That is to say, there is, in both, the creation of a relationship. So why do I go for a particular actor instead of another? Because in those first three or four minutes when I meet them, there are these knots, these secrets, this mystery, which I can feel will make my camera curious. What they will bring me, then, is much more than their technique. They will bring me their hidden identity, precisely the secrets that they are keeping, and that they are covering, by being actors. This is precisely what happened with Marlon Brando. At the beginning of *Last Tango in Paris* (1972) I said to him, 'Listen, my challenge here is trying to do a movie where you are not the mask that we have seen in all your great movies, but you are the person that I'm having dinner with now, at this very moment'. And he smiled one of his seductive and traumatic smiles and said, 'We'll see'.

Many, many years later, probably four or five years ago, I met him and said, 'So I was right, I made it. You took off the mask!' And he looked at me again, with the same smile, and said, 'And you think that that one on the screen was me? Ha, ha . . .'. On the experience with actors, Fiona Shaw can probably tell you things better than I can. What I know is that I float on the surface of this reality which is the – can I say *gestalt*? It is a word from the Sixties – and here are the greatest love stories, also, between me and somebody there, actors, electricians, script girls, etc. And what is tragic, and at the same time liberating, is that in that last hour, the last minute of the last day of shooting, magically, everything ends. All this fantastic being together, eating together, discussing together, all ends; and this community that is behind the making of a movie loves to be protected from reality, it's a kind of shelter.

I remember being in the Sahara Desert doing *Sheltering Sky* (1990) and one day I was kind of desperate. *Sheltering Sky* is a movie about an agonizing couple, and we were in the desert, and I felt miserable after a sequence of Debrah Winger and John Malkovich trying to make love, and yet they can't make love; it's finished, everything is finished. So I wrote a fax to my wife Clare saying, 'I'm desperate, I'm here shooting a couple divided by an invisible wall of glass. I'm suffering like a dog.' Two or three days later she sent me back a fax saying, 'While you are in the desert shooting a film about a couple divided by a wall of glass, the Berlin Wall has fallen.' And so I told everyone on the set, and they were amazed. But we were protected. I mean, it is difficult to say this today, but World War Three could happen at any moment, and I just feel really sorry that I am not on the shoot of a movie, as I would be in a kind of shelter. It's terrible but it's quite true, the kind of ecstasy you are in – at least in my position as a film-director. So there we were in the desert and what we did was to be frivolous. I went to John Malkovich and I told him what had happened and that the whole Soviet universe was fading, disappearing. And we looked at each other and said: 'I wonder what will they be wearing in two months' time when we go back?'

This is to highlight the extent to which you can tell the most deep and profound story, but the reality on the set is something else. It is like being on a Kubrick spaceship and being protected and distant, knowing that at the end of the eight, twelve, forty-eight weeks you will be kicked back into life and you will be happy.

I also just want to add something that I believe is very important. It would be really terrible to stretch all that happens during the weeks of the shooting of a movie outside of that context. This utopian republic exists, is born and it will die, *because* of that certain movie. In the case of *1900*, which is when I capitulated to the fact that a movie is made by everybody who is there and not only by the author, there were the farmers from Parma who were working in front of the camera as actors. Maybe it was coy, but there really was a big presence there, and they made me understand how much they had the movie in their hands. This presence of the peasants was incredibly important for the film, so I thought, 'Here we go, we have the real farmers and the real filmmakers, and together they make this kind of dream'. But dreams fade at dawn. And dawn is the end of the shoot.

Fiona Shaw (FS)   Chris Mawson had warned us that we might be very aware that we were speaking to psychoanalysts, and I was thinking about the fact that if psychoanalysis failed on the Irish, it certainly might fail also on people working on film because, as Bernardo said, there is a kind of magical world which is created which of course isn't just fascinating to the people involved, but is fascinating also to other people who aren't involved in it.

I cannot but see it as a family, a unit – as opposed to a school or a team or a spaceship. It is profoundly familial, and the reason that I feel that repeatedly is because most people on the film-set are, in fact, avoiding their families. Inevitably, therefore, they sort of create a new one, but the rules are, as Bernardo said, utopian, because it doesn't really matter who the father and mother are.

Last year I was in a film where Clare Peploe was the director and Bernardo was the producer, and although they were parental, I couldn't necessarily say which one was the father and which one the mother! They were nominally parental, partly because the set-up is almost medieval in its structure. At the beginning, in particular, as the entire behind-the-camera team were people that Clare and Bernardo seemed to have known for a thousand years, those of us who were just visiting were the flotsam coming in from England to Italy. We were like another family, we were very few actors, so we were a sub-family in this rather grand Italian family. And indeed, there were different age-groups and different desires: some people went clubbing till all hours of the morning, some people just ate. The eating aspect is enormous in an Italian film!

To add to Bernardo's comment on moments of happening, more recently I made a film in Ireland, on the west coast of Connemara, and I was in a caravan – you know, these habitual kind of prisons that we are given. They are prisons and they are terribly pleasant and you never want to be anywhere else – that is the really terrifying aspect of it because you have no history and you really have no future. You don't really believe that the film is going to end on the last day of filming, you feel it's all going to go on. At the end, people say things like, 'We must meet, I'll ring you on Monday!' And they do, or they don't, but it is important to say it. I think they can't bear too much reality and certainly cannot bear the reality of parting to that extent.

Yet that film was not particularly familial – it was an American film and, in the autumn of 2001, the Americans had come to this town on the very west coast of Ireland, so the next place was New York, but across the Atlantic – if you could shout loud enough they could hear you! This town had maybe only 100 people in it, and the film-people very cleverly buried all the telegraph wires which made the town look really fantastically old, and they painted the whole thing, so that it had sort of regressed into the nineteenth century in which the film was set. On the day after the terrible event of September 11th, what happened in the group – and I am being an amateur by putting this in – was that we had a discussion over dinner about what had happened in New York. Those on this side of the Atlantic immediately became profoundly alienated from the Americans, so that what had been an entirely unified group became suddenly divided into two very separate countries. The Americans, who were in a much more vulnerable state as they felt far away from their families and felt that they weren't in the right place when this tragedy had occurred, felt that they had been attacked by Martians. The lack of logic in their terror was hard to take in, unless one really absorbed their film culture. And somehow the kind of English and Irish liberalism of 'Ah yes, well, there's two sides to everything' was absolutely meaningless to them. So what happened is that this very benign dinner turned out to be very vicious, and it became quite difficult to go on filming the following day, as we were all playing lovers and friends of each other! In that way, despite what Bernardo says about people versus actors, real people I mean, I think that, because of the size of the event, the actors had to become real people, and of course became tribal people, they became absolutely representative of their own particular tribe, rather than being unified by any dizzy notion.

The other thing that happened on that set was that there was an enormous love affair that took place – and it is amazing! When love affairs happen on sets, people completely withdraw. Unlike in families, when there is a kind of ritual annihilation of an outsider, on a film-set there is a kind of target; and that, somehow, is the point, and so when a love affair occurs, people step aside and they allow it to happen; they sort of keep the secret openly. And of course the love affair itself is charged by the fact that it is built-on room service – you can see it all happening, notes being sent from one door to the other! In that way it is a sort of eighteenth-century existence, as it also was in Italy. It's terribly eighteenth-century, the whole courtly manner, and it is a kind of microcosm of the world. Well, it both is and isn't; it is a world in which anybody can cast themselves in any role and everybody will accept it.

Parentally, as I say, it doesn't have to be the director or the producer who are the parents, just because they are nominally. On other sets I have been on, for example when I worked on *The Butcher Boy* (1997), Neil Jordan could not in any way be seen as a father figure. He was completely uninterested in being the father. And if he were the father, then he didn't like any comfort on the set, he would specifically make sure that the set was uncomfortable because he felt that people worked better when they were uncomfortable. He certainly succeeded!! It's a very, very unusual place, really!

BB   You took up something I said about the real people and the actors. The reason I said that is because in my first movies the performers were not professional actors but, as we say in Italian, '*gente presa dalla strada*', 'people from the street'. Of course, then they are in front of the camera, and they have to be actors, but it is different. They are more vulnerable than actors who have a professional past, present, future.

FS   No, of course, you weren't insulting actors. But I would also add that the notion, the whole notion, that a film could be made like that now is blissful, but anathema. Most films now are often story-boarded and decided in advance of themselves, and where the actor used to be a creative person, one gets terrified that so many films are made where the actor is an absolutely secondary artist and that therefore they could be a 'person on the street' – and anyway, now there are almost an infinite number of actors, so there could almost be *an* actor for one film per life! Once it's over, you never use them again! Ideally, however, the actors hope that they are engaged in a slightly heightened creative activity of bringing some of their skill, and their personal history, I think, to films. But that takes time, and that time has been eaten into by financial producers, hasn't it, in the last few years?

BB   Maybe.

The audience

A1   The reference to family makes me think of an apocalypse. In the film colony, instead of the family dying off, one by one, over a period of time, the whole family dies at once. Only there is the potential in the inner family, as you say, to have a Big Buddha, to have a reincarnation. Your comment about absorbing the people round the camera, reminds me that on the set of *Stealing Beauty* (1995) at some point in time, we started asking everyone, 'If you were a person from Mars and had never heard of photography or film, what would you say was going on with these 125 people? What are they doing here?' One young documentary filmmaker from California came up with a wonderful answer. Referring to the black-and-white monitor that frames just above the camera, he said, 'Of course, it's a means of extracting the soul from the actors, and you see the image fleetingly in the monitor and then it goes into the black box'. So that's what filmmaking is about.

BB   Mmm. Thank you! [*laughter from the audience*] You mean that the actors are like kamikaze pilots! [*more laughter*]

A2   I was reminded of a film that was distributed some years ago that was called *Heart of Darkness*, which was made by Eleanor Coppola, and this was footage that she had shot over the notoriously problematic shoot of *Apocalypse Now* (1979). What I was recalling was the press conference that Francis Ford Coppola held at Cannes, when the film was first shown, and when he was asked to describe what had gone on he said, 'Well, it was a little like the Vietnam War, a group of people went into the jungle and went mad'.

It seemed to me, from what both of you were saying, that there is something that seems to be constructed on a film-set among the crew and everybody involved, which is like a temporary psychosis, really. It's either a refusal of, or a denial of, the ordinary stuff of the world outside, of life outside, of life as it ordinarily goes on. So what is perhaps then being deconstructed – to refer to the term that is in the title of this session – at the end of the shoot, is that temporary psychosis.

Again, in connection with Freud and dream, he described 'dream' as a temporary psychotic state, as an hallucination; so it seems to me that perhaps the phenomena are similar.

FS   I wonder whether it isn't temporary sanity, actually! [*laughter from the audience*] I mean, not to be in any way 'pollyanna-ish' about the state of affairs on a film-set, but there is often one person who is very difficult, as in all groups, and there is often a catastrophe. Often, in fact, it is the star himself who is that difficulty [*laughter at Bertolucci's reaction*] . . . often, I said!

I would say that the idea is that you very rarely see people getting out of life what they want, and living how they want to live; and it is remarkably that experience that they have the opportunity of practising for those weeks, and it is very challenging to the rest of their lives – and to everybody else's lives too! – that that can occur.

CM   That seems to connect with what you said about people getting away from their families, and something that was said in that last comment from the audience, 'Anyone can cast themselves in any role and everyone will accept it'. From one point of view that sounds like gross psychopathology. From another point of view it sounds like freedom, doesn't it? As long as there are certain other conditions that are obtaining, it is not psychopathology. It is the freedom to experiment and to use that freedom in the service of making a film.

What interests me in that is the question, 'What are those other conditions that prevent it from *just* being an escape?' Because a film that was the result of an escape, only, without a father who has got an eye on reality, as well as on the needs of the family, so to speak, would be likely to be a poor film, wouldn't it? And yet *1900* manifestly is not a poor film.

BB If you don't mind me adding a parenthesis, I was reminded from what was just said about *Apocalypse Now* that there is a link between *1900* and *Apocalypse Now*. The link is that Coppola 'borrowed' my director of photography. I had known Coppola since 1970, and it was 1977 then. I remember having dinner with Francis and Eleanor Coppola, I was with Clare Peploe, and we were all in a Chinese restaurant in Mott Street in New York. The following day the Coppolas were leaving for Manila in the Philippines to shoot *Apocalypse Now*. As they were having part of the crew which was going with Vittorio Storaro, I was telling them about *1900* and the fact that it was, in what they call now 'the first director's cut', five hours and fifteen minutes long. Then Francis excused himself from dinner because of their early departure the next day, and I remember him very clearly turning around, at the door of the restaurant, and saying: 'Ok, you made a five hour and fifteen minute movie; *Apocalypse* will be one minute longer than your movie!' [*laughter from the audience*]

And this was extraordinary because this was the complete acceptance of the fact that both Francis and myself, at that time, that is in the Seventies, were complete megalomaniacs! [*laughter from the audience*]

We could go further into the subject of the omnipotence of the film directors, and all that, the kind of childish omnipotence of the film director – and I know that Coppola experimented at least as much as I did.

A3 I was wondering how the theme of the movie, the script itself and the characters that the actors portray, inflicts or infects, or somehow creates, a different environment on every different set. What I mean is: does this little kind of microcosm which exists, differ from one movie to another because of what the movie is about? Do people take upon themselves characteristics from the film that they are at that point working on?

FS I don't think they do at all, but then I am not sure I should answer that! They *can* do, it depends on the type of film. If a film is very text-based, then it already has a musical notation that pretty well defines the attempt by that group to make that film. But if it is not very text-based – and *Apocalypse Now*, remarkably, was not, allowing itself to be made as it went along – then of course somebody has to join something. Either the people have to join the characters or the characters have to join the people. That is terrifying and, strangely, it is really not acting. What Bernardo said about *1900* is that, in a way, it is about capturing that, and if it is a psychotic state then it is very, very dangerous for all concerned. And of course the film takes no responsibility for people's recovery afterwards!

When working on *My Left Foot* (Sheridan 1989), Daniel Day Lewis lived in the wheelchair for pretty much the entire film, and the effect of his being in the wheelchair, of course, affected everybody else, made everybody feel slightly guilty about having a pint, and that kind of thing. But that was just necessary for that. Yet I think the overspill was that it took him a long time to recover from it.

29

A4   I want to come back to Bertolucci's *1900* which, for me, is one of the most important films I have seen, in particular as regards the way it was accurate, at the level of historical analysis, in its portrayal of social types, and the different roles that these figures played in the advent of Italian Fascism in the 1920s. Also, the way that it is accurate is as regards the level of individual class psychology, which is where perhaps psychoanalysis comes in, or more accurately, left–wing critiques of Freud that have been made. How far were you pursuing consciously this linkage of social class and individual class psychology?

Second, the film came out in 1977, at the time when, historically, the Left was being defeated, following its great upsurge in the Sixties and early Seventies. You spoke about the process of filmmaking being one in which you create a kind of sheltered world, but here to me there was a very close correspondence between the film and what was happening in the outside world, precisely the beginning of the collapse of the Left–wing upsurge and perhaps the threat of a resurgence of Fascism in Europe, as indeed we have seen.

BB   Yes. It was during 1974 and 1975 that we were shooting and I was very much elaborating my movies 'on the couch', in some way. I started being in analysis in 1969 . . . and it hasn't finished yet! So at that point, in the mid–Seventies, I was not conscious of everything that I was doing, but I was very conscious that one of my main duties was to let my unconscious help to create and to dig, in order to find out what the unconscious of the film was.

Plate 3   1900 (Bernardo Bertolucci 1976)

30

I like to think that I am always in a way extremely aware, but also extremely blind. Once I said that sometimes I like to move between the scenes of my movies like a blind person between the furniture of his own house. It is a balance between what you want and can control, and what you don't want and you don't have to control. The Renoir quotation was much about that. There are fantastic film directors, like the great Kubrick, who were complete 'control freaks'. Kubrick was sealed in his studio; I don't think they ever shot in real location, maybe when he was very young, but not in the famous last ten movies. He was sealed in his studio because he did not want reality to break into the movie, because he wanted to control everything. It occurred to me once that for Kubrick his going to work everyday was physically the only reality that he could allow to break into the movie – only him, only through him.

So of course I was, in a way, conscious of the fact that some of the characters were metaphors of what was going on in Italy in that period; sometimes I even think that they were too much metaphors of what was going on. I always try to find how to move between that excess of knowledge and control, and the very desired idea that it would not, in fact, be all that bad to allow, and to see, and to feel that the movie has an unconscious, and that this unconscious is coming from everywhere, just let it come, let it be.

During *The Conformist* (1970), for the last movement of the film, the last shot, we had to 'do a dolly' of the face of Jean-Louis Trintignant, and I was trying to explain to Alfredo (the head-grip, the guy who actually moves the dolly, which is the trolley the camera sits on to move it around) how to do it. You know, you have to explain how you want it to move, what speed, with what kind of feeling in the movement, and I think that I told him (and I only said this because I had just talked about it with my shrink) that he should imagine that a forward dolly movement is the movement of the baby which moves, starts to walk, towards its mother. And when the dolly goes back, it is the baby who has found the courage to move away from its mother. So the grip looked at me . . . [*laughter from the audience*] . . . but I think that the way that I told him made him swallow that kind of Freudian perversion!

A5   I just wanted to say something about seeing and the power of seeing, the power of the 'look'. The theme of this workshop refers to a 'colony' and there has also been a reference to prison, a golden prison even, which brought to my mind a short story by Kafka, *The Penal Colony*. It is the story of an inspector being taken to the site of this penal colony, where horrible machines have been devised in order to torture and create havoc. Yet, the reader is not so shocked by the machines *per se*, rather by the character of the inspector who looks, but is totally helpless. That is a helpless 'seeing' that in fact is quite tragic. In filmmaking there is not that helpless look, but quite the opposite: we spoke about the omnipotence of the director; are we also talking about the omnipotence of the look?

BB   I think what you have just said is something very beautiful and I think also that Kafka was living not too far from Freud!

A6   I am interested in what it is that connects the social structure of the team making the film, something that does not always happen in other work units. For example, you go to work very early, you work at least ninety hours a week, you do not get ill – it is fascinating that although you are working so hard you never get ill . . . maybe afterwards, but never during – you are all so addicted to making the film, whatever your role on the set may be – electrician, driver, make–up person, actor, and so on – and I ask myself: what is it that connects these people so strongly together? Perhaps in this sense there is a connection between filmmaking and other academic branches of work. One could identify a fascination with the text of the screenplay, which everybody in the team has in the form of a kind of 'book', the only book that they read in that period, and that is the basis of the whole film, that is what holds them all together. It is this fascinating creation of something human which in a way connects them all, to the extent that they really get addicted to this job (notwithstanding the reality that often they don't even get paid all that well).

BB   Personally I think that there is not a rule. Every case is different. Sometimes it is the screenplay that holds them together, but it is very rare. It is very rare that I have been able to force my crew to even read my screenplays! Perhaps I was once able to do it with the head of the electricians, but that is because he felt flattered that I was asking him to read it; usually they don't!

A6   But how are the people, the team, in this workplace different to others?

BB   That is why this festival is about cinema and not banking! [*laughter from the audience*] They are all in some way hypnotized and intoxicated, not by the screenplay but by the fact that as director, as producers, as actors, all together, you are able to seduce them into what you are doing. It is very much that, the atmosphere, as director, that you can create on the set. Unfortunately there is no one way that works every time. Every time you have to invent a different way. The same goes for actors, and these crews, the best ones, are working all the time, they are basically involved all year round. And yet every time they too . . . Maybe, it has come to me now! Maybe it is 'the compulsion to repeat'. It is this involvement which, if you succeed, without explanation, but just through your behaviour as director, in making them feel strongly, becomes extremely gratifying, in comparison with people working in banking, for example!

CM   I think that it is something to do with the inner and the outer world. Many other fields do not have this interchange between the inside world and the outside world.

FS It is to do with personal desire: everyone wants to be there, which is why they don't get sick. There is an element of healing in making something, but fundamentally it is an act of creation, not healing. It is you lot, the psychoanalysts, that have to deal with sick people!

A7 I wonder if you could say, for the sake of those of us who have not been on a film-set, something about what, I presume, has to be the discipline of the whole crew who are producing the film. It seems to me that one could draw a parallel between the intense discipline of a psychoanalysis, that allows something creative to go on in the analysis, and the intense discipline which must be there in a film crew, which allows something creative to occur within that crew. How do you balance this essential discipline without it becoming a dreadful, crushing, authoritarian control which would kill the creative process?

BB I think that the intense discipline of a psychoanalyis is the illusion of the psychoanalyst! [*laughter from the audience*] I know what you mean, but there are different kinds of analysts and the times have changed. I have been in analysis since 1969, so I have been witnessing personally the changes and from then up until now there has been a big change in what you call discipline. It is, I think, something that is very important, but often discipline is disguised, and it does not look like discipline. The same applies on a set. Sometimes you can walk onto one of my sets and think, 'Where am I? Am I on a choreographed set on Broadway of *Seven Brides for Seven Brothers* (Donen 1954)?' That is the feeling you get from it because everyone is moving as if in a choreographed ballet, especially when it is Monday and Roma or Lazio football teams have just won a match, and everybody is very happy! But I think that this kind of discipline is secret. It is something that, again, is a great balance of what you need.

Also, I was young in the Sixties, so the word 'discipline' is a word that I had to understand and accept later, because discipline was what we hated then!

A7 In fact what I meant was the discipline that was taken on by your crew. They have to turn up on time, they have to actually be there, spot on. Having a cameraman that turns up half-an-hour late – it just cannot be done. And I was thinking not of the discipline of the patient – I don't want to get in competition with you over when we started our own analysis and how many analyses we've had! – but the question of the discipline of the analyst, as represented in Nanni Moretti's *The Son's Room* (2001), where the analyst moves away from one part of his family home into another, the consulting room. It is that same sort of move into some other area, an area within which the analyst is disciplined in the service of the patient and what the patient then creates, within that setting.

FS Yes. It starts pretty early in the morning. The make-up people start at around four-thirty, five in the morning, particularly if there are a lot of people to get ready. That first hour is quite strange. It is often in the dark, and the make-up people are always very nice and there is coffee brewing or music playing, and then breakfast is served and the people are dressed. It's wonderful that it starts in the dark, I really love that. But people are on the set by nine o'clock, and of course they have to be, and the camera-crew have to have done their preparations by then too, or the thing would be chaos in a second! I think it is a very disciplined way of life, that is precisely why it is quite anarchic.

A8   An additional term to 'discipline' comes to mind, and that is 'boundaries'. If you don't respect the boundaries in psychoanalysis you will have enactments, you will have acting out, and they can be obviously destructive, so you respect boundaries which are fluid in some ways, in free association and in the transference and so forth. The same as keeping the door open on the set. And on Fiona Shaw's comment about the issue of sanity, I just wanted to add that Freud said that the dream within the dream represents reality, the play, the dumbshow, for example in *Hamlet*. So there is something very real. And psychosis does not seem to resonate, but again, just to throw out a term, a dissociative experience, an extreme form of which would be a multiple personality, some post-traumatic stress disorder where you don't have the psychotic aspect of denial – you know that you are there – it's more like avoidance for the sake of something going on internally.

BB   That last point reminded me of something I once mentioned to Andrea Sabbadini, a line of Dante from the *Commedia* (Inferno, xxx, 136–137), which I will here offer to the analysts, or those interested in analysis, who do not know it, because it is fantastic. Dante says, and it is a line that my father taught me, just as he taught me everything that I know:

> *Qual'è colui . . . che sognando desidera sognare*
> [Like he . . . who, when dreaming, desires to be dreaming]

That was said by Dante centuries ago, and if I was ever involved in a psychoanalytical institution it is this line which I would use as a motto over the door.

CM   And with that, very tellingly, we are going to have to end, since everything has to end, as Bernardo reminded us earlier about the film and the film colony.

ONE IN THE EYE FROM SAM

Samuel Beckett's *Film* (1964) and his contribution
to our vision in theatre, cinema and psychoanalysis

Ian Christie, Juliet Stevenson and Helen Taylor Robinson

Helen Taylor Robinson (HTR)   We have just an hour and a half to address
our interests in the author Samuel Beckett and his one venture into the creation
of a film, and I will begin at once by introducing our workshop panel to you.

We are delighted to have Juliet Stevenson, distinguished stage and screen
actor with experience, among much else, of performing Beckett's dramatic works
Not I and *Footfalls* for the Royal Shakespeare Company, directed by Katie
Mitchell. She also appeared in the recent Channel Four imaginative project to
screen nineteen of Beckett's dramatic works, acting in the screenplay version of
Play directed by Anthony Minghella, shown on television and also in a cinema–
screening at the Barbican earlier this year. Juliet, thank you for joining us.

We have also invited Professor Ian Christie, film historian and academic from
Birkbeck College, London University, who has a specialist knowledge of the
early development of cinema, as well as of cinema of the modern period, again
among much else. He is Irish and Beckett is very much his literary heritage and
interest. Ian, like Juliet, who discussed Beckett at the recent Barbican screenings,
also contributed to a BBC radio discussion of the same with colleagues from
the Gate Theatre, Dublin. Ian, thank you also for being with us today.

And I, Helen Taylor Robinson, will be chairing our workshop and also contributing from the angle that my experience of literature, and then psychoanalysis,
has given me. I am a member of the British Psycho-Analytical Society, a practising
psychoanalyst who also teaches at University College London and, among other
things, I have lectured and written on the work of Samuel Beckett.

After we watch *Film* all three of us will present and then invite you, the
audience, to participate with your thoughts.

The title of this workshop is intended to focus our attention on the assault Beckett makes on our conventional notions of what it is to see, to apprehend, to perceive and receive or take in. In all, his blow to our eye; capital 'I' as well as 'eye' selves.

He achieves this by his concentration of vision, his steady unrelenting gaze at one – one's self, the unit of self, the self isolated from all that might distract us, even as he shows us in the search, endlessly, for such distractions. Beckett stated about his creations: 'The end is to give artistic expression to something almost hitherto ignored, the irrational state of unknowingness where we exist, this mental weightlessness which is beyond reason.'

Imaginatively then, we might say that we are framed in the eye, suspended in the vision of one man, and must look at what he sees, which we might happily ignore, rather insistently *need* to ignore, and the tension in us, as we look, is part of the power of Beckett's vision.

Film, conceived by Beckett in words, was originally entitled *The Eye*. It is 21 minutes long; it is in the traditional two-reel black-and-white format; it is silent throughout but for the one sound – not word – '*shhh*', with a central protagonist played by the great black-and-white silent film star, here in his old age, Buster Keaton. It was written by Beckett in 1963 and directed in 1964 by Alan Schneider.

21-minute showing of *Film*

The protagonist, whom we always see only from the back until the last scene, shields himself from the perception of others, passing from a street to the stairwell of a building and finally to a bare cell-like room. All perception – whether coming from the eyes of human beings, cats, pictures (of God), mirrors or windows – is denied, removed or covered over. The protagonist then sits down to contemplate and tear up the photographs of his life. As he falls to rest, the camera confronts him with himself to denote that self-perception, unlike external perception, cannot be silenced.

Juliet Stevenson (JS) So where's the sound of a 'shhh' in it?

Ian Christie (IC) I think the projectionists hadn't turned up the sound by that time.

JS Where does it happen?

HTR When we see the woman in the street. It is very, very strange and very difficult, but I think we're going to make a go of our three very intermixed angles on it. First, Ian will set the film in some context, cinematically.

IC I am by profession a film historian, so my natural instinct is to try to place *Film* in some way, and I think it does need placing. It's an 'orphan' film, one that doesn't belong to any body of work or tradition. It has been very little seen, because it doesn't really fit into the normal process of distribution or exhibition, unlike even such avant-garde films as Buñuel and Dali's *Un Chien Andalou* (1928) or Genet's *Un Chant d'amour* (1950). It was Beckett's only acknowledged film project (although there was a version of *Comédie* made with Marin Karmitz in 1996, apparently with Beckett's blessing). *Film* was commissioned by Evergreen Theatre, an off-shoot of Grove Press in New York, which had been publishing and promoting Beckett successfully since the mid-Fifties as part of their avant-garde policy. Barney Rosset, the dynamic and ambitious head of Grove, had helped organize performances of the plays in New York and now wanted to expand into cinema. In fact, Beckett was one of three leading avant-garde writers invited to contribute to Grove's film initiative. The others were Eugène Ionesco, already famous for his absurdist plays *The Bald Prima Donna* (1950) and *The Chairs* (1952), and Harold Pinter, newly notorious after the success of *The Caretaker* (1960). Pinter's response was eventually realized for BBC Television in 1967 as *The Basement*; otherwise Beckett's script, directed by his regular American stage producer, Alan Schneider, was the only outcome, and was duly fêted at film festivals around the world in 1965 and 1966.

Despite this timing, what it immediately evokes is Beckett's early enthusiasm for cinema in the Twenties and early Thirties. At a time when he was in despair about his future, a not so young man with few prospects, he seems to have clutched at cinema as a way of overcoming these difficulties and offering a vocation. Extraordinarily, in 1935 he took the step of writing to Sergei Eisenstein, then the most famous filmmaker in the world, and asking if he could come to Moscow and study with him. Eisenstein received the letter, we now know, but unfortunately he was stricken with smallpox at the time and never replied! What would have happened if he had agreed is an interesting thought. A young New York film enthusiast, Jay Leyda, did travel to Russia around this time and became Eisenstein's pupil, and it changed the whole course of his subsequent life. So, Beckett's idea was not perhaps a total fantasy.

What we do know, according to Deidre Bair's well-authenticated biography, is that Beckett became very interested in film theory. He read *Close Up*, which was the only magazine that dealt with experimental film and aesthetics at the end of the Twenties, edited by a group of émigré intellectuals who lived in Switzerland; people like the American poet H. D. and the heiress and novelist Winifred Ellerman (known as Bryher), who were all fascinated by psychoanalysis. Both Bryher and H. D. had made the pilgrimage to see Freud in Vienna; and we know that Beckett saw the (originally) Kleinian analyst Wilfred Bion for some time in the mid-Thirties, and owed to Bion his life-changing encounter with Jung in 1935. So Beckett would have absorbed the psychoanalytic film culture which was very much the stock-in-trade of *Close Up* between 1929 and 1932 or 1933, although he seems to have felt that the Russian filmmakers, Eisenstein and Pudovkin, also championed in the magazine, were really pointing the way forward, and he was particularly interested in their theories of montage.

Film, then, evokes this period of enthusiasm on Beckett's part, which was already becoming anachronistic since this was the point at which synchronized sound and the 'talkies' arrived. By turning towards the Russian theorists, Beckett was aligning himself with the world of silent cinema that was already disappearing. We don't know in detail about his subsequent interests in cinema, but clearly this project of 1963 directly evoked the silent period, the world of the classic films built around silent comedians: Chaplin, Keaton, Laurel and Hardy, and many others. Beckett grew up seeing these, as everyone did, in the two-reel (20-minute) format which became the staple of that kind of film; and it is interesting that he chose to cast his film project in exactly that form when he conceived it many years later. It's like an exercise in personal and cultural retrieval, not unlike Sartre's celebration of silent cinema as 'a dubious phenomenon which I loved perversely for what it still lacked' in his exactly contemporary memoir *Words* (*Les Mots*, 1964).

But there is also another context for the project in the early Sixties. The final years of the previous decade had seen a renewed enthusiasm among artists for claiming the potential of film to realize *their* vision, rather than accepting the conventions of mainstream narrative. During the first phase of avant-garde film activity, in the Twenties, the painter Fernand Léger put it very well at the time he worked on his cubist film *Ballet mécanique* in 1924. He talked about artists' cinema being 'the revenge of the poets and the painters' on those who had taken cinema away from them and turned it into something commercial and routine. Around the same time, Virginia Woolf wrote inspiringly about a possible future cinema that would abandon banal representation in favour of 'innumerable symbols for emotions that have so far failed to find expression', giving as an example a fault that had occurred during the projection of a film she attended which produced a more intriguing image than the film itself.

Artists' films continued to be made, often in isolation, in many countries; but it was not until the late Forties that a new momentum emerged in America, initially due to the energetic promotion of a dancer-turned-filmmaker, Maya Deren, which brought such films to a wider critical and audience attention. Jonas Mekas would continue this work, so that by the early Sixties, filmmakers such as Kenneth Anger, Gregory Markopoulos and Stan Brakhage were recognized as major artists working directly *with* film in the way that painters and musicians did in their media. *Pull My Daisy* (1958) brought together many of the leading Beat writers and emerging New York artists to set the seal on film's place in the resurgent American avant-garde. In the following year, John Cassavetes' portrayal of the seedy margins of New York in *Shadows* (1959) seemed to provide an American counterpart to Godard's *Breathless* (*A Bout de souffle*, 1959), paving the way for the emerging generation of Martin Scorsese, Brian De Palma and Woody Allen, all of whom were active in the burgeoning New York film scene by the time Barney Rosset sought to bring Beckett to the feast.

Not that Beckett would have been unaware of parallel developments in France. He would certainly have known of the involvement of writers such as Jean Cayrol, Marguerite Duras and Alain Robbe-Grillet in French filmmaking of the late Fifties. All three had worked with the director Alain Resnais on films ranging from a meditation on the Nazi extermination camps, *Night and Fog* (1956), to the Franco-Japanese dialogue *Hiroshima mon amour* (1959) and the celebrated puzzle film *Last Year in Marienbad* (1961), which brought the challenge of the 'new novel' to a wide public, in a way not unlike the success of 'Godot' fifteen years earlier. Another writer that Beckett knew, Raymond Queneau, had seen his dazzlingly difficult novel *Zazie in the Metro* filmed with considerable success by Louis Malle in 1961. Absurdism and surrealism, however divorced from their subversive origins, formed an important part of the emerging popular culture of the Sixties.

Unfortunately, it seems that everyone who worked on *Film* was completely unaware of these traditions and new currents, because it seems to me a disappointingly inept and stilted film. The director of photography may have been the great Boris Kaufman, the brother of Dziga Vertov and a legendary figure responsible for all Jean Vigo's films, from *A Propos de Nice* (1930) to *L'Atalante* (1934), before coming to America; but I doubt if this would be apparent from what we see on the screen, which must surely be due to the actual cameraman. Schneider had already won approval for his obedient direction of Beckett's work on stage, but significantly this was to remain his only film.

If we turn now to thinking about what *Film* actually is, it doesn't only evoke the period of the silent two-reel comedies in terms of its length, but also in terms of a trope which is very common in, for instance, the Biograph films of D. W. Griffith. This is the idea of compressing a life into that short compass of between 10 and later 20 minutes; the sense of a life encompassed with such inter-titles as 'After many years . . .'. The violent ellipses that allow you to gallop through a life are here refigured as a lifetime telescoped into the series of photographs that Keaton shuffles through before tearing them up. In an interesting way this replays one of the early characteristics of cinema in a new form.

What seems to have intrigued Beckett most in tackling a film is the idea of cinema's essence as the 'look'. The script has, as an epigraph, the Irish philosopher Berkeley's famously paradoxical motto 'Esse est percipi', 'To be is to be perceived', and what *Film* proposes is a figure who is radically in denial of this principle, who refuses to be perceived, most of all by himself, until he is finally stalked and, in Beckett's curious phrase, 'investment proper' ensues. What I find most interesting about this is that Beckett sensed that you cannot quite do in film what he wants to do. If you compare the text of *Film* in the *Collected Works* with all the other play texts around it, they are much simpler, despite all their specification – 'like this', 'five second pause', 'ten second pause', 'lighting should be like this', 'absence of this'. *Film* is an equally obsessive text, but also an anxious one. A note warns us that the rich detail of the street scene 'about 1929', was dropped after being filmed, to be 'replaced by a simplified version'. Amid all his now habitual detailed prescription, there is a doubt – 'a problem of images which I cannot solve without technical help'. The intention is that we, as spectators, have two viewpoints through the film: the external E, or 'eye', and that of the 'object', O, which is in normal film terminology 'subjective'. Then, at the end, after falling asleep and so relaxing his vigilance, Keaton will be confronted by himself, and 'it will be clear . . . that pursuing perceiver is not extraneous, but self', or that O and E are the same.

But is it, and could it ever be? What is there in the film to suggest that the main narrating images *are* from a 'point of view', except that they are sometimes uneven and snatched? Through the conventions of cinema, we are all as trained as Beckett to believe that when you cut from one figure looking towards the camera to another figure, also looking, what we have is a second person, so if it is the same actor you are faced with a mysterious 'double' instead of another 'self'. I am not convinced that that was quite what was intended, which was that the denied full frontal view had been finally revealed to the horrified figure of Keaton, the self faced with the self. When it does not work, as I think Beckett knew it wouldn't, this is not a technical problem, but a fundamental conceptual problem about the nature of filmic language up to that point – although one that many gifted filmmakers were also intrigued by. On the other hand, there is no mistaking the character's desperate 'search of non-being in flight', as Beckett

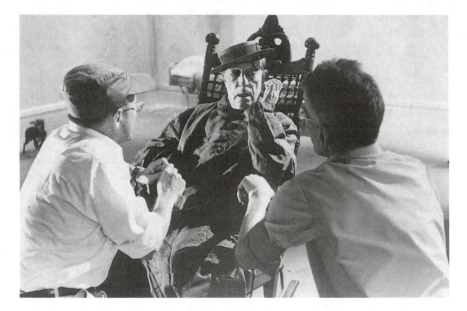

Plate 4 Film (Samuel Beckett/Alan Schneider 1964)
Source: bfi Collections

describes it; and it may be worth mentioning that a second version of *Film* was made in Britain in 1979, by David Rayner Clark, which brings greater technical sophistication to attempting to realize the film's crux, but also fails.

Interestingly, in creating the 'inadvertent' double, what Beckett and Schneider did was to go back to a key moment in cinema and psychoanalysis, their first point of contact in fact, because the very first film that attracted psychoanalytic interest was Hanns Ewer's and Stellan Rye's *The Student of Prague* in 1913, which is a film about a man who sells his soul to, effectively, the devil and is then haunted by his double, played by the same actor, who keeps popping up beside him and eventually kills him. Now this was the fictional *Doppelgänger* that the young psychoanalyst Otto Rank started from in his 1914 *Imago* study of doubles, which is what Freud talks about in his 1919 paper, 'The "Uncanny"'. So in a strange way, Beckett and Schneider, no doubt unwittingly, worked their way back to that understanding of cinema as a modern form of primitive magic, able to create a 'perfect' double and divorce perception from the perceiver, which might encourage us to ponder on the metapsychology of all film viewing, on its intrinsic voyeurism. This, of course, remains fascinating, even if what Beckett intended was merely a play within, or a rupture of, the familiar geometry of the look in classic narrative cinema.

HTR   We are going to turn to Juliet now who is going to discuss with us her responses to *Film* but also her experience from the theatre point of view. Juliet, did you have a significant something that you were feeling about something Ian said?

JS   I was intrigued by Ian saying that he thought that *Film* was badly made and badly shot. I thought it was brilliantly shot and I am intrigued by what you think is technically bad about the shooting and the camera work. It seems to me there is a fantastic harmony in the film between what the camera is doing and what it seems to me to be about. I know very little about film theory, but I thought there was a harmony between what *Film* is doing technically, in terms of the camera, and what I feel it may be about. So, Ian, why do you think it is badly made?

IC   It may seem an odd thing to say, but the circumstances were also odd. Schneider had never made a film before and never made a film subsequently, as far as I know. I think there is a kind of unnecessary intrusiveness of camera movement which muddies what the film is trying to do. I think it could have been more straightforward, and more effective by being simpler, instead of that incessant, unmotivated camera movement.

JS   I don't think there is a single unnecessary or excessive camera movement in the whole piece!

HTR   But Juliet, what are you thinking, feelingly, if I can put it like that, might have been evoked by the camera movement? The experience of watching the film? The feeling that something works?

JS   I think the whole thing works. I have no idea what Beckett or Schneider intended it to be about, I can only connect to it in terms of how I responded to it, and I suppose I respond to it partly through my knowledge of Beckett, though my knowledge of Beckett is fairly limited.

I have, however, spent a long time working on two small pieces and a short amount of time on a third piece. The two pieces I know very well, having played them nightly for months on end, are *Not I* and *Footfalls*, which constantly were echoing in my head as I watched *Film* because there are huge parallels, echoes. Beckett seems to me to be reworking similar themes again and again, though these are not identical.

I don't really understand why you feel that they have made a technical mistake in terms of the use of his second appearance up against the wall, because it seems to me that he is in refuge from himself, I mean that the camera is not us, exactly, it is him. It is him, he is observing himself, it is himself he is constantly in retreat from, as a character in *Not I* is, as to some extent the character in *Footfalls* is as well. He is a character obsessively in some form of very profound denial, so when finally sleep overwhelms him for a second and the camera creeps round and he regains consciousness and the camera scurries back, that is a brilliant moment. And I love the way the camera moves quite roughly, like a restless spirit or presence from which he is continually in flight. I love the way that he almost never settles, it is so like the dynamic of *Not I*, where the character almost never ceases to utter, and at moments when she does cease to utter, she is in danger of becoming completely uncoupled from any sense of reality at all, so she has to regain language again in order to maintain her very fragile hold on reality. The same is true of the character in *Footfalls*: she stops, she paces, nine paces, all the way through the piece. At moments when she stops she is at her most endangered because the rhythm of that pacing is somehow how she maintains her hold on reality, and on some fragile sense of safety. I thought that that was what the camera was doing in almost never resting, brilliantly, so that the actual camera work is some form of inner dynamic.

IC   I think that's what it is *trying* to do. I was watching some of Michael Colgan's Gate Theatre 'Beckett on Film' series, one of which you appeared in, and I was struck by a not very well known stage piece, *Rough for Theatre I*, performed by Milo O'Shea and David Kelly. It is really quite marvellously made, in black-and-white, with two derelict figures in wheelchairs, and it has many of the qualities I was thinking about. It is very interesting how *Film* re-creates that quality of dereliction, and yet there is also a sense in which the camera is both a part of the action but also subservient to the centrality of the performance.

What I think they were taking on in *Film* is inventing a language and making a work, all in one film, which is actually quite difficult to do. Many filmmakers spent quite a lot of time, right through the Fifties and Sixties, trying to invent new languages for cinema, and it's a pity some of this couldn't have informed the realization of *Film*.

HTR If we come back to the question of it working or not working, could we say that the whole issue of the technical business that Beckett engages with, is with things that don't work, can't work, things that stop you from working, stop you from functioning? I am just thinking about whether we can think of it not as a positive but as an absolute part of his vocabulary all the time, something that is not possible, the famous lines 'Fail again, fail better', which was what he saw the activity that he engaged in as?

Of course it is a conceit, of course it is an attack against how we think. I was trying to come to you, Juliet, not really feeling constrained by Beckett, although acting in Beckett is extremely constraining, constricting, narrowing. You said to me earlier, when we met to discuss this project, why you thought it was a good thing to be so held, in the way Beckett 'holds'. Maybe you've touched on it in a way, that the character has to be held by the movement, dialogue, as precisely as he determines. But is there anything more to say about that, just the difficulty of not being allowed to be you, yourself, one's self in a Beckett kind of a way?

JS I come as a convert to Beckett. For years and years, watching him, watching other people perform him, watching plays, reading him, I was always left outside, I never connected at all. I admired the work, to some degree, as an exercise in style, but I never connected to it in any way until I came to work on the plays, and then the very, very tortuous process of hacking a path through to the internal lives of those characters, coming to inhabit them, was a process of complete conversion, because I came to think and feel that he was, is, the great map-maker of internal landscape. There is simply nobody in the twentieth century, I don't think, who comes near him. He does what would seem to be the almost impossible thing of giving form to the totally incoherent experience of being alive, and he does that in all sorts of ways. The massive difficulty about performing him is in the parallel experience of playing characters who are so extremely chaotic, who are so marginalized, who are so right out on some edge that they are at times almost barely there. You feel that with May in *Footfalls*, that she is not quite there. Some nights going out on stage, and twice on Saturdays(!), I felt never quite sure that I was going to get out there or, in some odd way, who I was taking out there. You are held in this massive chaotically, violently turmoiled interior life, yet held and expressed by the tightest and most disciplined of forms. That is the genius of it, but that is also the difficulty of it. If you ignore the form and play with the form, pull it around and tease it apart and say 'this is driving me mad', and change it or say 'I don't like this, I think he's wrong about this', you just won't 'find', you won't make the journey. The pleasure and the torture of it is observing the score of his text – it is a musical score, to which you should be as obedient as you should be with music, and then allowing that, and only that, to express and contain and hold this kind of wild and internal life that the characters are coping with, and not coping with.

HTR   When you said you were scarcely sure you were there, 'she' (May) is there, when I quoted that bit about 'giving artistic expression to this irrational state of unknowingness where we are, this mental weightlessness', that is just what you have perfectly expressed. In other words, that what we call 'character', giving it such definition and form in the word and the meaning, is, for Beckett so not there, that is his trademark, '*not*' – *not* something, *not not not*, to get at that tiny area . . . Well, actually, he thinks it is a huge area, but an area that we make tiny in our lives.

JS   The difficulty in playing May in *Footfalls*, for example, is that I never felt I had succeeded – talk about always failing! I don't think I could ever make myself insubstantial enough, I could never reduce myself to the narrow point where she exists, enough. I was always, however much I reduced myself, however much I made the imaginary journey down to a place where no confidence exists, no love, no hope, no oxygen, no sexuality, no food, no nothing, no past, no future, however hard I tried to make that imaginative journey, I always felt that I had failed, so I was just another attempt.

HTR   That is a wonderful evocation of what is completely impossible to put into words but can be expressed in this very stylized dramatic form. Where can we go from there?

IC   I was just wondering what you felt about his exploration of radio. Already his discovery of film was a great liberation, it gave him a different way of communicating with an audience and I think Beckett became very interested in the possibilities of radio.

JS   How many forays into radio did he make?

IC   There are seven radio pieces altogether, from *All That Fall* to *Words and Music*. It is as if he was trying out all the new, and not so new, media after abandoning the traditional novel and poetry. There is also his gradual reaching out into television, with a whole series of specially written pieces. So theatre gets reconfigured; this very stylized, reinvented minimal theatre gets reinvented alongside forays into radio and television and this one venture into film.

JS   I think this film, Beckett's capacity to take a medium and write for it, is so much more successful and complete a piece of creative work than any of the

44

recent works that were made of his plays, for example. Somehow, they don't achieve what he is achieving here because they were for the theatre, and however interestingly they were adapted, I think that this is more completely a film than they were.

HTR   I will now tie in some of the things you have both been talking about. I have written something called 'As far as the imagination dictates: the form of the imagination, the form of psychoanalysis with reference to Beckett's "Film" and Freud's psychoanalysis'.

Prescript

'I have no way and therefore want no eyes / I stumbled when I saw'
(Famous lines spoken by Gloucester in Shakespeare's *King Lear*)

The opening sequence of *Film* raises, like Shakespeare's lines, the paradox of vision. The word 'film' itself, Beckett's choice of title, speaks the paradox. For film is a coating or fine covering, as well as what it has become, the name of the looked at, the engaged with, the perceived experience called 'seeing a film'.

The eye in *Film* fills the entire screen as an opening shot. 'All the world's an eye', for a long-held moment, but, to begin with, an eye unrecognizable as such, an eye shut, lidded, the heavy creases spread across our vision, blocking entry, to us and to *Film*, though this is the only way in.

Some start, some view!

Where Beckett starts always. The lid raises, the eyeball stares in silence and then the lid shuts fast. Only so much. And the shot conveys the act of looking, and of not looking, but not of anything looked at (except of course at us who look, as all will come to look in *Film*, at the agony of what's to come). So this is no normal sense of our eye, the aperture through which we come to know and be in the world, in fact the only way we can know, our eye, as the channel for our entry into. Beckett says 'No'. Because perhaps all looking for him is looking within the constraints of mentality, our mind, our mind as eye, our insides, where we are forever kept from seeing in any other than a sealed-off way. He detaches the eye from its function as our means to, and stares back at it, removed, to be studied for its doing, and its action of looking which becomes the process of *Film*. An impossible task, to study our organ of perceiving, apprehending, receiving, taking in – detached, dislocated from its place as part of us, looked at this way, which is apart from us and apart from the withinness of us, the unitary self-eye-self, 'sundered' to use his word.

And this done, a given, without sound, without explanation, without the usual and the familiar to help us. The eye on screen, full screen, staring, blinking fast shut, and taking up all the space we look at in an unrecognizable form. 'Not Eye' we could say, knowing Beckett. The Eye turned around.

Why? Don't know, can't know. (Except we know 'O Hamlet, speak no more! Thou turnst my eyes into my very soul; and there I see such black and grained spots as will not leave their tinct': previous and great artistic attempts to look within, in, at inwardness.)

The next shot is the entire screen black, slightly shiny and irregular, slightly marked, and slowly our eye begins to see another black film covering the screen, slowly, very slowly, taking definition as a surface, fronting us, black screen keeping out vision, not letting in much, and bit by bit our eye is allowed by the camera eye (has the eye we saw become the camera eye? How can we know, we can't, so much we can't . . .) to move across to an angle of white, or light, or space in the top corner. Black in plenty, light in only the corner. Formal division of our vision. To my eye, the black wall is pocked and marked and creased like the eye lid earlier; there is a similarity, both the lid and the wall keep us out, give us only a corner or so of vision through or vision to. They act as cover or film more than way through, except to 'no way through'. So what is an eye, seen like this?

We wait, we can't see, we can't know. Seeing in the trope of 'film' as 'not seeing', all this we are already in. Gradually the camera eye moves to take in buildings around the space of light and dark, black and white, to give us a modicum of hope that we are in a place, though no time (silence is time running, not time broken up into convenient sections), so still the eye here releases little to be going on with. Little to be going on with, little of mind, little of internal seeing and knowing . . . This is no sweeping eye of vision and understanding, breadth and knowledge. Centuries of seeing and knowing are out of our vision. This is eye bound, held, robbed of view. And the slow, rather aimless, forward-backward rhythm of the eye-camera, across the black wall surface and up to the corner of light, offers the circle of dark to light, in the silence, the given vision.

Jumps the protagonist into camera shot and the eye camera is galvanized, not aimless now, the figure pitiless, caught, huddled crouching away from the camera eye, a cloth covering his face, a hat over his head, a long dark overcoat concealing him, in the terror spotlight of the camera eye of knowledge. Would we want to 'be' if to be was to be perceived as this? Would we want to jump into frame, birthed into this squalid rubble of a black walled nowhere? Now there is the speed and movement of a kind of foundered 'precipitancy' (Beckett's words for the protagonist's movement across the screen) called life. The camera eye moves fast, the figure walks, falls, bumps into, scuttles away terrified, arms up to blot out the camera eye. On the way, in this race away from the penetrating eye, a couple are crashed into, the protagonist rushes past, the possibility of escape into word is 'SSSSSHed', not even words and their visions infinite, 'SSSSSH', the eye pauses and stares and horror stares back from the man and woman in eye view,

46

camera angle. The bungled chance we call human birth, intercourse? They run away from the eye. Why? Remorse? Anguish? The flight from God the creator as eye in the fall from grace, from paradisal not knowing? Who knows? The eye does not, the mind does not.

In the vestibule of the building, now in even narrower space, the protagonist pants and shakes and takes his pulse, cowers from the old woman, the flower-seller coming down with her tray of flowers; no eye sought here. She too sinks to the ground in the aftermath of the stare from the eye of the camera. The stare of blind creation destroys. The eye, when it is allowed to look head on, face to face, engenders agony, engenders collapse, presages fear, fear of looking, fear of seeing. All the opposites of the eye we know, yet true to the end, since we slowly as in *Film*, as through films of not knowing, uncover what the eye must behold, face on face.

In the cell of a room now, cornered, the protagonist covers and removes all possibility of looking and being looked upon, the camera eye remains watchful but quiescent. But by now the studied back view, and from slightly above, of the protagonist highlights the vulnerability, the attempts to protect the self from the act of closure, gives a child-like quality and pathos to our small freedoms. The despair of the protagonist's hands as he smooths his protective blanket and coat coverings over the offending eyes, mirror, window with tattered see-through coverings, eye-staring picture on the wall, creatures everywhere gazing.

No good though. No good. The circling of the camera round the pock-marked grey-white walls and the sudden coming into shot of the dark, black, malignant rocking-chair with the uncoverable eye holes set staring open in the headrest, strange black ornate foreboding in the middle of the room, that grim image of death around which the protagonist circles before settling finally, after interruption after interruption, to take his place, to review the photographs of life, the camera eye above him, in place ready for the kill, the tension of all not looking, not seeing, not wishing to look, looking no more, mounting the more we close in on the only thing we will never look on which is End, Closed Eye, or Death. Death we cannot look at with eyes (instead death eyes look on us, the two openings in the headrest unclosed) and all the speed of no time, the camera has time here, in the slow pointless manoevring we all go in for at the end – looking at and tearing up the past lookings of the eye, mother and baby, the birth of life (the hardest one to tear up and throw away), and all the while the camera waits, tries it on, penetrating the peace of sleep, and tries it on again, penetrating the rocking in peace, till up jumps the protagonist to face full frontal, full face the eye turned in on the I, the self, the full gaze of self-knowing which takes shape in the final agony of perceivedness, no escape, the unitary self, or One in the coming together of what has been sundered to allow the petty reel of black film called Life, the full coming together of Death with Life, the vision in which Beckett's eye has given imaginatively so much in so little, his artistic eye transcending.

The traditional catastrophe, as in *Oedipus Rex*, is that full knowledge is death, partial patch over the eye vision is life, and the all-seeing eye, death, takes in all. And here I would say the artist's imagination takes all, goes the full distance in 21 minutes. And creates the eye as closure, or death, where we might want to stop at the eye as opening, or life.

Psychoanalysis, Freud's imagining eye on the inner world, goes only the temporal distance we call life and reinstates what we might call the reverse, the play back of *Film*, offers the benign eye of the self looking upon the self at the chaos of internal imagery, the falsity and misconstruction of fantasy, not vision, puts the photographs back in loving order, suggests the ways of seeing once again, reinstates the flower-seller to life, woman who loved and wooed us with flowers from birth into adult sensuality, repositions the man and the woman who engendered us, Father and Mother, and kindly sets us back on the road to light, insight with the eye of self knowledge, we could say, filmically reruns, rewinds the inexorable Beckett movie we have just seen to give us another chance. And one is the mortal eye, and the other the eye immortal. The one, psychoanalysis, restores Life, the other, the artistic imagination restores Death. We are grateful in different ways to the working eye of both. But perhaps the terror that art assuages in its eye on Death brings us the peace we can only behold when we look on its creations. And without art we cannot see that we cannot see.

The audience

A1 When you spoke about the non-being, the negative, I associated Bion, and I wondered why had you not referred to the fact that, as probably many of you know, Beckett was analysed by Bion in the Thirties, when he was a young man, and I wonder also who had taught whom about the negative experience?!

A2 In discussing that last point with Bion's widow, it seems that Beckett felt it had helped him to see (be treated by) Bion but that it was not an analysis; it took place well before Bion qualified as an analyst, and Bion himself was practising at the Tavistock at the time and was functioning as he would have done, highly individualistically. Both of them probably learnt a huge amount from it. The bit of Bion that I am reminded most of, interestingly, is echoed by these masks, the one eye! [The speaker refers to the gold BAFTA Masks, one eye a hole, one eye an eye, an interesting conception for the British Academy of Film and Television Arts (BAFTA) emblem of seeing and not seeing, in the auditorium of the 'Princess Anne Theatre' where the event took place.] Bion wrote about binocular vision and how the lack of the depth produced by binocular vision can produce psychotic despair.

I was unsure about whether to see the camera as representing death, because although it is a beautifully portrayed film, as an analyst I also saw in it the most incredible malevolence in the looking. The part where we all smiled is where the living creatures were pushed out of the room, like the patient or ourselves who want to get rid of something – we open the door and something else comes in, and that happened a few times and it was also reminiscent of a lot of the early comedy, the genius of Chaplin.

The tearing up of these things, the photographs, you could see it as in the end it is all dust, and in the end all these pictures we have of our lives, but I can also see it from the point of view of the poor psychotic despairing patient who has got a severe superego, who is saying your marriage, it means nothing; your baby, your babyhood, the breast, it means nothing. Now that kind of superego that the analyst sees in the consulting room, may masquerade as telling you the realistic hard truth about life. Funnily enough, I see Beckett as *not* doing that. Even in the most apparently despairing, I don't see him identifying himself with the superego triumphing over life. What I see in the film is a psychotic hatred of life being portrayed when he is tearing these things up. I do not know how the decision was made to have him with the eye patch, but I thought that was one of the most interesting parts (monocular vision).

A3 It's a tribute, surely, not just to Chaplin, but to Buster Keaton himself, the comic bit, and I just wanted to say I also found that a great relief – and we know that Beckett is also a humorist – that this is one of his great things, that humour is also a relief from the essentially tragi-comic elements.

HTR Yes, the film is meant to be comic and seemingly unreal. But Beckett did say: 'Nothing is funnier than unhappiness'.

A4 I didn't see the end as a hatred of life. I felt that it was beautifully and symbolically a persistent pursuit of 'ceasing to exist' and there is also the metaphor of him using this silent film technique at the point at which silent film is about to die. From the breaking through of the couple, and every so often through the film the testing of the pulse (the protagonist feels his pulse throughout) it felt as though, with the cloth over his face, he could break the couple. Similarly, it was almost as if the woman coming down the stairs – because she was old – could be a mother figure, and he destroyed the maternal gaze and that every time he managed to get rid of a gaze, he would test it to see if he himself had ceased to exist. In the end, he did what children do, which is to cover his own eyes – thinking that if they cannot see anybody then they cannot be seen. At every point it was as though he was making an attempt not to be seen and therefore ceasing to exist. There was a kind of triumph in the end, and I found it quite calming that at last, in a restful way in this chair, he had managed to cover up every possible gaze, including the photographs, which would somehow keep him going, at a point where he was ready to stop.

JS I thought it was interesting that the photographs were all, in a way, conventional photographs of those periods, those rites of passage in your life, but not quite. For example, the bride was not looking out at the camera, as you might expect her to she was looking at him. Always, all the characters were looking at him, holding him in their gaze in the photographs.

A5 I felt very moved by the film and I thought not so much primarily of malevolence, but of terror. One could talk about the psychotic, but it is also like bits of ourselves which are like that, terrified of being looked at, terrified of being seen, in any way. I think that that terror turns into a sort of murderous look because it is destructive of life at the same time as being terrified; it is a sort of destruction of life, a *destroying* of life. At the end, I was impressed by some sort of peace in the rocking, but then when the camera sees him, when we see him, he too is horrified – he is horrified again. I thought it was completely ambiguous, as far as I could tell, in the end.

IC We have this extraordinary text of Beckett's, and this is a case where you can look at the text and see what the ambitions of the piece were, and you can look at the film, and there is a space between them. [The audience were given Beckett's text alongside the seeing of the film.]

The mysterious thing I find about the film is this term Beckett uses: he calls the final moment, the apotheosis of the film, the 'investment'. He speaks about the approach to the 'full investment', and the 'full investment' is, as it were, the separation of the 'E' and the 'O' (the Eye and the Object). It is the character seeing himself, it is us seeing him, it is all of those things, but why does he call it the 'full investment'? It is a very mysterious and strangely powerful concept.

A6 I wanted to say something about discovery and what is being discovered in Beckett's *Film*. A lot of people have remarked on the fact that things are not seen – things are also, of course, not spoken. But I put it another way, and that is that what we are looking at, paradoxically, is something that is both unseeable and unspeakable. In a sense what we are discovering through the clarity of our vision, and the blurring of his vision, is something that for him is unspeakable, for him is unseeable. There are all sorts of interpretations of the last confrontation, it is obviously some sort of self consciousness, but at the same time we are becoming conscious of something that hitherto has been in this blurred, unspeakable or unseeable, place.

HTR Beckett says that the first stage – the camera eye – is inadvertent; the second stage – the catching of the protagonist outside of the angle of immunity – is also inadvertent; but that the final one, the full investment, on the other hand, is deliberate.

50

A6   But, as the audience, we are also put in the position of being in a state of tension because we don't know what is being discovered by people who are actually seeing him in the film. One might talk analogously about the tensions in the consulting room, of something being there to be discovered but that is as yet undiscoverable or unseeable or unspeakable.

A7   Ian, you talked about placing Beckett historically, and the influences which led up to him. I wondered what you saw as the things that came *after* him? Do you think that Beckett has contributed to film development or do you think that he is too much of a one-off to have done that?

IC   I think there are several possible answers. In a sense this film was ahead of its time, it was an orphan film, shown briefly at festivals and then it disappeared; but I think that Beckett's influence is very pervasive in all sorts of ways. There is a very interesting book by an English filmmaker (American-born, resident in England) called Peter Gidal, a remarkable, very idiosyncratic book, that explores Beckett's influence on late modernism and minimalism, and clearly a lot of what Gidal and his fellow independent filmmakers were doing in the Seventies and Eighties was strongly motivated by Beckett. I do not think we should look for literal correspondences. For example, a comparison with David Lynch is very interesting and very apposite, but a great pervasive influence rather than a point-for-point correspondence, and Gidal as one of the channels through which that flowed.

A8   I feel that this film is to other films what poetry would be to the novel, in terms of how closely and how economically the technique echoes the message and the content. I noticed this, for instance, in the way that the camera creeps along the character in the same way that the character creeps along the walls, both the external and the internal – when he gets into his room he skims the room, to discover all the things that make him uncomfortable.

In terms of the meaning of the last scene, I share the view of people who don't think that this is the final shut-down, that this is the destructive end, in a similar way to how sometimes we would view a psychotic breakdown as an end of something, but also a beginning of something. For instance, when he was shredding those pictures, I fully expected him to shred them to such tiny bits that nothing would remain or that he would then follow it, because he is looking at the floor and we are looking at the floor as well, and we see those fragments, and that he would go and turn them in a way that he has covered all the mirrors and all the eyes, but he has left us with those remnants of photographs. I think that there is enough of an ambiguity there to say that we do not know whether that is a moment of end, of the brutality of seeing that he is killing something, or that it is actually a resolution, because after all there is the tension of not seeing we are seeing, but we do not know what that insight is going to lead to.

51

IC   It is perhaps worth remembering that the motto of the piece is 'Esse est percipi', quoted from Bishop Berkeley, philosopher and fellow Irishman, which implies that continued being depends upon perception. So one could see it as a moment of affirmation and of overcoming the terror of being looked at.

A9   To go back to Ian Christie's question about 'investment', I am of the view that there is a terror to releasing, and it seemed that in *Film* Beckett was trying always to remove the object. That was a very poignant effect, and it goes back to Juliet Stevenson's point about the feeling she had when she would go on the stage of 'was May there?' and 'was there a presence?' Without relating to an object, there is an endless sense of emptiness and there was an anxiety about having to retreat, this endless retreat, with a sense of terror, from the object – a retreat that perhaps also in clinical practice one can see in such a poignant way.

I also thought that seeing a film by Beckett, and not just the film of one of Beckett's plays, really did bring something different, something extra, that I thought was really very moving.

HTR   We could conclude by saying that undoubtedly Beckett's contribution to our vision is not in question. What we then make of it, and that is what we have tried here to do, from some specific angles of our own today, is up to us.

Reference

Gidal, P. (1986) *Understanding Beckett: A Study of Monologue and Gesture in the Works of Samuel Beckett*. London: Macmillan.

Working through trauma

3

SONS AND FATHERS: A ROOM OF THEIR OWN

Nanni Moretti's *The Son's Room* (2001)

Nanni Moretti, Paola Golinelli, Stefano Bolognini and Andrea Sabbadini

Andrea Sabbadini (AS)   In 1936 Freud wrote a paper, it was in fact an 'open letter' to his good friend, the French writer Romain Rolland, on 'A disturbance of memory on the Acropolis'. About thirty years earlier, Freud recounts, he went to visit Athens for the first time in his life and he remembered how, as a child, he knew everything about Athens and Greek culture and the Acropolis; and, because he was from a rather impoverished family, he considered going to see Athens and the Acropolis to be an impossible dream, one that could never be achieved. When, as a mature and successful man, he finally managed to get there with his brother Alexander, the shock of seeing something which he had almost believed could not exist, other than in his mind, was such that he underwent an experience of 'de-realization', or 'de-personalization' – as if it was not really happening. Indeed, he 'felt' it was not really happening.

Nanni Moretti is not the Acropolis! But, sitting next to him, I now have a similar sense of unreality, of de-personalization, as Freud did at the beginning of last century. It is not the first time, of course, that I sit next to a film director, but because of the quality of Nanni Moretti's films, one is, or at least I am, left with the sense of knowing him very personally, and very intimately through them. We know all about his character, his personality, his idiosyncrasies, his neurotic traits, his skin problems and so on. To add to the 'uncanny', '*unheimlich*' feeling that I was describing, there is the added dimension that this is a film about a psychoanalyst, like myself, and like so many of you in the audience. On an even more personal note, the son of the protagonist is called Andrea, like myself.

Furthermore, as you might know, the film takes place in the city of Ancona, and my mother's maiden name is Ancona!

This film, *The Son's Room* [*screened for the first time in Britain the previous evening, as one of the special events of this* First European Psychoanalytic Film Festival], is very different from all Nanni Moretti's other films. I consider Moretti as one of the major contributors to contemporary Italian cinema, and for our festival we could hardly have chosen a better film – both for its quality and its subject – than this one.

Now let me invite Dr Paola Golinelli, the psychoanalyst from Padova who is our Italian consultant for the festival, to say a few introductory words.

Paola Golinelli (PG)   Over the years I have looked forward to Nanni Moretti's films expecting to see, as always, an intelligent, acute, ironic and amusing presentation of a generation which proudly reflects upon its own image, putting to one side the generation gap. With this, his latest film, Moretti dramatically introduces into his representative world the theme of generation differences, and of the inevitable bereavement opened up by conflicts in the encounter between the self and the other, between father and son.

As a psychoanalyst, the strong feeling evoked by the film made me think of the opening dream in Chapter 7 of *The Interpretation of Dreams*, a chapter that is central to this text, which, in 1900, launched psychoanalysis. Who dreamed that dream, and who reported it, is not known; it is a sort of urban myth of *fin-de-siècle* Vienna. Freud takes it to illustrate his theory of dreams as wish-fulfilment, perhaps because of its moving universality and dramatic character. As you will recall, a father who has kept vigil that day over his dead young son, and later entrusts the vigil to a reliable old man, dreams that his son, now alive, wakes him up telling him to hurry because the candle has fallen onto him and is burning him. In the oneiric dimension, the 'son of the night', as Freud called him, revives, summoned back to life by his father's wish. The father thus gives him a second birth, having contributed to his first emergence with precisely his wish for fatherhood. The wish *par excellence* brings about the dream, that is, the wish that sons will survive their fathers, giving the latter a promise of eternity.

So, two themes intertwine: life and death, wish-fulfilment and frustration, pleasure and reality. The first theme concerns the birth of the son forming part of the fantasy of immortality, and as such the son must correspond, as far as possible, to the image the father has of himself, otherwise he clashes and comes into conflict with the other's diversity. The second theme concerns the son's death and poses the problem of the impossibility of working through such a loss because it signifies having to put an end to one's own desire for immortality. It is impossible to work through such a bereavement, in the same way as it is impossible to work through the bereavement of one's death, that is, to place an insurmountable limit to one's own omnipotence. This is the irresolvable, infinite, analytic task which Nanni Moretti takes on in his latest work, even giving the father in his film the occupation of psychoanalyst. Over and beyond the universality of the theme of grief, the film deals with the relationship and conflict between father and son, it unfolds its dramatic nature and its eternal topicality, and turns the death, which overwhelms this particular father and son, into the representation of a sadly lost opportunity to meet and get closer.

I shall now ask our colleague, Dr Stefano Bolognini, to present his paper on *The Son's Room*.

Stefano Bolognini (SB)   How is the work of a psychoanalyst affected by the events, vicissitudes, joys and sorrows of his or her private life? What happens in the analytical setting when an analyst falls ill, undergoes a bereavement, or any other event which makes harsh demands on him or radically alters his existence?

Nanni Moretti, the movie director and intellectual from Rome, is known internationally for his films, which deal, largely, with the conflict between late adolescent, self-centred individuals, rather unwilling to adjust, on the one hand, and conformist social environments on the other. For this, his latest film, Moretti has surprised his devotees by choosing a strong, dramatic theme: the effect of the sudden loss of an adolescent son on a hitherto serene and cohesive family.

What sets this film apart is the fact that the boy's father is a psychoanalyst, and the story unfolds, closely following the repercussions of the trauma on relations with patients currently in treatment, as well as on the family and the

Plate 5 The Son's Room (Nanni Moretti 2001)

main character. Therefore, 'the person of the analyst', or perhaps 'the analyst as a person', is at the centre of a heartbreaking, but generally realistic story, in which the exploration and representation of grief is so intense that the United States Board of Film Censors banned it to those under 17 years of age.

When the first official meeting between the Società Psicoanalitica Italiana and the British Psycho-Analytical Society took place in London, in March 2001, on the theme 'The Analyst as a Person', I deeply regretted that, since I was co-organizer on that occasion, I could not present this film, which deals extensively, and far from superficially, with precisely this matter. The film goes to the crux of the relationship between intra-psychic life, family life and the professional life of someone who has chosen such a demanding and involving occupation, where the technical aspect is inseparable from the relational context and from the analyst's own internal world.

The first part of the film presents the everyday life of the Sermonti family in Ancona, a typical provincial city, in tune with the idea of a peaceful, comfortable, routine existence. Dr Sermonti (played by the director himself) appears in the first scene as he jogs around the city. While taking a break for breakfast in a coffee shop, significantly, he is attracted by the passing of a small, colourful group of Hare Krishna followers who sing and dance seraphically, symbolizing the dream of an ideal life, proof against sorrow. In his daily life, which takes place entirely within a large apartment containing both his consulting room and the family home, Dr Sermonti alternates between the treatment of patients and the affectionate contact with his wife and children, two athletic adolescents well settled in the social context.

We are given the impression of overall harmony, perhaps even a little too much so: there are no aggressive undertones in their conversations, and the only disturbing element is an accusation by the son's headteacher that, as a joke, together with a school-mate, the boy stole a fossil during a lesson. The father's doubts on this matter – an act so out of character for this docile, well-adjusted boy – disturb him slightly and remain suspended in the otherwise virtually conflict-free atmosphere. The boy initially denies the theft, but later admits and minimizes it; and so his gesture could readily be interpreted as an expression of preconscious aggression by the boy against the institution/family, against the headteacher/paternal equivalent, and fundamentally against certain 'archeo-paleological' aspects of the father's profession itself.

The situation takes a turn for the worse when the psychoanalyst, breaking with the therapeutic setting, decides to make a call to a patient at the patient's home. This is in response to great pressure from the patient, who is in an anxiety crisis following a cancer diagnosis. As a result, Dr Sermonti decides to cancel the Sunday morning run he had planned to have with his son, and the boy then sets off to go diving with his friends. The subsequent, tragic announcement of the son's death traumatically ushers the audience into the painful second part of the film, where, scene by scene, we discover that, faced with bereavement, people have widely differing ways of reacting and working through. Thus, family bonds are in jeopardy. Bereavements do not unite but divide, Moretti says.

Parallel with events within the family, we see the psychological continuum of the working through of Dr Sermonti, the analyst, crushed and stunned by a traumatic event which has heavy repercussions on his relationship with his patients, to the point of inducing him to suspend his activities (temporarily, perhaps). One of the film's merits, therefore, is the way it represents the complexities of identity and function – the person and the analyst – which are here not dissociated. For once, the image of the therapist is neither idealized nor second-rate. The film avoids the distortions which have packed so many movies, with analysts seen as detectives, perverts, murderers, madmen and even the most unlikely of comic characters. Here, we breathe a more truthful, human atmosphere. Leaving aside the criticisms which have been levelled at the plausibility and technical orthodoxy of the analyst presented in the film, Dr Sermonti is a great deal closer to the reality of the everyday life and problems of our profession than the analysts portrayed in many other films.

The corridor Dr Sermonti walks down within his apartment, his soul increasingly burdened with grief and tension, to go from the family's rooms to the office where he works, and vice versa, symbolizes, both tangibly and spatially, the inner journey which each of us makes, day after day, session after session, to keep *separate*, yet at the same time *connected*, our personal world and the analytic function practised with our patients. This is done with humanity, and therefore *without splitting*, but with professional order and competence, and therefore *without confusion*. This is a difficult and highly refined formula which can be reached only if the analyst is well trained and is in good enough shape. The trauma which affects Dr Sermonti is more than a bereavement, and it ends up occupying much more of his heart and mind than can be accounted for by the painful loss, terrible though it is. In the labyrinth of deep fantasies, the persecutory register emerges ever more frequently than the depressive one. Sermonti's growing intolerance towards his patients is only partly explained by the fact that, this time, his grief is really much greater than theirs. Nor can it be explained fully by the analyst's perceiving the extent of his patients' regressive claims to have their needs considered, before anything else in the world. It was precisely this that had forced him to make a house-call instead of going for a run with his son.

The obscure area which Dr Sermonti seems unable to make sense of is the enigma of his son's fatal accident. Dr Sermonti makes a desperate effort to explore how the accident effectively happened, examining the nozzle, the aqualung and the valve, which his son wore when he drowned, to see whether it was jammed. A partial key to understanding this obsessive urge emerges from the film. We realize he is rejecting the irreversibility of what happened and, in a split, delirious and omnipotent manner, is cultivating the fantasy of a return to the previous situation. Incredulous, when faced with this loss and his own impotence, he longs to be able to re-decide not to go, or rather, not to have gone to the patient's house. Similarly, alongside the more mature grief for the loss of his son as a separate object, we gather the intolerability of the narcissistic wound to the family/self object conveyed in the scene with the 'unacceptable' broken teapot. Here, his inability to accept something damaged in himself, displaced onto an everyday object, is depicted with great skill.

But, on a more disturbing and obscure level, we have the psychoanalyst's constant busying himself with the dynamics of the accident. It seems to me that Dr Sermonti is tempted, and tormented, by the possible danger of an intuition: the son, who was more fragile, mild-mannered and irresolute than his sister, drove himself beyond his own capacities, forcing his way into a dangerous tunnel to chase his prey ('into the depths', perhaps like his analyst/father), to challenge his own limitations. The likelihood of this challenge is indicated after his father had given him a sharp pep-talk about aggressive determination, and the will to win. This comes at the end of a tennis match which the irresolute son had lost. It is as if, in the subsequent diving expedition, the son's attempt to regain his self-esteem, faced with an ambitious and critical paternal superego, had pushed him beyond his limits.

Reading between the lines, it is as though the illusion that Sermonti had in fact managed to defuse, or at least mitigate and check, the fearsome potential of the Oedipal bombshell, which had long lain dormant in his soul, is now broken and seen for what it is: an illusion. The dramatic refutation supplied by events only just enables him to glimpse the true, deep-seated reasons for his present inability to take on the illusions, resistance and blindness of others, even more than their sufferings. The disquieting doubt (in symmetry with the fact that his son might 'incredibly' have stolen the ammonite from the school) is that the happy, loving Dr Sermonti 'incredibly' might have in some way, through his own excessive narcissistic expectations, contributed to pushing his son into challenging his limitations.

Is this perhaps one reason why Dr Sermonti can no longer stand the inevitable immersion in the preconscious process during his analytic sessions with patients, to avoid inner contact with a thought of this nature? This 'insight' is mostly avoided, and the tension rests on the obsessive question of being 'guilty or not guilty' of paying the house-call to his patient, so that the internal persecution becomes associated with patients in general, whom the analyst can no longer stand. In my opinion, his resistance to the deep insight can also be seen, significantly, from the somewhat superficial way he asks a colleague for help. Indeed, for advice on how to deal with his professional block, Dr Sermonti does not turn to a more experienced psychoanalyst (such as his analyst or one of his supervisors), a figure of authority in an appropriate situation for considered inquiry. Instead, he goes to see a friend and colleague who has a more-or-less similar level of experience to himself, within what is presumably a public institution, who gives him some rough-and-ready, common-sense advice on how he should have a 'frank' talk with the most problematic patient (the one he visited at home). He makes no attempt to begin a true exploration of his troubled soul. Dr Sermonti, the professional man, will have to wait until Sermonti, the man, is able, with the passage of time and, presumably, with a great deal of suffering, to get into contact again with this darker side of himself.

The last part of the film is devoted to the different ways the three main characters in Sermonti's family work through their bereavement. A girl, who used to be friends with the son, appears on the scene, and the dead boy's mother, in particular, places great hopes in this meeting. But when the girl, who is in fact willing to remember her deceased friend, turns up with her new boyfriend, the parents, who had deluded themselves that they could at long last put a halt to their grief and hold on to something in their dead son's life, suffer another hard blow. Nonetheless, this meeting proves useful. Amid very human disappoint-ment, stress and embarrassment, Dr Sermonti, his wife and their daughter offer to drive the girl and her boyfriend as far as the motorway. Moved by the young couple's obvious lack of resources and the late hour, the family extend the lift from one motorway service station to the next, until they end up driving them all the way to their holiday destination, over the border in France. They say goodbye with an air of sorrowful but more integrated acceptance of the limits of their relationship (the 'border' recalls the unmentionable border between life and death which separates them from the dead boy).

This tender and extended leave-taking seems to correspond to the main characters' need to find a different time-span and way to work through the separation and loss of the object than that dictated by the trauma. The final scene, in which the father, mother and daughter separately venture onto the beach, each at his/her own pace, following a different trajectory and with different thoughts, places a question mark over whether their paths will flow back together or move apart. However, it also confirms the need of each one of them to be aware of, and follow, their own individual time-scale and way of working through, to carry out the process of reparation in search of a new internal order, by means of an effort which we realize must be considerable.

The film has a great emotional impact, as one can imagine, through a specific, powerful affect: shared emotion. Moretti seems to me to have avoided expres-sionism, and to have allowed the facts and events to speak for themselves, calling upon the spectator, in a natural and instinctive way, to be moved.

In our work, this happens when a patient provides us with elements which enable us to share profoundly what he is experiencing, in a manner which avoids two conditions: first, when the patient *does not completely empty his experiences into us*, thus *remaining himself exempt*; second, when the patient does not carry out in advance, and on his own behalf, the entire working through process, but comes into contact with us with an *unsaturated potential* which requires to be at least partially experienced and understood together.

The representation of grief in this film is powerful but not mawkish, realistic but not expressionistic, pressing but not intrusive. In psychological terms, it does not replace the Self of the main character with our Self, through an alienating psychic contagion, but leads us to share the universality of grief for the loss of a child, by means of an unavoidable 'co-emotion', which is a natural emotive development, unless certain defences come into play.

I remember a patient of mine, with her sardonic smile and a constantly derisive expression on her face, who, whenever faced with a chance to be moved or share intense emotions, would immediately say: 'What's all this tragedy? I'm not a cry-baby. We can do without all this pointless mawkishness. And now am I supposed to dissolve into tears like some child in a nineteenth-century novel?' and so on, and so forth. At the end of a long period of analysis, she no longer expressed herself this way. I believe that 'co-emotion' is blocked when it is induced and wrung out of us with manipulative techniques, to enslave us emotionally, by someone who means to control and exploit our emotions, without however sharing them in the least. On the contrary, when authenticity is perceived, our ability to be moved (to experience inner emotions with others) is a living thing of great fecundity, something to be allowed to happen within us, protected by reserve, but free from any sense of shame. It is in this perspective, as well as for its specific professional setting, that *The Son's Room* must involve us directly, both as analysts and as people.

Nanni Moretti (NM) [*his contributions are relayed by an interpreter from Italian into English*] First of all, I would like to say good morning, and although it does happen that analysts can sometimes fall asleep during sessions, I have had a cappuccino brought to me here this morning just to avoid this problem! And naturally, I have already noticed, and interpreted, the lateness with which certain people came in to attend this session!

I would like to pick up on a few of the points that have been made so far. For example, at a certain point you [Dr Bolognini] mentioned the corridors which Dr Sermonti has to pass along in order to go from his patients to the apartment and vice versa. From the very outset, from the very first moment when I started to conceive this idea, to have these thoughts, I had always planned for this proximity between the analyst's place of work, his consulting room, and his family home. Almost always, the analyst's consulting room is in one building and his home is elsewhere, often in another part of the city, perhaps in a completely different area. But I specifically wanted to have this proximity, the fact that the two places should be on the same level, even on the same floor, although naturally with two entrances (the front door of the apartment is separate to that of the office/consulting room). It is a choice which I perhaps have difficulty in explaining rationally, but thinking about it now, in hindsight, after making the film, it is perhaps that Giovanni Sermonti felt that, in order to confront the part of his place of work where he had to confront the pain and suffering of his patients, he needed that proximity, to feel close to the support of his family life and his own domestic environment. And perhaps, in the same way, the fact that the place of work is so close to his domestic environment reminds us that when he goes back to his family, notwithstanding the fact that his hours have finished, and his work is done, Giovanni brings with him the experiences, the things that he has heard, that he has lived throughout the day.

And then I wanted to say something about that sharing of emotion as discussed by Stefano Bolognini. I have had a few encounters with the public in France and in Italy, and a few people said something to me which, twenty years ago, when I started to make films, might have offended me, but, instead, now it gives me pleasure to hear: and that is that this feels like 'more than a film', that this is 'more like real life'. At the beginning of my so-called career, that sort of comment would have offended me, for the reason that, at that time, I felt that I was very much a director, that my role was that of not afflicting the public with reality, but very much reminding them that what I was doing was making a representation of reality. Instead today, this observation pleases me because I know how much work lies behind the film in terms of the work and the style that is conveyed in all that is done through the writing, the way in which it is directed, the acting and the editing.

And then lastly, I wanted to say a word about Stefano Bolognini's comment that the son might have actually brought about his own death by overdoing, going beyond his own capabilities, as a result of his father urging him to be more competitive after the tennis game. As *The Son's Room* has yet to be launched and

Plate 6 The Son's Room (Nanni Moretti 2001)

screened in many countries, I will certainly use this comment as my own in many interviews to come!

The audience

A1   First of all I would like to say how much I liked the film, which I found to be, echoing Dr Bolognini's comments, the most honest portrait of a psychoanalyst that I have ever seen represented in cinema. With regard to the proximity between the apartment and the consulting room, I thought also that what *The Son's Room* did very well was to portray the analyst's own need to understand, as well as being something which he can put to the service of his own life. The life of the analyst's patients can be structured in his psyche as a defence *against* human suffering. I am referring to the way in which Giovanni Sermonti reacts to his son's misbehaviour at school, the stealing of the stone. At no point can he just let go, like his wife does, and just say, well, '*È una ragazzata*', 'Kids do these things', but he needs to go further and further to try and understand. Similarly, there is something somewhat heroic in the way in which he approaches the suffering of his patient with cancer. What I am trying to get at is that, as I said, the film portrays that attempt to understand everything about suffering, coupled with the feeling of being wholly helpless when something beyond one's capacity to understand actually happens to oneself.

NM   With regard to the representation of the analyst, I have tried, and I hope to have succeeded, in giving him a credible character. Very often my choices as a director are influenced by my 'job' as a spectator. I will give you some examples, just dividing my films up into stages. When I was younger, initially, I was much more cerebral, I had a more arid approach to viewing films and so perhaps this transformed itself into a more formal sort of rigour and perhaps even a certain rigidity in my own work. Later on, as a viewer, I started to take a different approach, I stopped reading the critics before actually seeing the film, I allowed myself to be transported, to be moved by the films, and that gave me more space in my own work, that allowed me to give more place to 'intrigue' and to 'plot' in the story, and this can be found, for example, in *Bianca* (1984) and in *La Messa è finita* (1985) where there is much more of that.

   At the end of the Eighties, and this is speaking as a viewer, there seemed to be a return to a somewhat undervalued aspect in the cinema, which was a return to the screenplay. However, in a rather academic sense, it seemed to be that there was a return to trying to portray stories which had actually been told rather better, perhaps twenty or thirty years earlier; in other words, that this attempt was a formal way of telling stories, of giving attention to the screenplay, which lacked personality to a certain degree. Now that is a certain viewer's approach to it, therefore as a director I tried to find a freer way of describing a narrative, and so it is that in *Palombella Rossa* (1989), in *Caro Diario* (1993) and in *Aprile* (1998) I was attempting to get away from the linear narrative and to give freer rein to my feelings.

As I was listening to the comment just made about *The Son's Room*, I was reminded of the many stereotypes, those many caricatures of analysts that have recurred throughout the many, many films that I have seen in my life – and I have seen many bad films! I really wanted very much to avoid falling into that sort of stereotype. In order to give that authenticity, that credibility, to my analyst, I did have to confront a problem in terms of screenplay and direction of the film. I wanted to respect the setting, I wanted the analyst's work to be carried out in his consulting room, whereas, for example, an American screenplay-writer would tend to feel that this might be a boring thing to represent: those walls would be broken down and a scene would be presented in which the analyst takes his patient out to the park and they sit in front of a little lake, and the patient tells him about his problems with his wife, and so on and so forth. I was thinking about *Good Will Hunting* (Gus van Sant 1997), a film with Robin Williams, which was not a bad film at all, and for better or worse, right or wrong, American screen-writers and filmmakers have this fear of boring their public if they stick to those decisions. But I wanted my film, the work in my film, to be carried out within those walls, within the consulting room.

And then, with regard to the early part of the film in which the father is continuing to worry about the problem of the theft in the school, he doesn't really believe his son, and so on, I wanted with this to try and describe my character, and to describe those somewhat obsessive traits which unfortunately are part of my own character, and which burst out in the second half of the film. This was therefore a way, in the first part of the film, of giving an indication of those differences between the mother and the father.

A2   When listening to Stefano Bolognini on the issue of the passage (and the corridor) from one role to the other, I was reminded of George Orwell when he tells of his experience of restaurant work, which for him served as a representation of the passage from a period of turmoil to a public state. In Orwell's case, there is a kitchen in turmoil, and all sorts of confusing things happening, but at the moment of passing the doors, the waiter acquires a certain attitude, and then he makes his entrance onto the scene. I thought that in general what you, Nanni Moretti, have most at heart in your films is the exploring of this passage which leads from turmoil, uncertainty and rage to, at a certain moment, coming out into a public space. In this passage, what you are looking for is authenticity, and for me this search for authenticity is one of the leading missions of your cinema; that is, to be indignant and to be enraged at all the falseness that surrounds us. It is for this reason that your films have this feeling of confusion, of some kind of never-ending discussion, and then, finally, at the end of the film comes a certain perspective, and a certain opening, which is your search for authenticity.

NM   On the question of authenticity, I just wanted to add a parenthesis. I like very much the directing, how to direct actors in a film, and I also like the directing of people who simply have minor roles. In directing the extras in that basketball scene, when there is that sort of riot afterwards, I wanted to be in there too, and I was very concerned to reassure the extras not to have any concern for me, and so it was that we were all in there battling away – and we even got quite hurt! And, in the same way, I wanted to achieve that authenticity from the extras in the scene of the funeral parlour in which the coffin is closed. When I speak of authenticity, naturally, at the outset of embarking on any scene, there is the question of style to be dealt with. In that scene, where the coffin containing the body of the son is sealed, I wanted specifically to avoid a couple of short-cuts which directors typically use in confronting and dealing with death and dead people. On the one hand what tends to happen is that there is a sort of sensationalizing of death by external, affected shows of emotion. On the other hand there is the use of slow-motion techniques, or things which, in some way, neutralize, or create a sort of closing off of that experience, or else they take the option of going into the grotesque. For example, there might be a death in the family and while the body is in the bed in one room in the house, in another room there is the rest of the family arguing about money, discussing questions of betrayals and infidelities, with mobile phones ringing away, and all the rest. I even saw a French film where a burial was taking place and the mobile phone actually went off from within the coffin because the dead person had forgotten to switch it off! And so there is this simultaneously cynical and infantile approach by the director. As for my own film, once I had chosen this subject, I wanted to make a full-frontal attack on the subject. When people ask me the reason for that scene, my reply is that that scene is important, it is important for the director, for the actors, for the characters, but all as non-believers.

A3   I was thinking about the meaning of the theft of the fossil, and the way that it created a conflict between the father and the son, as it was a disappoint-ment for the father who, from the start, was unable to believe that his son was innocent, and after all he was not. When the son died then, there was this conflict, still, between them, and that made it even more difficult for the father to mourn his son. Also, I thought that in the film the daughter's part was very well done. So often in families when there is a child who has died, or one who has become seriously ill, the healthy child – or the living child – is forgotten, and I thought that in some way this daughter too was forgotten. At the end of *The Son's Room*, when the death of the son, Andrea, is better accepted, the daughter, that is, the reality of the daughter being alive, is also accepted and the three of them form a family once more. That, I thought, gave hope to the ending, and to the film.

NM   Well, the story of the fossil in the first half of the film is in order to introduce into the representation of the family and its normality, with its

Plate 7 The Son's Room (Nanni Moretti 2001)

conversations and its daily life, something different, something which would contrast with the apparent or real – or unreal – harmony of their domestic life. It is not explicitly told to the viewer, but perhaps something is about to happen. People have asked me whether, after the son's death, Paola (Sermonti's wife) involuntarily tells Giovanni, her husband, that it was in fact their son who had stolen the ammonite. I think not, I think that it remains a secret. And in the second part of the film, that obsession that Giovanni has of 'if on that Sunday I had not gone off to see the patient', 'if I had stayed with my son', 'if I had gone running with him' – all this series of ifs – if, if, if – all of that may be connected with the guilt that he feels at having doubted his son.

With regard to the daughter, I do not think that she is put aside. I think that there is one bereavement, and that there are three different ways of dealing with that grief. Her way is different to that of the father and that of the mother. Very often there is this idea of grief uniting people, bringing solidarity where there is pain, and I wanted to make a film about grief which divides people who love each other. And in fact Giovanni and Paola go into marital crisis and separate in the second part of the film. The film ends with two question–marks really, because we do not know what will happen to Giovanni and Paola, nor do we know whether Giovanni will ever be able to resume his work. I wanted to say something about the daughter, particularly, that it was a very happy encounter between the girl that was created in the screenplay, and the girl who played her, who understood the part immediately, unfortunately also for personal reasons of her own, and who brought to it that sort of immediate understanding coming to it from a more real standpoint, not just as an actor – in fact she is not a professional actor. In the school-year when we were shooting the film she missed many days of school, but I have to say, with the pride of a father, that she took her final high school exams at the end of the year and passed with flying colours! And if this can be of any interest in those resemblances between reality and film, the son had significantly fewer shooting days, and yet, on the other hand, failed his exams and had to repeat a year!

A4 *The Son's Room* had a great impact on me when we watched it yesterday, and, in fact, last night I dreamt about it! The question I wanted to ask is a very simple and in a way banal one, compared to these great questions of grief and authenticity that have been raised so far. Being, as a young boy, very fond of cars, there was one detail I did not understand in the film, and that is: why as a director did you choose (and you spoke about all those decisions you have to make as a director) the make of car that you did?! There are so many more powerful cars, especially in Italy where they produce such wonderful cars, that I would have expected the analyst to have, if not an Italian car, then at least a Volvo or something! I apologize for this egocentric question.

NM Aagh, the question of the car! It is not something I particularly boast of, but I do not give a great deal of importance to cars in my life. In one of my films, in *Caro Diario*, I made a sort of involuntary praise – or publicity – of the Vespa, the scooter. For *The Son's Room* I did not want a car that would be too ostentatious, I did not want the latest model of any given car, in order not to give any publicity to these recent models, nor did I want too much of a 'film emblem' car, like the Volkswagen 'Beetle'. So, as in my life, I eventually chose the car basically on the strength of the body-work, of the appearance, the design!

It was a little bit the same as my choice of the city in which to base my film, for that was also a choice which was made by elimination of other factors. From the very beginning, when I had the idea of making this film, I had always thought that I did not want to make it in Rome where I had set my previous movies, but that I wanted to locate it in a small seaside city. There were other possibilities, for example, a city like Trieste, but that turned out to be too big and important: Trieste has a symbolic aspect, it is a border town, it is of importance in terms of the history of psychoanalysis – it has all these characteristics. Then there was another seaside town, but this was too pretty, too picturesque, so that was ruled out. Another city in question was already the territory, the domain, which was associated with another film director who always based his work there, so that too was ruled out, and in the end it was Ancona.

I also wanted to add a last point on the humane nature of this analyst. It was of importance to me that he should not only be a credible character, but also that there should be a sense of connection of emotions, which connected him to his patients . . .

A5 [*interrupting*]   You say that you wanted to make a credible character. I have one very big objection: in Germany, psychoanalysts would not go to visit a patient on a Sunday. They would speak to them on the telephone, or maybe give them an extraordinary (extra) hour in their consulting room on a Sunday, but never would they go with them to their own house. I think that it is a problem for the son and the father, that the father does not allow his son to grow apart from him. The son said to the mother that he was unable to tell the father about the ammonite because 'daddy is so happy' and he did not want to disturb this happiness of the father. In my view this aspect too is a difficult character-trait of a psychoanalyst who is far too sympathetic.

NM   Perhaps in another country an analyst would never go and visit his patient on a Sunday; instead in Italy, in a film of mine, he would! I am sorry for those people in other places, I am sorry for the analysts there also, and I am above all sorry for the patients! My analyst does his work with humanity, and he knows that there are some situations when one makes exceptions to the rules and that there are situations that are urgent situations.

Anyway, to go back to humanity, which I was speaking about before I was interrupted, when I was writing the screenplay some Italian analyst friends of mine brought to my attention an essay, written by an Italian analyst called Luciana Nissim Momigliano, entitled 'Two people talking in a room' which deals with the human relationship between analyst and patient and the nature of the feelings between these people. This essay highlights some very beautiful and very important things, but I was astonished nonetheless to find that, in the history of psychoanalysis, these things were only being written about in 1983 and not a long time before.

A6   There is a sense of the future at the end of *The Son's Room* which we have perhaps not yet underlined, and that is the scene where the two young adolescents, Arianna and Stefano, take off at the end of the film.

NM   As regards that sense of future and the two adolescents, it is clear that Andrea's father, mother and sister will never be the same people again. They cannot forget, and nor do they want to forget; their life will never be the same. And yet, at the end of the film, something moves, something has become unblocked. Until the end of the film they had been closed up in their rooms, closed in with their suffering, and then there is a movement, both in physical, geographical terms, and in psychological terms. Now, something begins to unblock, there is the beginning of an opening up to others and to the outside. Their pain, too, is perhaps beginning to change into something else.

A7 I also felt that at the end there are two question-marks regarding the future, but I think that *The Son's Room* supplied more clues as to a possible reconciliation and rearrangement of the family than it did to that of Giovanni's return to work. There was something a bit more fatalistic about the work issue and, paradoxically, I think it was related to the scene where the protagonist consults a colleague who suggests to him that he must speak with the patient – the particular patient whose house he went to, which made him cancel the jogging plan – and Giovanni says to him 'No, I cannot do that'. What we are encountering here is a certain confrontation between two theoretical trends in psychoanalysis. The consultant's suggestion is closer to the paper you, Nanni Moretti, just quoted, to the Ferenczi tradition, to the intersubjective trends of psychoanalysis, to a feeling that, at some moments, the roles are erased and that there is a necessity to share something very personal in order to allow the analytic process to re-emerge. The protagonist, on the other hand, for very understandable emotional reasons, but maybe also for professional or theoretical credo, feels that without the role and without a certain objectivity, work cannot go on, and thus he laments his loss of objectivity. My feeling, again as an analyst, is that only at the moment when Giovanni could acknowledge what he went through to his own patients, not just factually but, in some way, acknowledging his experience emotionally and hence allowing *them* to help *him*, only then can he, too, allow himself to start helping them again.

NM In the scene of the teapot, for example, after the priest's rather unfortunate comments, what we understand is that Giovanni is not just cross at the priest, who might have uttered a clumsy phrase, but that he is expressing his rage at the fact that here are two parents who have survived their offspring.

A8 I wondered whether you could tell us something about the experience of being an actor and a director and a screenplay writer all at once: how do you manage to change into these roles – I suppose they are all part of yourself – and what do you think that you gain by taking on all of these roles? Secondly, I wanted to ask you how you put together this work in practical terms, for example: do you make story-boards?

NM For those who do not know, many directors actually go on set with a story-board, which is a set of drawings in which the director has already drawn out the scenes which he will shoot in still images: there are the story-boards for the long shots and the close-ups, and so on and so forth. The answer is no, I do not prepare story-boards. I do not do my homework, I just turn up at school in the morning and, depending on the context I have chosen for my scene, I go through everything with the actors, rehearsing and deciding things there and then.

In terms of the way in which I perform the three separate roles of actor, director and screenplay writer, what happens is that, already at the initial stage of writing the screenplay, I am envisaging and incorporating into that the decisions that will be director's decisions and decisions related to the acting.

A9 I wanted to congratulate you on the simplicity of your films and the truth with which you agree to answer our questions. Let us put aside the theft of the ammonite, and the issue of the boy not being competitive enough and his father's suggestion to him that he play more sports. The point is that the son goes out with his friends, and then that he dies, and only here, now in the film, do we discover that he was in love. Given all this, it becomes clear that central to this film is the theme of adolescence, the adolescence of the son being that which the father found so difficult. Is this what you had in mind when you made the film?

NM For what my opinion is worth, no, I did not consider this aspect. And I am not just making a light-hearted joke when I say 'for what my opinion is worth', for paradoxically, the more one is inside, immersed in the film and as author of the film, the more one loses detachment and objectivity.

One of the issues between the father and the son, for example in the dialogue about the tennis match, is that the father fails to understand how his son does not have the competitive streak that he himself has – and this is speaking myself as someone who is extremely competitive – I am possibly the most competitive tennis player ever, and all within the boundaries of the rules of the game, for I have never taken a point illegally from my opponent! In any case, this failure to understand the son, and the way the son is not competitive, can be brought out further, in order to highlight how the father cannot understand how his son is different from himself.

As regards the question about the director – actor – screenplay writer: when I started making films, and at the time this was with a Super Eight, a camera which these days is rarely used any more, from the very beginning I always felt it natural to be both behind the camera and in front of it – in front of the camera not so much as an actor, but rather more as a person. From those very first short films, three things came very naturally to me: the first is this fact of being both behind and in front of the camera, another is that of being able to talk about my own environment, my own political and sociological milieu, and the last is being able to poke fun at that very environment, and also at myself.

A10 I wanted to highlight a couple of more general aspects of guilt that follow the death of someone beloved. One is the sheer exaltation, pleasure, relief, that one is alive oneself – this creates a great deal of guilt. The other is that you are extremely angry, somewhere, if your mourning will permit it, that your beloved person has died, and you feel very guilty about that too.

NM In reference to these senses of guilt, I – and note that when I speak about my characters I always speak in the first person – so I, the character of

Dr Sermonti, give up my work. However, this is not a defeat, any more than the fact that being able to do that job before is a victory; it is simply a question of awareness, of becoming aware that I am simply not up to doing the job. I attribute to myself a fault that I do not have, I have a far more cerebral way of dealing with these things, a much more consciously worked way than that of Paola, the wife, for example, a more male response perhaps. Paola's expression of her pain is more natural, organic, carnal even, while for me this sense of guilt is so enormous that I, the character, feel the need to unload a part of it and thus attribute it to the patient whom I had gone to visit on that Sunday, and it is in this way that I begin to feel rancour towards him. As regards the fact that Giovanni is unable to accept this death, this film is not about destiny, but about something much more terrible than destiny, which is chance.

SB Going back to an earlier point, I just wanted to reassure our colleague who spoke earlier about the Italian analyst's methods of practice: yes, usually they are human and affective, but they do not go to the home of the patient! Through all these comments it has come to me that, like after the delivery of a son, Nanni Moretti's *The Son's Room* now belongs to all of its audience. We can now not only ask questions, but also fantasize about it and reconstruct our own personal version of this story which is, ultimately, a universal story. The theft of the ammonite stone, for instance, can be understood in so many different ways. One of these could be that of an attack on the headmaster of the school, who is – as his son comments in the film – an equivalent of the father. As the father is an analyst, and in this role therefore an archaeologist, it then becomes an attack against the relationship between the father as analyst and his patients, the rivals of the son.

As regards the ending, with the two young kids, Arianna and Stefano, I think that Paola and Giovanni feel some liberation through this experience, because they need the time for some company, for greetings and comings together and separating from taking sides, they need to be in a different time and a different way to that of their traumatic reality with their son. And so on: we can fantasize, we can interpret and construct all we like, but ultimately this film moved us, touched us and I am very grateful to Nanni Moretti for this experience.

4

WITNESS AND PERSECUTION IN TWO SHORT FILMS

Miguel Sapochnik's *The Dreamer* (2001) and Lindy Heymann's *Kissing Buba* (2001)

Jed Sekoff

The Dreamer

Evolution Films, 2001. Screenplay by Ivor Powell and Miguel Sapochnik; directed by Miguel Sapochnik; produced by Ivor Powell; starring Joerg Stadler, Indra Ove, Stuart Bowman, Will Tacey, Sam Spruell.

In a world of the near distant future, clones have come to serve as servants, companions, lovers and soldiers. When they have outlived their usefulness, disposal centres 'decommission' these creations, a process akin to being hung on the factory line of a slaughterhouse, or crossing through the gates of a concentration camp. One clone, a former military model, a bred killer, seemingly breaks free from his disposal. He kills two of his tormentors, watches another knock himself unconscious and flees to a beach at Land's End. Alas, the freedom is fleeting. We recognize the beach as a picture hanging on the wall of the decommissioning chamber. His escape has been a dream. Full of promise, yet stillborn. The final image, sand pouring from his now dead hand.

Kissing Buba

First Take Films/APT Films, 2001. Directed by Lindy Heymann; produced by Marilyn Milgrom; starring Miriam Karlin, Philadelphia Deda, Carol Been, Raffi Columbine.

73

Two children, Tamar, a girl about 12, and Daniel, her brother, 6 or so, accompany their very pregnant mother on a visit to their grandmother, Buba. They have come for tea, cake and company. Instead they find an old woman narrowed and frightened, huddled in a small apartment whose doors and walls she has splashed/slashed with red paint to keep away unnamed dangers. Daniel notices nothing, tucked safely within the oblivious envelope of his exuberance. Tamar has no such luxury, she is leaving the blanket of childhood, peering out into a widened world that is now full of strangeness, full of pain. We see it feels too much for her. She does not want to kiss her Buba. Yet, alongside the fear and confusion, she finds sympathy and curiosity. A suitcase of old photographs becomes a meeting place, between a past in Odessa laden with lost relatives and untold tragedies, and the present in London, still haunted by old ghosts, yet ripe with the signs of renewal. A history is shared across generations, and so in the end is the kiss.

> *By twos the dead are swimming,*
> *by twos in wine they flow.*
> *On you their wine is pouring*
> *the dead swim two by two.*
> (Paul Celan, 'By Twos')

> *Both doors of the world*
> *stand open:*
> *opened by you*
> *in the twilight.*
> *We hear them banging and banging*
> *and bear it uncertainly,*
> *and bear this Green into your Ever.*
> (Paul Celan, 'Epitaph for François')

Torn

Two doors open. Two portals, two passages into a oneness, or rather into a place where we lose count, where we begin to lose heart. Our eyes walk us through the doors. One, the paint-splashed shield of a council flat; the other, a grim centurion vault that reeks of camps and ovens. Each the entrance into a kind of hell, an all too conjurable hell. What would we give to be able to look away? What would we give to have never heard the hinges squeak, to have never felt the shudder of the metal clanging?

'No one's here, I've got nothing' is the desperate plea of the grandmother, who has clearly seen too much of those who break through the doors to render something into nothing. The MX318 series clone can make no such plea. A steely, piercing silence is the only sound appropriate to the leaden indifference of the abattoir. 'Quick, inside, they get you', the Buba begs. And no amount of reason, no hardened words of a worn down daughter, no sweet sounds of grandchildren, can convince us that this is wrong. Clearly, they do get you, inside or out.

And once gotten, once the trauma of history has visited a door where no ram's blood kept loved ones safe, what then? The doors of these two films open us precisely, incisively upon this question. A question of the gotten and the forgotten. A question of mourning and remembrance. A question of persecution and witness.

Another few lines from Paul Celan, this time from the stunning poem, 'Death Fugue'.

Black milk of daybreak we drink you at night . . .
he sets his pack on to us he grants
us a grave in the air . . .

I want to think upon two films, *The Dreamer* and *Kissing Buba*, as meditations on this theme of 'graves in the air'. That is to say, I hope to pause with you to reflect upon the proper burial of the defamed and the desecrated. To ask the question through the imagery of Paul Celan and our two films, how do we quiet the banging doors? Or should the question be precisely reversed, how do we dare open the doors, open our ears and our eyes so that we might in some small measure answer the call of the dead for remembrance and release?

It may very well be that it is only in the small measures, the incidental details, the momentary glances, that we may grasp the answers to such questions. Lives, as well as God and truth, exist in the details, not in grand or abstract themes. A photo pinned on a wall, becomes a promise of sea and sky, of freedom, of love. A piece of cake eaten loudly, lustfully, gratefully, becomes a link for a frightened grandmother and grandchild each famished for contact and connection. Such moments, finely observed, lingered over, taken up, lead us both outward and inward to fuller worlds, to a fuller grasp of the particular.

Each film illuminates such detail. A boxed cake, brought by a dutiful daughter, may lead us to the tea rooms of Odessa, or dark cafés off Finchley Road, to childhood memories of sweets and grandparents, or to echoes of hunger, desperation, fear. A pin-up photo glanced by a desperate prisoner offers us a life beyond prison walls where movement and daylight and kindness still exist, where struggle and freedom await.

For psychoanalysis, this movement of the particular is the dream of free association. For our films these detailed movements generate an association between dreaming and imaginative illumination. *The Dreamer* and *Kissing Buba* 'dream back' against the distortion and obliteration that accompany ruptures in our personal and collective lives.

Each of these films touches us with the poignancy of the particular, and from these poignancies we may risk, without quite knowing that we are assenting to the task, an engagement with the painful work of mourning. For all mourning, as Freud finely observed, begins in the evocation of the particular, in the bit-by-bit return of traces of lost loves, hates, experiences and imaginings. Mourning draws upon the paradox of memory, for we are haunted by what we fail to remember and released only through what we dare to recall.

Perhaps that is not the best way of putting things. What is at stake is not some ideal of grieving, but the very possibility of grief itself. How do we grieve what we cannot adequately translate, comprehend, or locate? Especially we who are not among those who suffered, who are bystanders to wounds and experiences that may be too much for memory or understanding to sustain. Pogroms, ethnic cleansing, genocide – signposts of pains unimaginable. We face at best a 'torn mourning', a grief that cannot suture such damaging wounds, but that comes to live with the tears and ruptures of traumatic experience. Each film reveals this tension and contradiction at the centre of grief and loss; each evokes for us the frayed and fragmented testimony of unassimilable suffering.

In the face of such testimony, we must admit the inadequacy of our capacities to mourn. Our grief and recollections do not bring one soul back to life, do not undo one suffered pain, one act of injustice. Yet, if we face this fundamental impossibility, rather than turn our backs, we may find something vital and sustaining. We turn with our incomplete 'torn mourning' toward an act of bearing witness. A witness who may stand against the erasures of time and injustice. A witness who speaks back against persecution and forward toward a time, as the author Christa Wolf (1977) named it, of the 'remembered future'. A future, that is to say, infused with a past that we dare to recollect and engage.

To put this still another way, we come to face mourning not as an ending, but rather as an ongoing condition. A mourning alive to the experience of suffering, but poignantly attuned to the possibilities of hope and renewal. All this is dependent upon our fragile, compromised capacities to connect to the fullness of our experience, despite the suffering, despite the risk. To mourn, we depend upon infusions of experience, upon the fullest evocation of memories, emotions, wishes, and dreams. We need the complexity of our life stories. We cannot forgo the twists without twisting and constricting ourselves in the process. And so we need stories, experiences, memories, films, that invite us towards complexity, towards an imaginative quest that turns towards rather than flees the shadows of our all too abundant pain and loss.

Dreaming

These two films bear witness for us, with us. To witness is to make visible. To bear witness is to carry the burden of such vision. Bearing witness is not simply observing something, or testifying to what has been seen – though it may often include these things – bearing witness ultimately involves accepting the emotional and psychic burden of refusing to let experience, however rupturing or painful, evaporate or disappear.

The troubling magic of films is such that we are quite vulnerable to the shadows and light that flicker by. Films enter us at multiple levels: sound, image, music; narrative, dialogue, gesture; viscerally, emotionally, intellectually, phantasmatically. And films are complicated acts of witness. Psychoanalytically, we may speak of multiple identificatory processes, that is to say, as a viewer we take up positions aligned with various levels of a film. On the one hand, any and all characters may speak to us and through us, not just the protagonist whom we are given to focus our love and identity upon. At the same time, the camera itself becomes the centre of a fundamental identification, as we look on the unfolding drama with an omnipotent, omnipresent eye.

In *The Dreamer*, we are swiftly wrenched away from the frothy, saccharine contempt of the Clone World commercials, into the unobscured coarseness and violence of the disposal process. Each shot hits its mark, and we are held fast, the doors closed firm behind us, our heads clamped tightly, anxiously awaiting the next moment, a moment that arrives in devastating, quick, electric bursts.

The Dreamer takes us, indeed shakes us, forces us to accept but not to choose (in the manner of a 'torn mourning') between several oscillating identifications. We take up the plight of two doomed clones, a hapless and helpless woman drenched in dread and sweat, and an avenging and dreaming military specimen, whose spasm of violence and imagination evokes in us the necessity of hope and emotion as well as of redress and revenge. We identify then with an experience of utter helplessness, as well as the variegated currents – love, dream, aggression – that spark a sense of power and freedom.

More complexly still, we are called to contend with less pleasurable identifications. (And we must first admit the utter pleasure of cinematic experience wherein we are offered access to danger, conflict, suffering, as well as romance,

Plate 8 The Dreamer (Miguel Sapochnik 2001)

violence, and sensuality, all from the safe confines of our seats – with food and drink to boot.)

What part of us recognizes ourselves in the anxious and guilty new 'recycler'? Do we know our own capacities for compliance, for being an accomplice, for hoping it is our good intentions, not our actions, that absolve us? (Perhaps, the filmmakers let us off the hook here, when he/we are knocked unconscious out of fear and out of harm's way.) And then, vile as it may seem, we look upon even if we try and refuse a connection with the wily old technician, and the crude, abusive, violent torturer. When films work, as *The Dreamer* surely does, they do so by enabling a deep journey through a range of identifications with victims and victimizers, through the gamut of human possibilities.

In *Kissing Buba*, we receive another gift of a textured journey, an elaborative and jagged arc that takes us through fear, trembling, and incomprehension toward the possibilities of forgiveness, remembrance and love. Again, the setting is its own character: the small room, echoing previous shelters, havens, traps; the mad paint, spewing out from some gaping wound, a life's blood of sanity and security. The grandson, sweetly oblivious to the faltering of those about him, sheds his sweater, but retains his innocence. When he jumps upon the bed, we want to jump with him, forgetting all the lumps and broken springs. We also feel the weariness of a daughter who has seen too much, and perhaps understood too little. She hopes a good nosh and a quick visit could cover the wear and tear of her own life as well.

And then we come to inhabit the place between Buba and Tamar. A fraught and fragile place. A place redolent with the risks of connection, thick with the dangerous threads that tie us to one another. It feels as if both Buba and Tamar, grandmother and granddaughter, have looked past the surface of the world, deep into the fissures that crack its calm, and both wish to look away, to not see the fracture in each other's eyes. Yet, and yet, something, something about our wish to look, our wish to connect, our wish to heal and to love and to remember, calls them back to one another. First a plate of food, then a plate of memories, and then that forgiving, linking, kiss.

Each film offers a kind of kiss as a fleeting but compelling gesture against the unfathomable pains they recall. *The Dreamer* reaches past the destructive flow, to find the momentary succour of a laughing face and a loving look. *Kissing Buba* also trusts that affection and connection are potentially restorative. We might think of these gestures as underscoring the centrality of what Bion (1967) called 'linking', here thoughts made thinkable, made 'linkable' through the restoration of emotional bonds.

Yet, two by two these films take us as well into a terrain where the very possibility of linkage collapses upon itself. The clone's escape is a dream after all, in the end he must awaken from it, back into the no-thing of the unsymbolizable, the unsayable, the unthinkable. The Buba is left in the end in the same apartment, with the same red paint, the same demons at the door, the same memories stored

78

or lost in the old and crumpling suitcase. Links form and dissolve, much as the lines between phantasy and reality, dreaming and wakefulness, the past and the present, become blurred and uncertain.

It is intriguing that such oscillations and uncertainties are inherent in both the pathological effects of trauma, as well as the potential healing that a 'torn mourning' may offer. On the one hand, trauma has the devastating impact of collapsing poles of experience. For example, in trauma reality comes to match or surpass even the worst of our phantasies, blotting out the space between psychical life and external world necessary for creative, generative imagination. On the other hand, it appears that only through a process capable of imaginatively playing with the boundaries of reality and phantasy, or those of time and space, may we restore our capacities to encounter the world as a place awaiting our engagement and response.

The power of persecutory regimes emanates not only from their capacities for physical violence, but also through their distortion and disruption of the generation of imaginative symbols. All totalizing powers demand control of the basic symbols of life – what clothes are to be worn, what art is to be displayed, what music shall be heard, what words and ideas may be spoken or thought. The banishment of space for imaginative living is the necessary vehicle for terror regimes to colonize social and psychical space. At heart, they seek to collapse a self capable of generating its own textures, so as to write their own phantasies unimpeded onto the world. Internal regimes of persecution depend as well upon a narrowing of imagination, reflection and consciousness. As Eric Brenman (1988) points out in his essay on cruelty, 'narrow-mindedness' is the necessary accompaniment to the suppression of our inherent movement towards reparation, emotional contact and concern.

Dreaming is at the heart of our capacity for generating textures. In the dream we think our way back to the world, while shielded for a time from the world's imperatives. Or to put this another way, through dream-work we weave a usable fabric out of the torn and tattered remnants of our psychical experience. We create – not out of whole cloth, but out of the psychical materials at hand – the possibility of a new thought, of a fresh message from the unconscious (hence the disturbance of repetitive dreams that keep us ever at a distance from the renewing aspect of dream life). Dreams should not be seen as alternatives to reality, but as a gathering place and process that mediates between reality and phantasy, between memory and perception, between the wish and psychic pain.

In *The Dreamer*, the dream-work offers not simply a temporary escape, or the enactment of a violent wish, bur rather releases fresh possibilities of emotion, of laughter, of love. Even as he enters the endless repetition of death, the dreamer's face alights with the spark of the new. In *Kissing Buba*, we find memory as the constitutive dream-work. Sheaves of photographs, images from the past, a record of lives gone, places once lived, celebrations once held, poses once offered. The photographs are a portal, a prayer, a search for lost time (Proust). Buba and Tamar

Plate 9 Kissing Buba (Lindy Heymann 2001)

gather together the pieces of the past, assembled as a memorial to things lost and perhaps found again.

Jean Altounian, a Parisian analyst, whose Armenian family suffered the genocide of 1915 and the historical erasure that followed, has noted that 'the capacity to symbolize and to conceive of oneself as belonging within a line of descent is surely the privilege of privileges' (1999, p. 444). Clones have no descendants, and their 'contained life-spans' and 'emotion inhibitor chips' cut them away from their progenitors. Granddaughters who shun their frightening elders lose the threads of connection that tie one generation to the next. The threat of erasure, of lost ties and bonds, stands out as starkly as the overwhelming disruption of trauma. We need means to 'dream-back' the strands that hold us to one another, strands that reach back across generations, and forward to those to come.

I have called this privilege of gathering up our memory, our suffering, and our dead by several different names: 'linkage', 'torn mourning', 'bearing witness'. Perhaps we need different names and myriad forms to face the burdens of appropriating traumatic history. Warren Poland (2000) has emphasized the silent witnessing that analysis offers to the patient's self-reflections. In Poland's version of bearing witness, we stand (or sit) alongside our patients but are not one with them. This picture of what might be termed, 'alone in this together', reflects both the unsharable otherness of tragic trauma and the transformative value of comprehending witness. At the same time, to borrow from Francis Tustin, the search for sharable or usable forms is also at the heart of the psychoanalytic process (see Milner 1989). Psychoanalytically we try to create an intimate space wherein two people come to live a life together, where two minds occupy a shared arena, and a joint set of experiences unfold.

The Dreamer and *Kissing Buba* create intimate arenas in which to explore the complexities of 'bearing witness', of 'making links', of risking a 'torn mourning'. They ache with an essential aloneness that stays with us, long past the ending credits. They each demonstrate knowledge of aloneness as an intimate possession, of aloneness as both curse and creative process. And yet each film goes further, elaborating a series of tentative, but still deeply poignant moments, where two people meet, look into each other's eyes, touch their hands to one another, and know that they have both seen and been seen.

References

Altounian, J. (1999) 'Putting into words, putting to rest and putting aside the ancestors: how an analysand who was heir to the Armenian genocide of 1915 worked through mourning', *International Journal of Psycho-Analysis*, 80(3): 439–448.

Bion, W.R. (1967) 'Attacks on linking', in *Second Thoughts*. London: Heinemann.

Brenman, E. (1988) 'Cruelty and narrowmindedness', in E. Bott Spillius (ed.) *Melanie Klein Today, Vol. 1*. London: Routledge.

Celan, P. (2001) *Selected Poems and Prose of Paul Celan*, trans. J. Felsiner. New York: W. W. Norton.

Milner, M. (1989) 'Autistic areas in all of us?', *Winnicott Studies*, 4: 4–10 [a celebration of the life and work of Francis Tustin].

Poland, W. (2000) 'The analyst's witnessing and otherness', *Journal of the American Psychoanalytic Association*, 48(1): 17–34.

Wolf, C. (1977) *The Reader and the Writer*. New York: International Publishers.

5

A POST-POSTMODERN WALKYRIE

Psychoanalytic considerations on Tom Tykwer's *Run, Lola, Run* (1998)

Annegret Mahler-Bungers

My first viewing of Tom Tykwer's film *Run, Lola, Run* left me feeling uncomfortable – a reaction shared by many of my friends and colleagues. However, to my surprise, the film proved at once to be a great success with the younger generation, not only in Germany and other European countries, but also in the United States: in the third week after its start, the film had already topped the charts. The considerations that follow are based on my own sense of frustration at the obvious discrepancy between my generation's reception of Tykwer's *Run, Lola, Run* and that of the more welcoming younger generation. Implicitly (or unconsciously), rather than explicitly (or consciously), the film seems to be aimed at young people, addressing their specific problems through aesthetic means which are part of their culture and which articulate the particular desires of that generation.

A second starting point of my considerations is to be found in the impression the narrative structure of this film leaves on the viewer, turning *Run, Lola, Run* into a cinematic event in which the very medium of *film* seems to recall its origin and its own semiotics. What remains impressed on our memory is the moving body, with Lola's permanent running and her fiery red hair recalling the origin of the 'moving pictures', which can be seen in the context of the revolution of movement, for example through the development of the motor industry at the beginning of the twentieth century (Kittler 1985, p. 125). While 'movement' itself becomes central to the film's aesthetics, the striking colour of Lola's hair, the three repetitions of the story, the flashbacks, flash–forwards and the particular locations in which the action takes place, all play with the special denotative and connotative power of cinematic art on which the similarity of cinema and dream technique is based.

Cinema and dream technique

Run, Lola, Run can be seen as corresponding closely to the ambitions of the young generation, presenting, as it does, both a wish-fulfilling dream and a nightmare. The fictitious dreamer, dripping with sweat, will wake up reluctantly after each of the first two sequences of the dream, only to fall asleep again and to dream the story once again in order to find a better ending to it. He does this until he finds a wish-fulfilling ending which will enable him to sleep on. With respect to the typical repetition compulsion it expresses, this 'dream' has the characteristics of a trauma dream: in the film, the young car racketeer Manni loses the 100,000 Marks which his boss expected him to deliver by a 20-minute deadline. This can be seen as a shocking initial situation: scared to death, Manni calls his girlfriend Lola, who promises to provide him with the money in the limited time left. In the first sequence Lola runs through Berlin to see her father, a bank manager, to ask him for the money. However, occupied with his lover and hard-pressed by Lola, her father reveals to her that she is not his real daughter and turns her away without further ado. Desperately, Lola and Manni raid a supermarket, but while running away, Lola is shot dead by a policeman. Before the story begins a second time with Manni's telephone call, we see Lola and Manni lying in bed talking about love. In the second sequence or rerun in the film, Lola manages to get the money out of the bank by kidnapping her father. This time round it is Manni's turn to die, run over by an ambulance in the excitement of seeing Lola as she runs towards him with the money. Once again we witness a dialogue between Manni and Lola in bed, serving as an interlude to the story being told with yet another ending. In this third version, Lola will single-handedly win the money in a casino while Manni accidentally bumps into the tramp who had made away with his money in the underground, gets it back, and eventually delivers it to his boss. Manni and Lola are now happily reunited and 100,000 Marks richer – a perfect fairy-tale ending.

The film demonstrates once again the similarities of cinema representation and dream technique, both being basically endowed with endless possibilities of representation and special effects. Tykwer's own explanation of what film-work means for him (for example his creation of *Run, Lola, Run*) shows an astonishing similarity with what Sigmund Freud called dream-*work*. I emphasize the word *work*, because Freud's crucial interest lay in the *way in which* the dreamer transforms his or her unconscious thoughts into visual pictures. He thus initially investigated the *means* of this transformation which he found, as is generally known, in the codes of ancient rhetoric (metonymy, metaphor, synecdoche). In 2000, Tom Tykwer wrote in an article that his films are an attempt 'to find out how to film the pace of thoughts' (Tykwer 2000, p. 3), that is to say, how to transform thoughts into moving pictures. What he is describing here may be thought of as essentially pure dream technique and, in my opinion, *Run, Lola, Run* realizes this concept almost to perfection. In watching this film we are not only confronted with a series of flashbacks and flash-forwards and associations which cross our mind – or rather, cross the screen – at a neuronal speed, but we are also placed in a surreal location and time structure. Quintessentially, what Tykwer has done with *Run, Lola, Run* is to make a screen adaptation of a special way of thinking, a special pace as it were, in which a dramatic initial situation triggers off the dynamics of accident with a variety of consequences. In this way, *Run, Lola, Run* is 'a film about the possibilities of life' and at the same time 'a film about the possibilities of the cinema' (Tykwer 1998b, p. 131).

The sense of possibility

This way of thinking has a forefather in Robert Musil's (1933) novel *The Man without Qualities*, a character he invented almost a century ago and whom he introduces as a *Möglichkeitsmensch* (possibility man) in the fourth chapter of his book:

> If you want to pass through open doors you have to respect the fact that they have a fixed frame: this principle is simply a prerequisite of reality. But if there is a sense of reality then there must also be something that you might call a sense of possibility. Someone who possesses this sense of possibility does not say for example: here this or that has happened, or it will happen, or it must happen. Rather he invents: here this could or should happen. And if anybody explains to him that it is as it is, then he thinks: well, it probably could be otherwise.
>
> (Musil 1933, p. 16)

As we can see, for those equipped with this sense of possibility the thinking process does not take place in the indicative form. Instead, the grammatical form used is that of the subjunctive, more specifically, the *conjunctivus potentialis*. This thinking does not apply only to events of the external world; the man of possibility also conceives the subject itself as being subjunctive as a mode of a self-reflective position. He considers identity not to be fixed but rather a creation in process, and furthermore he accepts the unpleasant and sometimes dangerous possibilities and uncanny abysses of his own internal world. He enjoys experimenting, he doubts what seems to be fact, he is willing to try out alternative ways of thinking and he believes in accident instead of fate. In this sense *Run, Lola, Run* is a filming of this subjunctive pace – or grammatical mode – of thinking: what would happen if Manni lost the money in the underground? How would things turn out if there were only 20 minutes left to get the money? What would happen if Lola avoided rather than bumped into the woman with the child? What would happen (flash-forwards presented in a rapid succession of slides) if this woman won a huge amount of money in the lottery or the authorities took her child away, etc.? This is a playful and experimental way of thinking, typical of children's games: 'I could be the robber and you could be the policeman . . . I could be the mother and you could be the father'. The two dialogues between Lola and Manni in bed, which take place between the three versions of the event, put across exactly this kind of thinking: 'What would you do if I died?' 'I wouldn't let you die'.

The adolescent structure

Although Lola and Manni are no longer children, they are also not real adults. As a pan shot on Lola's puppets and cuddly toys shows us, Lola still lives in her nursery, in contrast to her boyfriend Manni, who finds himself caught up in a dangerous and very tough underworld. In short, they are adolescents, and their adolescence represents the narrative and aesthetic structure of the film, as long as adolescence is understood as being, according to Julia Kristeva (1994), less as an age group than as an 'open psychic structure'. In literature (for example in the *Entwicklungsroman*), as in other forms of representation, growing up has become the figure of the uncompleted, the unfinished *per se*, for all possible identifications and drive developments, all sexual orientations, all possible courses of fate, are still imaginable.

From this viewpoint we can take Musil's sense of possibility to be the basic condition of the adolescent, a condition which the film then uses in order to experiment with the subjunctive mode of play-acting – all of which takes place within this potential space. This not only applies to the mechanics of the plot, but also to the use of different aesthetics and techniques: *Run, Lola, Run* presents us with different formats, colour alternating with black-and-white, slow motion, fast motion, cartoon film, hand-held camera and fixed camera, video and digital techniques (Tykwer 1998b). Similarly, Lola's different running scenes could be seen as corresponding to the three different modes of the subjunctive which Albrecht Schöne (1961) identified in Musil's novel: *Potentialis*, *Experimentalis* and *Utopikus*. The first part puts the question to the test: 'Can love really solve everything?' (*Experimentalis*). Since this experiment ends fatally, the question then arises of 'How could it have gone otherwise?' (*Potentialis*). Finally, the third run shows us the fantastic and omnipotent wish-fulfilment with its happy fairy-tale ending (*Utopikus*).

The '*Lola*' thesis on a synthetic background

Here we encounter a characteristic of the film which may account for the irritation I experienced on my first viewing of the film. For while its aesthetics experiment with an incredible range of media possibilities and its narrative structure offsets the space–time continuum (and thus operating with the subjunctive mode of the sense of possibility of *anything goes*), at the same time a subjectivity is being narrated which is almost diametrically opposed to Musil's man of possibility. In *The Man without Qualities* a self-definition of man is brought in via literature – in parallel with the ideas of structuralism and critical theory – which is referred to as *postmodern* in that it unmasks the bourgeois self-confident subject to be a mere surface and thus dismisses it. The Ego is understood as a void synthesis of anonymous structures by which it is crossed (Foucault 1974), as an imaginary distorting mirror (Lacan 1973) or as a marginal fact which may simply occur peripherally in the streaming of our wishes (Deleuze and Guattari 1974).

And yet it is exactly this postmodern self-definition of subject that Tykwer contradicts in the figure of Lola. The cinematic techniques that represent the sense of possibility – the artificiality of its aesthetics, the 'syntheticality' of the city, the 'museality' and 'surreality' of the locations (bank, casino), and the free play with real time, merely serve as a background against which Lola, a character who is fully identical with herself, is positioned. As Tykwer explains: 'The artificiality of the construction must be wedded with the authenticity of the figures' (Tykwer 1998b, p. 136). In a number of articles and interviews, Tykwer has repeatedly emphasized the importance for him of the authenticity, vigour and emotionality of Lola's character. In the film script she is characterized as a person who is

Plate 10 Run, Lola, Run (Tom Tykwer 1998)
Source: bfi Collections

mistress in her own house: 'Lola is blessed with a stout sense of self-confidence which is only irritated if a situation gets out of hand. This happens rarely, but if it does she breaks out into hysterics. But normally her self-image is determined by her creed: I am in charge of my life (I have my life under control) even if everything is still open and possible' (Tykwer 1998b, p. 119).

The figure of Lola seems to offer a deliberate *thesis*,[1] by which the film opposes not only the philosophical self-definition of subjectivity in postmodern times, but also more importantly the social and psychological condition of humankind in the post-industrial and late capitalistic world which, also as regards mass media, could be characterized as a synthetic, imaginary and totally other-oriented interface world.

All this serves to highlight, in my opinion, the conflicting desires of today's young generation: how can (adolescent) individuals in an adolescent society of imaginary self-definitions define themselves so as to overcome their passive role as mere objects of social forces and, at least partially, develop into self-determined subjects?

Lola seems to be opposed to the 'dangerous' aspects within the creative strength of this adolescent 'open psychic structure'. I am referring here to the danger of going off the rails when the fact of a 'fixed frame', to use Musil's terms, is ignored. In the grammar of thinking, the loss of a sense of reality would be represented by the loss of the ability to determine, identify and reach a 'truth' of some kind. Lola and Manni demonstrate such a derailment in a playful way during their first dialogue in bed. Manni's simple and clear answer to Lola's question: 'Do you love me?', namely his 'Sure!', will then be taken apart during the following dialogue. The more Lola questions Manni's metaphorical use of words (utterances which, within a common accepted discourse, would make sense), the more Manni gets confused. Lola exposes Manni's choice of words by turning their symbolic meaning into a symbolic equation,[2] so that Manni loses the subjective certainty which the frame of symbolization of language usually provides. Through the representation of these details, the film demonstrates how a subject can lose his footing by the dissolution of such reliable frames. In both dialogues, however, it is Lola who eventually clarifies things. The first exchange ends with her resolution that she must come to a decision as a *thesis* of her self. The second dialogue (in which they use the subjunctive form to play on the possibility of Manni's death) ends in the indicative with Lola's statement: 'But you haven't died, Manni' – thus bringing them back to reality.

Lola is the figure of limitation, framing and structure, and therefore represents the defence mechanisms of the Ego; Manni, her antithesis, on the other hand is 'chaotic, without orientation, instable' almost the 'perfect counter-programme' (Tykwer 1998b, p. 119). In dream theory terms, Lola and Manni can be read as two aspects of one and the same person, as Tykwer himself suggests when he writes that Lola's 'secret notion of the world's chaos is virtually embodied by Manni' (ibid.). In her desire to save Manni and 'to set up this unsteady, beloved narcissus again' (ibid.), the film articulates the wish to somehow redirect the narcissistic self-definition of the postmodern 'fun' society, to a self-definition that is more object-related.

An important motif in Tykwer's earlier films is the obsession for collecting things, as seen in several of his characters. Asked about this in an interview, the director explained:

> Yes, it's a way for me to master the chaos which is surrounding us all the time. I'm very much fascinated by every kind of system we are rigging for ourselves in order to manage all the impressions that are pelting down onto us . . . [when you are filming] you have to deal with the problem of how people are systematising their look. I have to do this with my camera, too. The gatherers in my films have such a system.
>
> (Tykwer 1999, p. 29)

This statement can be read as a definition – at both a basic and more complex level – of the workings of art: art giving a new order of reality to the chaotic impressions and experiences of our external and internal world by the means of its *form*. In this sense, the *form* is the frame of the door through which the potentially infinite possibilities of imaginable contents enter. The 'system of the look' (ibid.) – like Tykwer's principle of filming – thus is structurally the same as the containing (or the alpha-) function of the mother (or the analyst) (Bion 1962): gathering, keeping, containing, systematizing chaotic elements and giving them back to the world in an (artistic) form that frames and limits them, hence giving them coherence and meaning.

All of Tykwer's films, and in particular *Run, Lola, Run*, seem to articulate the young generation's desire for a bonding system of orientation, in order to deal with the chaotic world of possibilities – first and foremost as created by the mass media – which deeply frustrates the adolescent need for identification. Instead, the open psychic structure multiplies by almost boundless imaginary proposals of identification. In Freud's understanding of human socialization the law of the father was crucial for drive development and the establishment of a Superego (as a result of the Oedipus and castration complexes). And yet the only valid value that society seems to make available is, from this critical point of view, that of money. Today, people have the feeling that they are ruled by economic laws with principles quite different from those of the Oedipal parents, forcing the incestuous wishes towards repression and sublimation.

Through aesthetic means, above all, *Run, Lola, Run* shows the experience of the loss of a stable object within a traditional family setting. While Lola and Manni are filmed with a fixed camera, the other characters, namely Lola's parents, are shot with a hand-held video camera. The figures in these scenes are shaky and uncertain (such as in the sequence with Lola's father and his lover and in which – to add to this effect – her father's verbal manner seems to be uncertain and adolescent). When Lola begins her run, she passes her mother: the camera catches this figure of the mother by circling around her, a woman addicted to alcohol, telephone and TV. Her glance – or rather, the glance of the camera – turns Lola into a cartoon character on the television screen, as she runs down the spiral staircase. Lola seems to vanish through the void gaze of her mother as if she was losing her footing by her mother's absence (or rather by her mother's failing to be a mother). In this way, the objects are shown to be uncertain, decentred and psychically absent, a motif that is continued in her father's confession that Lola is not his real daughter.

The perversion of the man of possibilities

While the bourgeois self-definition of subjectivity is conceived as a frame, into which an intrinsically contradictory 'patchwork' psyche projects itself in order to find its identity within this image, the concept of postmodern self-understanding deconstructs this frame and unmasks this image as mere delusion. Undoubtedly, it makes a great difference whether the subject conceptualizes and reflects itself in this way and whether this self-understanding also includes the sphere of acting or self-experiencing. However, as long as the subject remains within the framework of *thinking*, framelessness and *anything goes* remain only a *thought* or a mere *reflection* – what in psychoanalytical terms would be referred to as belonging to the secondary process. Yet as soon as it starts acting out this *anything goes*, the subject is likely to disregard reality and the social and moral frame of reference, while – in the sphere of self-experiencing – it is likely to become psychotic, that is to regress into primary process.

In the latter cases we are confronted with a problematic version of the man of possibilities, in other words, a version which would disengage itself from Musil's sense of possibility. We might note that this version became alarmingly prominent in what was called the New Age Movement of the Seventies and Eighties, when our society as a whole culturally drifted increasingly into a superficial world in which, due to the mass media, the difference between the real and the virtual became decreasingly discernible.

This interpretation of society's development is a point of reference for the analysis and criticism of the young French author Michel Houellebecq, whose novels and essays are immensely influential for the youth cultural scene of western countries (Houellebecq 2000, 2001a, 2001b). Even if Tom Tykwer may not share Houellebecq's pessimistic world-view, he nevertheless appears to agree with him in the analysis of our society as it is latently represented in *Run, Lola, Run*. For both, the world of unlimited possibilities is, at the same time, a limiting world of rigid compulsion.

Houellebecq regards the world as 'a supermarket and an insult' (Houellebecq 2001b, p. 67) providing us with all the possibilities of wish-fulfilment which compel the subject to succumb to multiple, superficial, narcissistic and object-unrelated satisfaction (note the place where Lola and Manni end up: it is, of course, a supermarket). In Houellebecq's view, the virtually religious promises of the culture of advertising constitute a

> frightening, hard-hearted Superego which is far more inexorable than any commandment of duty that ever existed. It sticks to the skin of the individual, repeating to it over and over again: 'You must desire. You must be desirable. You must participate in the competition, in the fight, in the life of the world. If you stop, you don't exist anymore. If you lag behind, you are dead'.
> (Houellebecq 2001b, p. 73)

Similar utterances might be heard at the beginning of *Run, Lola, Run*. The Superego in a world dominated by a culture of advertising, as Houellebecq describes it, is persecuting, compulsive and sadistic; in short, it has the traits of the primitive, early Superego. Tykwer disguises this haunting Superego with a variety of representations of time; for example at the beginning of the film in the opening titles, the cruel face of time is presented first in the form of a pendulum and then in that of a clock which draws the viewer into its dark mouth, reminding us of the god Chronos as he gulped down his children. During the film, time and time again the hands of clocks can be seen, mercilessly ticking away as signs of the inexorable, chronological time which – in the psychopathology of everyday western life – has become what we might call a persecutory object.

A film-opera as an initiation

In the view of Houellebecq the 'logic of the supermarket leads inevitably to a scattering of desire' (Houellebecq 2001b, p. 68). In this era of *anything goes* then, we could view the wish as losing its determinable aim which, in line with Freud's drive theory, is the incestuous love object. Houellebecq recalls Schopenhauer's concept of *the will* as a 'force being organically, totally, and stubbornly aimed at completion' as a 'desire for being' (Houellebecq 2001b, p. 73).

Lola, an incarnation of this determined and lively will-power, concentrates the forces of the dispersed desires within herself. With this concentration, she puts up a resistance against the indecisiveness of the decentred *Möglichkeitsmensch*, as presented in the parental figures who, as Musil puts it, 'live with unconnected ideas sprawling out without a centre' (Musil 1933, p. 20). Lola's wish does not revolve narcissistically around the Ego, as is the thinking behind the culture of advertising, but rather around her object of love: Manni, whom she wants to save. She thus incorporates an 'altruistic morality' (Houellebecq 2001b, pp. 88–89), an attitude which Michel Houellebecq would like to see replacing the *laissez-faire* selfishness of the parental New Age generation, constantly in danger of drifting into degradation and loss of the object in question.

As a vision of an active will and a dynamic force, and being equipped with the violent emotions of fear, passion and love, the figure of Lola becomes an allegory. The symbol of the fiery hair, which marks her out, has its own cultural history in the childhood of this generation. It reminds us of the strong and independent *Pipi Langstrumpf* (Pippi Longstocking), of the stubborn little ship's *kobold Pumuckl* (another cartoon character!) and of the self-confident, free and resistant *rote Zora*. All these characters are able to resist and are equipped with a strong will, and yet they are also without parental roots. As is the case with Lola, their parents are absent and it seems that only they themselves are able to create themselves. Lola's strong will and her lively ambition are at the opposite end of the spectrum from externally manipulated desire (for example, as can be seen in the mentality of advertising), for it is her own deliberate decision to help Manni. The passionate movement of this young body, driven from the outside as well as from the inside, displays the dramatic dialectic of the subjective wish and the cruel, externally determined compulsion.

The ending

The young author Helmut Krausser writes that *Run, Lola, Run* could be interpreted as an opera, given that the music of the film is – unlike in many other films, one could argue – an indispensable part of the picture–sound synthesis and that 'here, via such cinema, many young people for the first time can experience the powers of great opera. The audience becomes a sound-box for the soundtrack, the music is no longer just a background whispering; it is experienced not only with the ears but directly with the whole body' (Krausser 1999, p. 35). Krausser goes as far as to compare the suggestive and powerful attraction of this music to Richard Wagner's 'Prelude' to the First Act of *Die Walküre*. The comparison with Wagner fits all the better if we remember that Tom Tykwer is, like Wagner, a *Gesamtkünstler*, being the soundtrack composer and writer, as well as the director of his film. Why, though, does Krausser specifically refer to the *Walküre* when there are examples of this kind of power everywhere in Wagner's operas? In my opinion, he unconsciously struck the right note with this choice, for Lola can be understood as a postmodern – or rather a post-postmodern – Walkyrie, a woman *with* qualities, with a strength, resolution, firmness and love with which the young generation can fully identify. This might well be the reason for the successful reception of the film: the possibility of identification with a subjectivity that feels *real*, alive and sure of its own existence. 'For me, the challenge of filming is to tell a subjectivity, that means to make something imaginable. To produce identification means to produce a subjective impression' (Tykwer 1999, p. 27).

Run, Lola, Run has this effect, not least, because of its picture–sound synthesis, which pervades the viewer from head to toe. In this way, the bass drum scans the uncanny outside compulsion of progressive time, as well as Lola's heartbeat, together with the text which is breathed in the pulsating beat of her desire: 'I wish I was . . . , I wish I was . . . , I wish I was'.

To some extent, then, viewing the film becomes something of an initiation rite, if we take initiation rites to be an inscription of identity onto the body (and let us not forget that Lola and Manni both have prominent tattoos!). In *Run, Lola, Run*, it is the music which engraves the strength of a will-driven, strong subjectivity onto the body of the viewers, so that their heartbeat will become unified with that of Lola.

Aesthetically, this film operates in a playful way in the imaginary realm of the postmodern adolescent 'open psychic structure' as well as in the realm of possibility by playing with the potentials of fate and accident. It dismisses the 'grand narrative' (*one* beginning, *one* climax and *one* ending) and plays with an amazing variety of film techniques as well as with quotations from the thousands of films Tykwer had seen as a boy and adolescent. To add to this, the whole ensemble is conveyed with an incredible wit. In all these ways, then, it is clear that the narrative structure of *Run, Lola, Run* operates in the mode of the *conjunctivus potentialis*.

Yet, beyond this potential space of the imaginary we can feel the latent wish to frame and to contain the *anything goes*, that is to concentrate on the essential, acting and thinking – at least sometimes – in the more decisive grammatical form of the indicative tense. This, in a dialectical movement, will open new and alternative options, such as the possibility of feeling real and alive and strong.

Limitation, in its unconscious meaning, is nothing but death itself, and vice versa: death is the unconscious meaning of limitation, framing our life and, in the film, confining Lola's grandiose rescue fantasy. Even the last part of the film and its conclusion – with the fulfilment of Lola's omnipotent wish – deals, in my view, with death, for every realization of a utopia means that the wish's movement comes to an end, and therefore life, too, comes to an end. At the close of the film, we see Lola and Manni walking alone on deserted streets, no people, no cars, no life. This is death, or perhaps just a dream, for only in a dream, or in a film, *anything goes*.

Notes

1   Julia Kristeva (1978) uses Husserl's concept of 'thesis', though without its latent theological meaning, to mark the coming into being of the subject as a result of the castration complex, which she calls a breaking or 'border'.
2   Lola: 'Your heart says: Hello, Manni, is that her over there?' Manni: 'It certainly is'. Lola: 'Then you say: Oh, thanks a lot for this information, catch you later?'

References

Bion, W. R. (1962) *Learning from Experience*. London: Heinemann.

Deleuze, G. and Guattari, F. (1974) *Anti-Oedipus: Capitalism and Schizophrenia*. London: Athlone Press, 1983.

Foucault, M. (1974) *The Archaeology of Knowledge*. London: Routledge.

Houellebecq, M. (2000) *Ausweitung der Kampfzone*. Reinbeck bei Hamburg: Rowohlt [*Extension du dumaine de la lutte*. Paris: Editions J'ai lu, 1994].

Houellebecq, M. (2001a) *Elementarteilchen*. Cologne: DuMont [*Les Particules élémentaires*. Paris: Editions J'ai lu, 1998. *The Elementary Particles*, 2000].

Houellebecq, M. (2001b) *Die Welt als Supermarkt*. Reinbeck bei Hamburg: Rowohlt.

Kittler, F. A. (1985) 'Romantik – Psychoanalyse – Film: eine Doppelgängergeschichte', in J. Hörisch and G. C. Tholen (eds) *Eingebildete Texte: Affären zwischen Psychoanalyse und Literaturwissenschaft*. Munich: Wilhelm Fink.

Krausser, H. (1999) 'Lola: ein Nachwort, viel zu früh', in M. Töteberg (ed.) *Szenenwechsel – Momentaufnahmen des jungen deutschen Films*. Reinbeck bei Hamburg: Rowohlt.

Kristeva, J. (1978) *Revolution in Poetic Language*. New York: Columbia University Press, 1984.

Kristeva, J. (1994) 'The adolescent novel', in *New Maladies of the Soul*. New York: Columbia University Press, 1995.

Lacan, J. (1973) 'The mirror stage as formative of the function of the I as revealed in psychoanalytic experience', in *Ecrits: A Selection*. London: Tavistock, 1977.

Musil, R. (1933) *The Man without Qualities*. London: Picador, 1997.

Schöne, A. (1961) 'Zum Gebrauch des Konjunktivs bei Robert Musil', *Euphorion*, 55: 196–220.

Töteburg, M. (1999) 'Run, Lola Run: Die Karriere eines Films', in M. Töteberg (ed.) *Szenenwechsel – Momentaufnahmen des jungen deutschen Films*. Reinbeck bei Hamburg: Rowohlt.

Tykwer, T. (1998a) 'Ich will Authentizität und Leidenschaft: ein Gespräch mit Tom Tykwer', *Junge Welt*, 24 August.

Tykwer, T. (1998b) *Lola rennt (Drehbuch)*. Reinbeck bei Hamburg: Rowohlt.

Tykwer, T. (1999) 'Generalschlüssel fürs Kino. Tom Tykwer im Literarischen Salon Hannover, moderiert von Michael Althen', in M. Töteberg (ed.) *Szenenwechsel – Momentaufnahmen des jungen deutschen Films*. Reinbeck bei Hamburg: Rowohlt.

Tykwer, T. (2000) 'Den Gang der Gedanken filmen', *FAZ*, 2 December: 3.

6

THOMAS VINTERBERG'S *FESTEN* (1998)

An attempt to avoid madness through denunciation

Liliana Pedrón de Martín

Festen is one of the productions of the Dogma 95 Group.[1] Thomas Vinterberg, the director, together with Mogens Rukov, co-author of the script, created an aesthetically relevant production, as much from the point of view of sound and image syntax, as from the argument itself. In the light of psychoanalysis, *Festen* clearly shows the conflict between the intention of denouncing and revealing the actual deeds versus the intense mechanisms of disavowal and denial that hide what is known individually and socially. This intention is reinforced by a special filmmaking, that comes out from Dogma 95's ideology, especially in relation to the use of the technological resources. The hand-held camera technique compromises the spectator and forces him or her to see and hear without avoiding the facts. In the same way that the argument proposes that the spectator be a witness of the battle against denial, the cinematographic language proposes, in an analogical order, a battle against superficial action.

About 'Dogma 95'

In 1995, in Denmark, four filmmakers – Thomas Vinterberg, Lars von Trier, Soren Kragh-Jakobsen and Christian Lebring – created a Manifesto called 'Dogma 95'. With the use of ten rules, called 'the vows of chastity', Dogma 95 demands a very special aesthetic realism in cinema and a precise search for aesthetic truth. Avoiding technological sophistication the filmmakers go back to basics. Dogma 95 is interested in leaving aside every possible convention in filmmaking involving the use of technical resources and film style. The Dogma filmmakers are almost religious in their intention of going back to basics to obtain a break with cinematic convention. Their polemic is introduced in cinema media when what is hidden behind the formalism is revealed. They believe subjective matters are not solved by technological efficiency. Some of their specific rules of film syntax are: use only sound images available live at the shoot, use a hand-held camera, shoot in colour with no special lighting, avoid superficial action, focus on here-and-now (no period pieces), and adopt Academy 35 mm as the film format.

The Manifesto gives the movement a publicly shared character creating the expectation of change. This kind of cinema may produce a feeling of discomfort but, for those who believe in it, it is alive. Richard Combs (2000) states in his 'Rules of the Game' that these rules emphasize more than the basics, the way in which these resources may be used. I think that Dogma 95 succeeds in keeping its vanguard style every time it makes us become conscious of the 'subject's manipulation' because of the indiscriminate advance of technology. Their permanent intention of transmitting ideals renews polemics in the media. Their last vow says: never credit the director. This defiant and contradictory proposal invites us, the audience, to assume a creative and critical position with responsibility.

About *Festen*

In Vinterberg's *Festen*, it is summer in Denmark and in 'The Great House' a feast is about to start. Helge Klingenfeldt, patriarch and lord of the family, is 60 today. The invitations have been sent out and the film starts as the guests are arriving home. All the film takes place in the mansion. Helge's wife Elsie and their two sons, Christian and Michael, daughter Helene, friends, relatives and of course next of kin attend the party. Christian, the one who denounces the patriarch, is the eldest son and twin brother of Linda, who committed suicide a short time before the party. Linda was the only one of the four children who continued living with her parents. Christian lives in Paris, where he has two restaurants.

Helene, the only surviving sister, expresses throughout the gathering the necessity of remembering and investigating her sister's suicide. Her partner, a black man, symbolizes her intention of disrupting the family's status quo. Michael, the younger brother, is an alcoholic who treats his wife and children brutally, while idealizing his father's prestige. In this character, the tension generated from 'finding and hiding' the truth is taken to the extreme.

The formal and conservative tone, created through the costumes, the songs and folk scenes, contrasts with the necessity to denounce suicide and incestuous perversion. The argument links the past, through the parents' perverse enacting and condoning incest in what is now a decaying kingdom. Nobody will be the same after the feast. The celebration, intended to uphold power, topples it. Father

Plate 11 Festen [*The Celebration*] (Thomas Vinterberg 1998)
Source: bfi Collections

and mother are accomplices of the crime. The father as the chief and the mother as helper and ally, outlive filicide (Freud 1913). Each one of their sons and daughters, including Linda with her suicidal denunciation, decries the outrage and demands the incest be publicly confronted. The employees, especially the chief cook Kim and Lars the valet, foment the rebellion to uncover the incestuous horror.

Rebellion against the father is a classical theme in literature. We can find it in mythology, Shakespeare, Kafka, etc. Let us remember Cronus' myth. Cronus, the son of Uranus, wrested power expelling his father. Cronus had many sons and then ate them, in this way avoiding succession. By means of this process he managed to keep time in an eternal present.

In the sense of the film's argument, Dogma 95 is not in the vanguard, but it is in the aesthetic field. Using image and sound without sophisticated technical resources points out the essence of the argument.

Collision between the two realities

Festen shows with a clear aesthetic conviction the social structure of perverted, addictive, maniacal and omnipotent pathologies. From a psychoanalytic point of view the film is significant. It materializes the 'uncanny' (Freud 1919) and reaches artistic expression.

I will now turn to the concepts that pertain to the functioning of the psychical apparatus in perversion. Freud (1924a, 1924b) describes the mechanism of splitting of the ego, blocking the circulation between two worlds, two realities that disavow each other. In his article 'Fetishism' (1927), he refers to the coexistence of knowledge of castration and its disavowal as a prototype of perverse functioning. In the same way the film shows two realities fighting against each other. One recognizes neither loss nor mourning, and the other denounces barbarity. The camera, as if it were a witness, a hidden camera, reinforces the intention of unmasking the defence.

Perversion requires subjugation of the object. The perverse social frame reinforces the narcissistic relationship where extreme dependence is involved. The film illustrates many perverse mechanisms of this sort.

Christian's speech must be disavowed because it attacks the stability and credibility of the corrupt system. From the moment of his denunciation of the father, disruption of two realities ensues. Those who try to silence the denunciation become more and more intense. Though Helene, the intermediate daughter, does not want to forget her older sister's death, she declares openly that Christian is confused. In an 'uncanny' speech, their mother asks Christian to apologize and admit that everything was a product of his fantasy. The speech is uncanny because it is familiar as well as threatening, like a bedside story that contains the naïve and the well known. The certainty of the mother denying what her children have denounced represents the return of what has been repressed.

Michael, the younger brother, in his desperate attempt to maintain the family idealization, takes the extreme position: he who denounces should disappear.

Linda's suicide letter, however, proclaims the limit to parental omnipotence. With it, all resources to hold the truth hidden vanish. Death and suicide cannot be denied anymore. No one can go back. The obstruction of the escape mechanisms (the car keys metaphor in the film) confronts everyone with reality. In spite of the fact that the truth may not be accepted, it produces a collision effect.

Like a trap, the 'celebration' gets the characters in contact with the disavowed facts, but there is no space for the moment of elaboration. The subjective transmission of the truth does not take place within the film.

Denunciation and madness

The title of this chapter alludes to avoiding madness. The term madness seems to me the most illustrative to explain the affective manifestation that comes from the state of dependence shown by the film characters. André Green (1990) conceives of madness as related to the passional affective component, that modifies the subject–reality link. The chosen object, total or partial, becomes unique and irreplaceable; it fascinates the ego and alienates it, creating an over-estimated internal representation. This affective manifestation originates in the early relationship between mother and child and therefore it inhabits the heart of man from the very beginning.

Madness coexists with passion; passionate love of pleasure is joined to suffering. Madness does not only belong to a psychopathological structure in itself. It can exist in neurosis, perversion and psychosis. According to Green (1990), madness can be expressed in neurosis when, in spite of suffering, love is 'related to the object', it interplays with the other. When the relationship with the object is disturbed, madness is the expression of the enclosure of narcissistic perverse pathologies and falls into extreme isolation in psychosis.

In the film, madness is represented as tied to extreme ambivalence that permanently reinforces the mechanisms of splitting and disavowal. When the object of passion becomes impossible to manage, the intention of disavowing reality increases. In that way each one of the characters in the film tries to avoid extreme dependence. It is interesting to point out that none of the characters could build a 'healthy' exogamic relationship. The servants also feel confined and for that reason they support Christian's rebellion.

In spite of the fact that the celebration goes on, when the disavowal weakens madness becomes more evident. Helene shouts desperately that she can't put up with it. Narcissistic passion invades the scene. Linda, the suicidal daughter, assumes, through her acting out, a crisis that in her other siblings takes on a defensive role, facing both parents. The suicide, in the film, has the value of a protest. Linda, the victim, cannot tolerate continuing to be a subjugated object in her father's incestuous hands and, through drowning herself, denounces him.

In 'Mourning and melancholia', Freud (1917) explains the identificatory mechanisms that produce alienation in the one who incorporates the 'other'. Paraphasing Freud in his well-known phrase '*the shadow of the object falls upon the self*', we could say that the shadow of Linda falls on Christian. He is the spokes-man of the message which his sister, in the enclosure of melancholia, can express only through suicide. The protagonist, instead of remaining in the arms of Thanatos, frees himself from the deadly link by means of the incest denunciation and vindicates his sister's death.

The spectator identifies with Christian and supports his wish not to give up. This is Vinterberg's gift. Nothing is more important than denunciation. Nothing can move him away. Heterosexual love will make sense to Christian only when his desperation eases by revealing the horror of incest.

Cinematographic speech enables Vinterberg to express these states of mind with a language that can be compared to the one that rules our dreams. The metaphor that the director uses in his film is the image of Linda overlapping with the image of the family waitress. This young girl is in love with the protagonist. They have been lovers for some time. The image of Linda drowning in the bathtub becomes a brilliant 'condensation' of the 'double' phenomenon, based on Narcissus' myth, which Otto Rank (1914) uses to explain this concept. Vinterberg seems to choose this psychoanalytic resource (cinematically in the seductive play-drowning of Christian's girlfriend, the waitress/sister double, in the bathtub). The shadow, the image of his dead twin sister, overlaps with the image of his lover. In this image of the double, love and life are intermingled with death. Life and death are, once more, considered as two sides of the same coin. The spirit of death, which the image suggests, could also be associated with representations intended to exorcize Christian's feelings of guilt for fraternal rivalry.

When Christian suggests to his lover that they should go together to Paris, could we think of this as an exogamic ending where Eros achieves his linking function? Or, perhaps, could we think that through this choice the protagonist remains tied down to his past?

The Double reappears as an epilogue: the double image of the dancer in the music box constitutes the syntax through which image, sound and argument are articulated to achieve a poetical representation of Renaissance.

Note

1   The original Danish title of the film is *Festen*. While in Britain the film is known as *Festen*, in the USA the title has been translated as *The Celebration*.

References

Combs, R. (2000) 'Rules of the game' (Dogma 95, cinematic movement), *Film Comment*, September–October: 28–32.

Freud, S. (1913) 'Totem and taboo', in *Standard Edition 13*. London: Hogarth Press, 1953.

Freud, S. (1917) 'Mourning and melancholia', in *Standard Edition 14*. London: Hogarth Press, 1957.

Freud, S. (1919) 'The "Uncanny"', in *Standard Edition 17*. London: Hogarth Press, 1959.

Freud, S. (1924a) 'Neurosis and psychosis', in *Standard Edition 19*. London: Hogarth Press, 1961.

Freud, S. (1924b) 'The loss of reality in neurosis and psychosis', in *Standard Edition 19*. London: Hogarth Press, 1961.

Freud, S. (1927) 'Fetishism', in *Standard Edition 21*. London: Hogarth Press, 1961.

Green, A. (1990) *On Private Madness*. London: Hogarth Press.

Rank, O. (1914) *The Double: A Psychoanalytic Study*. Chapel Hill, NC: University of North Carolina Press, 1971.

7

ISTVÁN SZABÓ'S *SUNSHINE* (1999)

The cinematic representation of historical and familial trauma

Diana Diamond

Sunshine is the central signifier as well as title of this luminous film that at once affirms what is timeless and universal in the individual psyche and what can be configured by historical circumstances and cataclysms. This multigenerational family saga depicts the lives of the members of a Hungarian Jewish family as they unfold against the shifting historical backdrop of the Austro-Hungarian Empire, the rise of Fascism, and the Stalinist and post-communist eras. As we watch the spectacle of history filtered through the individual personalities and fates of four generations of Sonnenscheins, we realize that *Sunshine* does what few films accomplish: it shows how history reverberates in and is resisted by the individual personality and psyche, whose conflicts are configured out of the social and political fabric of the time. In *Sunshine* many individual narratives are threaded into a text constructed largely by one family member, a fourth generation Sonnenschein, one of only three to survive the Holocaust. This monologic voice is embedded in a polyphonic text where sight and sound, image and narration, the lexical and the symbolic converge to create multiple channels of meaning and commentary.

'Sunshine' refers to the 'Taste of Sunshine', the tonic distilled from local herbs, which forms the foundation for the family fortune, and which continues to function as a talisman or symbol of family unity long after the recipe for it is lost; to Sonnenschein, the family's original name (Sonnenschein means 'sunshine' in Hungarian), which is eventually changed to Sors (which means fate) as the subsequent generations of the family assimilate into the upper echelons of Hungarian society; to the power of Eros which in each generation

Plate 12 Sunshine (Itsván Szabó 1999)

ensures the family's survival at the same time that it wreaks havoc with family relationships beginning with the quasi-incestuous marriage between first cousins raised as siblings; to the family ego ideal, that is to the cultural and religious traditions of its elders and the ways that they are alternately embraced or betrayed, forgotten and rediscovered by subsequent generations; and finally to the good maternal introject epitomized by the central female figure of the film, Valerie, the matriarch and photographer, whose portrait of herself sitting in the family courtyard filled with flowers functions as a recurring icon of renewal and redemption in the film. It is the latter two aspects of *Sunshine*, the core good objects in the family and the family ego ideal, which enable this family – bisected by religious persecution, incest, adultery, poverty, incarceration by both fascists and Stalinists, murder and death – to survive.

Trauma, familial and historical, and its enduring impact on the psyche is a recurring theme in *Sunshine*. The circularity of universal family dynamics, such as Oedipal and sibling attachments and rivalries, as well as the ways in which the family progresses or is broken on the wheel of history, is depicted cinematically as one generation turns into another, father turns into son, mother into daughter (in this film literally as well as figuratively since Ralph Fiennes plays three generations of men in the family, while Rosemary Harris and her real-life daughter Jennifer Ehle play the Sonnenschein matriarch Valerie as a younger and older woman). This chapter focuses on the transgenerational transmission of trauma within the family, in particular how incest and murder of family members during the Holocaust overwhelms and challenges the representational capacities of the subsequent generations in ways that lead them to re-create, re-enact and rework aspects of their traumatic history even as they attempt to master it. By making the spectator witness scenes of incestuous sexuality, as well as scenes of unspeakable violence, the film recapitulates primal scene fantasies in which intense eroticism and aggression are often confounded (Laub and Auerhahn 1993; Knafo and Feiner 1996). The identification with the persecutions and transgressions of previous generations privileges ties to internal objects, curtailing individuation and impoverishing the object relations of future generations, often creating a sense of living simultaneously in the past and the present (Laub 1996; Kestenberg 1993). The latter is depicted in *Sunshine* not only through the use of the same actor to represent three generations of Sonnenscheins, but also through the admixture of archival documentary and fictional film footage, and through the interpolation of imaginary characters into newsreels. The film's use of sight and sound including the *mélange* of fiction film and documentary blurs the distinction between past and present, actual and fictionalized events, giving the film quasi-mythic status at the same time as it affirms the realness of historical trauma.

In its blend of sight and sound, verbal and visual modes of representation, *Sunshine* epitomizes the ways in which film is uniquely suited to capture historical and individual traumas that often strain or overwhelm the limits of representation. The visual mode conveys aesthetically the full force of what is often unspeakable and unrepresentable through lexical and symbolic means. Further, the visual mode conveys experience with an immediacy that places the spectator at the heart of the action; for the imagistic mode of representation encapsulates both self and other, fostering, and even demanding, shifting identifications between subject and object, victim and victimizer (Horowitz 1972; Diamond and Blatt 1994). By contrast, the verbal or narrative mode allows for the restructuring of trauma by recovering the subjective meaning of experiences that defy signification. Narration also counters the ruptures in the self and in human connections that are the legacy of trauma; for narratives are not told into the void, but presuppose a listening resonating presence (Rose 1995). But perhaps most important, narration fosters the resolution of trauma because it allows for the creative manipulation of categories of time, space, the self and other, enabling traumatic events to be explored metaphorically and even playfully. In *Sunshine* the narrator serves as a witnessing presence, which not only catalogues the impact of the Holocaust on the family, but also interweaves familial and historical traumas in ways that illuminate the subjective meaning of both. The depiction of trauma through sight and sound, image and narration enables the spectator in *Sunshine* to experience the 'black hole' or 'empty circle' of trauma (Laub and Auerhahn 1993; Rosenblum 1999), while it also challenges the spectator to situate such traumatic events in the chain of images and signifiers that make up the complex tapestry of this multigenerational family saga.

Sunshine, like many historical films, begins with a traumatic event, the death of the narrator's great-great-grandfather during an explosion in his distillery while manufacturing the 'Taste of Sunshine'. This explosion functions as a prolepsis, that is, both a prediction of the tragic events to come, and a preview of survival. Emmanuel, his 12-year-old son, survives the disaster, and with the cloth-bound book containing the secret recipe for the herbal elixir hidden in the lining of his coat, he leaves his village ghetto for Budapest. There he sets up his own distillery and manufactures the 'Taste of Sunshine', which is an 'instant success'. Emmanuel has two sons, Ignatz, who becomes a lawyer and supporter of the liberal monarchy of the emperor Franz Josef, and Gustave, who becomes a doctor and communist who deplores his brother's monarchism. The rivalry between the brothers is played out in part over politics, and in part over their love for their cousin Valerie, the daughter of Emmanuel's brother, who was adopted by the family after she was orphaned in infancy. When Ignatz asks his father for permission to marry his sister-cousin, his father forbids the union, insisting that it is against Jewish law for first cousins to marry. 'Mighty God has created nature and the laws of nature forbid marriage between brother and sister. Want is not a word of ours . . . God wants, we wish for . . .' he admonishes his son. But the erotic connection between the cousins prevails over the law of the father. In marrying his cousin, Ignatz turns his back on Jewish law, which forbids such a union, instead affirming the secular law of Hungary, which does not. Henceforth his allegiance is as much to the emperor Franz Josef, whose liberal empire allowed Jews to flourish economically and socially, as to his own father. Indeed, he changes his name from Sonnenschein to Sors (fate), and fulfils his ambition to become a high court judge and then, during the First World War, a military court judge. But with the collapse of the empire and his marriage to Valerie, which we are told 'fell apart in the same way', he retreats into isolation and an early death. From its inception, the quasi-incestuous union between Valerie and Ignatz sets up contradictions and conflicts between the couple and within the family that ultimately lead to its demise, contradictions that are conveyed as much visually as verbally in a number of scenes.

In one scene, we see the three sibling cousins lined up in a row on the potty as infants. This sibling scenario is re-evoked later when Ignatz and Valerie first make love in Vienna, and then dissolve into giggles as Valerie admits, 'I have to pee'. 'When I'm in your arms, I feel like I've finally come home', states Ignatz. 'No kidding', quipped one reviewer (Scott 2000), who like a number of reviewers was either discomforted or baffled by the incestuous and often graphic sexual scenes in the film. The incestuous nature of their union and its potential impact on the family comes home to Ignatz and Valerie when she becomes pregnant. 'But you're my sister', he protests, 'My mother will murder me.' 'Me too', replies Valerie. Although the couple's marriage and the birth of their two sons restores family harmony and leads to the suppression of such primitive fantasies and fears, the essential confusion and tensions in the relationship endure and ultimately lead to its demise. When Ignatz returns to his family after a long absence at the end of the First World War during which he served as a military judge at the front, Valerie tells him that she is planning to divorce him because she finds him to be a 'man without feeling'. 'I am your sister and will always be your sister', she tells the stunned Ignatz, who replies, 'You're not my sister, you're my wife . . . I'm not your brother, I'm your husband.' But Valerie protests that he has never really loved her and replies, 'I loved you, I seduced you – you knew I was safe and would always stand by you because I'm your sister.' Valerie's betrayal resuscitates old Oedipal rivalries as evidenced by Ignatz's fantasy that it must be Gustave who has seduced her, despite Valerie's insistence that this is not the case. Overcome by fury and despair he rapes her in a scene in which the former eroticism between the couple is eclipsed by aggression.

In these scenes, which feature the development of an incestuous and forbidden relationship, Szabó plays with reversals of the gaze in ways that heighten the primal scene implications of cinematic viewing (Metz 1982). Psychoanalytic investigation reveals that primal scene fantasies are often characterized by split identifications in the viewer that 'involve figuratively being in two places at once, as both the observer and the observed' (Knafo and Feiner 1996, p. 556). Just as these scenes break down the split between observer and observed, so also do they subvert the typical scenarios of active male/passive female as they have been constructed in film (Mulvey 1989). Valerie functions not only as the target of the male gaze who fulfils the voyeuristic and scoptophilic desire in the male onlookers, but also as a woman who herself controls the gaze (ibid.). As a photographer, Valerie participates in the creation of the spectacle. She is the *metteuse-en-scène* who directs the actors and the action, epitomized by the many scenes of her photographing the family at crucial moments in the family's history. Hence Szabó inverts the specularizing of women, even as he affirms it. In keeping with her role as the subject as well as object of the gaze, Valerie acts on her passion for Ignatz. In fact, the discomfort which the sexual ardour and aggressiveness of the women in the film has engendered among a number of reviewers may well devolve from unconscious resistance to this redirection of the gaze, whereby men are as much objects positioned for their erotic impact and women the ones who project their fantasies onto the male figures as vice versa. One reviewer, for example, commented on the relentless pursuit of the men by the women in the film and on 'the great many gratuitously predatory sex scenes in which three generations of gorgeous women become so attracted to three generations of Ralph Fiennes that they virtually rape him' (Deak 2000, p. 30). Ironically, the only rape in the film is that of Valerie by Ignatz, which may signify the attempt to reinstate Valerie as the object rather than the subject of desire. That ultimately aggression eclipses the eroticism between the couple also foreshadows the impending violence that will befall the next generation.

In *Sunshine*, the dialectic between sight and sound, image and narrative replicates the tension between conscious and unconscious experience. For example, after Ignatz fulfils his ultimate ambition and is made a circuit court judge, Emmanuel presents Ignatz with a pocket watch that belonged to his grandfather, advising him to 'take nothing on trust, see everything for yourself.' This scene is immediately followed by a long aerial tracking shot of lush and bucolic fields and forests with the camera slowly zooming in on the naked Ignatz and Valerie making love. The gradual revelation of the couple's nakedness and abandon, reminiscent of primal scene knowledge, provides an ironic counter-point to the verbal advice of the father as he presents his son with a family heirloom, his grandfather's pocket watch. This heirloom, the only item that survived the explosion in the distillery, signals the consolidation of identification between father and son. But the couple's sexual banter ('the judge imposes stiff sentences') suggests a playful inversion of paternal law, which is not simply inherited, but subverted and then created anew with each generation. Further, these scenarios which juxtapose the fulfilment of ambition with the gratification of sexual curiosity and expression are also reminiscent of primal scene fantasies and scenarios; for an essential component of ambitious strivings is thought to be a quest for primal scene knowledge and participation (Knafo and Feiner 1996). Ultimately, Ignatz's ambition to create his identity anew fails. When his father and the emperor die on the same day, 'Ignatz took the coincidence . . . as a strange and significant omen.' We are told that 'the empire and his marriage to Valerie fell apart in the same way', and Ignatz withdraws into isolation, his early death emblematic of his irresolvable conflicts between devotion to family tradition and allegiance to an obsolete monarchy.

As Ignatz devolves into Adam in the next generation and Bela Kun's brief Soviet republic, led primarily by Jewish intellectuals, yields to the right-wing, anti-Semitic military regime of Admiral Miklos Horthy, the intrafamilial conflicts over incestuous and forbidden sexuality, over loyalty to family and Jewish tradition versus assimilation and professional advancement are intensified and reconfigured. Adam, Ignatz's son, turns his back on Judaism altogether when he converts to Catholicism in order to gain admittance to the elite officers' club, where he fences in his quest to become the Hungarian national champion. He marries another Catholic convert, but reluctantly allows himself to be seduced into an adulterous affair by his sister-in-law. Up to this point, *Sunshine* has focused on the everyday life of the family with most of the action taking place in the grand bourgeois family apartment, around the family dinner table, or in the family bedrooms. But in the next generation, as we watch the family relationships and fates reconfigured by the rise of Nazism, the recurrent images of family artifacts and rituals (e.g. the china, furnishings, portraits, photographs, dinners and weddings) are eclipsed by the homogenized and monumental imagery of Fascism.

Adam Sors' meteoric rise to national fencing champion and Olympic gold medallist occurs in the shadow of Hitler's rise to power. The scenes of Adam Sors fencing at the Berlin Olympics in 1936 are intercut with archival newsreel footage of Hitler introducing the ceremonies. The orchestration of sounds and images in these clips, including colour intercut with black and white newsreels, Hungarian hymns and flags juxtaposed with Nazi anthems and iconography, links the characters to the national contexts and political conflicts that define their fate. The choreography of sabre fencing with its combination of grace, physical power and dexterity connects Adam with Hungary's military and national traditions, while his participation in the Berlin Olympics dominated by Nazi symbols and pageants links him to the aesthetics of Fascism. As we watch the Sors/Sonnenschein family and other Hungarians watch Adam win the Olympics, we also watch them become bewitched by what Sontag (1976) has called the spectacle of 'Fascinating Fascism'. The shots of Adam receiving his gold medal reveal an admixture of pride, triumph and incredulity, and such scenes, which blend close-ups with Nazi iconography, serve to cement our identification with Adam at the same time that they connect him to historical characters. We know, for example, that Adam Sors is based in part on a real character, the Hungarian national fencing champion Attila Petschauer, who won several gold Olympic medals and who, like Adam, was subsequently beaten to death in a Hungarian labour camp in 1942 (Deak 2000).

After the Nazis invade Hungary and Jewish deportations begin, even Adam's celebrity status as an Olympic fencing champion, which briefly provided a bulwark against the rise of anti-Semitism, cannot save him and his family. His interchanges with his sister-in-law with whom he has become involved in an adulterous liaison are increasingly overshadowed by murderous fantasies, which reflect their impending fate as Jews in the Nazi-occupied Hungary. 'You want me to kill my family?' asks Ignatz at one point, as Greta urges him to run away with her, leaving the others to perish as the Nazi's assume power. 'Yes', she replies, 'Kill them. I wish Ivan were dead. I don't see anyway out.' 'I never want to see you again', replies Adam. Shortly thereafter, Adam, like many Hungarian Jews, is drafted into service into a Hungarian labour camp along with his son Ivan, while the other family members are initially confined to the Jewish ghetto and either go into hiding or are taken to concentration camps.

It is in the Hungarian labour camp that Ignatz/Adam/Ivan meets his fate; where the denial of his identity consolidates his identity. 'I believe this will be a century of love, justice and tolerance', proclaimed Ignatz in a toast to the dawn of the twentieth century. Less than half a century later, his son Adam is stripped and beaten to death as his grandson Ivan watches, a horrified and helpless witness. In the labour camp, Adam Sors' Hungarian officer's uniform and white as opposed to yellow armband, signalling that he is a Christian Jew, almost immediately captures the attention of the military sergeant; for the white arm-band, the ultimate sign of assimilation, constituted the 'ultimate provocation' for the true anti-Semite (Deak 2000, p. 31). That Attila Petschauer, Adam Sors' real-life model, was tortured and killed in a Hungarian labour camp in a similar

106

fashion because he was a Christian Jew (Deak 2000) lends an air of historical truth to this scene.

The scene begins when the captain in the labour camp rips the white band off Adam's arm with the demeaning comment, 'What is this? A Christmas tree ornament?' and demands that Sors identify himself as a Jew. 'What are you?' he barks. Sors repeatedly replies, 'Adam Sors, doctor of law, officer of the Hungarian army, Olympic gold medallist.' 'You're garbage, you are a stinking Jew', reiterates the captain. This brutal, stereotyped interrogation continues as we watch Adam stripped naked, repeatedly flogged, and bound by hands and feet onto a pole, all the while affirming that he is the Hungarian fencing champion and an Olympic gold medallist. As they string him up on a tree and spray him with freezing water, we watch his face congeal into a frozen mask as he utters his last words, 'Olympic gold medallist'.

This scene, perhaps as much as any scene in fictional film, convincingly depicts the horrors of the Holocaust, its power deriving from the tension between image and sound, dialogue and silence, action and inaction. The prolonged close-up of Adam's frozen visage and broken body forms a Christ-like spectacle at the end. The use of such Christian images and motifs functions as an ironic commentary on Adam's steadfast refusal to affirm his Jewish identity, and on the assimilationist strivings of his forebears. In its use of Christian symbolism and iconography, *Sunshine* follows many Holocaust films in which Christian values or heroics have sometimes distorted or even eclipsed the identity and experience of the Jews, as was the case in *Schindler's List* (Spielberg 1993) for example (Brown 2000). However, by depicting the Sonnenschein/Sors family's progressive assimilationist strivings, including Ignatz's repudiation of his name, Adam's conversion to Christianity, as well as the irresolvable contradictions engendered by these strivings evident in the crucifixion-like scenario of Ivan's death, Szabó makes imaginative leaps that lay bare rather than distort the authentic details of the historical experience of assimilationist Jews. The man whose father changed his name from Sonnenschein to Sors (fate) in order to consolidate his position in the Hungarian judiciary, who himself converted to Christianity in order to be able to fence at the officers' club and become the national Olympic fencing champion (a sport that symbolizes Hungary's Christian warrior knight past), himself is executed by the Nazis in a labour camp run by Hungarian fascists in a manner that replicates the crucifixion. We watch Adam's identity being shattered along with his body, the mixture of Christian and Jewish iconography functioning here not as a glorification or obfuscation of the family's identity, but as a bitter commentary on the contradictions inherent in their choices and fate

In depicting the brutal murder of Adam Sors, and the response of his fellow inmates and son to it, this scene takes on the near impossible task of simulating the horrors of the Holocaust – the second source of its power and efficacy. A number of Holocaust scholars (Laub and Auerhahn 1993; Laub and Podell 1995; Rosenblum 1999) have suggested that there may be something inherently deadly in attempts to use illusion and metaphor to deal with trauma. Knowledge of real atrocity eclipses and paralyses the functions of fantasy and representation, creating 'an empty space, a black hole, with no outer reference point from which to view it or take refuge' (Laub 1996, p. 42). For example, writing of his mother's death in the Holocaust, Aharon Appelfeld affirms, 'It is just impossible to deal directly with the nakedness of the deaths. It's like looking at the naked sun on a clear summer day. You couldn't stand the temperature. You can never understand the meaning of the Holocaust. You can just come to the edges of it' (quoted in Alter 1986). Some theorists, however, believe that film may be uniquely suited to represent scenes of massive trauma such as Holocaust experiences (Insdorf 1989). Kracauer (1960), for example, wrote that filmic images, like Athena's polished shield which reflected but contained the horrific image of the Medusa, allow us to view 'the reflection of happenings which would petrify us were we to encounter them in real life' (p. 305). The final close-up of Adam Sors encased in ice, surrounded by silence, serves as such a petrifying timeless image. In his clinical work with Holocaust survivors, Laub (1996) found that such searing time-less moments are often those involving the witnessing of the deaths or public execution of loved ones. Such traumatic separations or losses may create a cleavage in the psyche of the survivor, laying down a set of parallel if shadowy experiential tracks that may coexist with or derail the experience of living in the present.

The power of the scene of Adam Sors' death further resides in its depiction of its impact on the survivors. At the same time that we witness the chilling execution of the father, we observe its impact on the son. We see him being initially restrained by those around him and then succumbing to silence and immobility, only his anguished expression and quivering body registering his full horror and inner resistance to the event. In the silence and inaction of Ivan and his fellow inmates, we see human beings surrendering to psychic numbness. These scenes also illustrate the subversion of the normal generational patterns of parental care and protection of children that took place in the camps. For as Wilgowicz (1999) points out, the camps embodied 'the pure culture of the death drive . . . based on infanticide and parricide' (p. 429). In watching Ivan bear helpless and silent witness to this grisly and almost unbearable scenario of torture and execution, we ourselves momentarily become complicit witnesses to the simulated events. That two prominent Holocaust scholars with whom I discussed this film initially forgot this scene altogether speaks to the extent to which even filmic representations of Holocaust atrocities may activate defences that screen out direct knowledge of trauma. Ultimately, the final solution was an assault against 'genealogy, filiation and individual and collective memory' (Wilgowicz 1999, p. 249). The difficulty in viewing and recollecting this scene may also be attributed to its primal scene implications. In psychoanalytic work with Holocaust survivors, Laub (1996) has observed, 'being present at or vicariously participating in scenes of massive aggression is the equivalent of the primal scene fantasy, which likewise involves forbidden knowledge' (p. 301).

108

Perhaps the most crucial aspect of this scene is its identification of Ivan as the witnessing presence at the core of the film. It is at this point that we understand why the film takes the form of a family history narrated by Ivan. The central significance for Holocaust survivors of remembering and bearing witness has been articulated by Primo Levi (1969), 'Precisely because the Lager was a great machine to reduce us to beasts, we must not become beasts . . . even in this place one can survive, and therefore one must want to survive, to tell the story, to bear witness' (p. 233). On the one hand the scene presents the father encased in ice, signifying the timeless petrifying moment of the trauma; on the other, it depicts the living presence of the son whose object loss and sense of objectlessness generates his compulsion to bear witness to these atrocities through a number of narrative modalities. The trauma, then, becomes the site of engagement, the jump-off point for the creation of a series of successively more integrated and coherent narratives, ranging from overpowering narratives that subsume all current realities, to life narratives in which the trauma is repetitively re-enacted, to fully realized or witnessed narratives characterized by more integrated and subjectively realized ways of knowing (Laub and Auerhahn 1989, 1993).

Ivan's first narrative of his father's death is an overpowering one, told after the war to his great-uncle Gustave and his grandmother, Valerie, the only two other Sonnenscheins to survive (Gustave in exile as a communist in France, Valerie in hiding with a Christian family in Budapest). 'What did you do?' asks his great-uncle Gustave, who returned from France to serve under the new communist regime. Ivan replies, 'Nothing. I just stood there. That's all I could do. I could do nothing.' 'You just stood there and watched them kill your father?' Gustave asks incredulously. When Ivan tells him that there were over 2000 inmates and only 20 guards, he wonders why the prisoners did not run at the Nazi guards and disarm them, or try to escape. 'People would have hidden you', he insists. Ivan's reply, 'There was nowhere for us to go. . . . People either hated us or were scared of us', reveals his image of self as degraded or condemned, and an image of others as unresponsive or malevolent. These clips also illustrate how these malignant self and object representations come to form a core part of his identity, which is then transmuted into a life script, involving the re-enactment of endless scenarios of hunter and hunted, persecutor and persecuted through his work with the secret police.

Almost immediately the imago of his murdered father is reprojected onto his mentor in the secret police, Andor Knorr, a survivor of Auschwitz, who encourages him to avenge his father's death by bringing Nazi war criminals to justice under the new communist regime. 'There can be no forgiveness for what happened here. . . . We're going to get every one of those fascist bastards . . . it can't be fobbed off on those Germans. . . . You think about your father, it's your job to find his murderers', Knorr tells Ivan. In a reversal typical of survivors, Ivan assumes the role of aggressor, evident in his interrogations of Nazi sympathizers shown in the foregoing film clips: 'I suppose that you just stood there and wrote poems while your friends did the killing', he accuses a famous poet, after finding evidence of his fascist collaboration. In similar fashion, he accuses a filmmaker who made fraudulent newsreels for Nazi propaganda in terms redolent with his own self-accusation: 'you did nothing . . . you just watched while your friends did the killing. . . .You just fucking filmed it'.

Laub (1996) has observed that this so-called identification with the aggressor may in fact be based on a misguided attempt to reconstitute a depeopled internal object world, for in the camps such internalizations serve as a bulwark against states of utter objectlessness and aloneness.The assumption of the role of aggressor also devolves from splits within the superego, particularly between the ego ideal and the punitive aspects of the superego, which has been observed to be the psychic legacy of Holocaust survivors (Kestenberg 1993). The degradation and annihilation of the parents caused them to be simultaneously idealized and deprecated by their children, leading to distortions in self and object relations.

The way in which Ivan's memories are enacted at the level of object relations is also reflected in his affair with a colleague in the secret police, the beautiful young wife of a leader of the Hungarian resistance, who was reputed to have saved hundreds of Jews in France during the war. Significantly, this man is absent from the film, an absence reflecting that of Ivan's own father. Colonel Knorr, Ivan's surrogate father, explicitly warns Ivan that such a liaison could be ruinous for him, while the woman herself repeatedly reiterates that if her husband learned of the affair he would 'shoot them both'. Ivan's pursuit of this woman is both an act of Oedipal defiance *vis-à-vis* a devalued paternal imago and an act of identification with an idealized paternal imago, and also to some extent a re-creation of the debased object relations of the camp. In the atmosphere of suspicion and surveillance that pervades postwar communist Hungary, the affair is short-lived and degraded, consisting of furtive couplings in parks and offices, the lovers always fearful of being followed, watched and exposed. His lover, although beautiful and ardent is also coldly ambitious and exploitative, and she ends their affair abruptly for fear that Ivan's increasingly vocal criticism of party policies might imperil her career or safety.

In its depiction of the relationship between Ivan and his lover, and in fact in its depiction of the erotic and Oedipal scenarios of three generations of Sonnenscheins, we see the ways in which history leaves its imprint on the nature and resolution of infantile conflicts. For example, the relationship between Ignatz andValerie grows in the dense soil of a close and extended kin network, in which intense Oedipal conflicts and rivalries flourish.We see this in the vivid depictions of the rivalry between the son and his father (Emmanuel) who specifically forbids his son's passion forValerie; between siblings, e.g. Ignatz and his brother Gustave, who also desiresValerie; and between mother and daughter (Valerie and Rose) who endlessly battle for primacy in Ignatz's affections. AfterValerie and Ignatz marry, these tensions and rivalries continue to erupt periodically, but are generally contained or sublimated in the interests of family unity and harmony. By contrast, for Adam, who begins a quasi-incestuous affair with his sister-in-law Greta in the shadow of the rise of Nazism, the forbidden sexuality is from the start tinged with aggression, and the affair ends with fantasies and overtones of matricide and fratricide. Finally, for Ivan, the incestuous and parricidal wishes of the Oedipus complex (Loewald 1980) are heightened by his guilt over surviving and his sense of complicity in his father's execution, by virtue of his helpless acquiescence during the event. This sense of complicity fuels his affair with his married co-worker in the secret police, an affair which begins in an indiscriminate and almost instantaneous manner, and which in its emotional bankruptcy, its connection of closeness with potential injury, its merging of intimacy with paranoia and betrayal, reflects the political climate of the Stalinist era in which it flourishes. Ivan's clandestine and compulsive attachment to his lover is also infused with fantasies and re-enactments of the destructive scenario of his father's execution in the camps. Psychoanalytic investigation has revealed that for Holocaust survivors, primal scene and sexual fantasies are often infused with descriptions of violence and destruction (Kestenberg 1993; Laub 1996). Indeed, Laub (1996) has written, 'being present at or vicariously participating in scenes of massive aggression is the equivalent of the primal scene fantasy, which likewise involves forbidden knowledge' (p. 301).

However, it is in his relationship with Andor Knorr that we see most directly the re-enactment of the scenario of his father's death and his own sense of guilt and complicity. With the rise of Stalinism and its resuscitation of anti-Semitism, Knorr becomes a suspect in a supposed Zionist plot to overthrow the communist regime, and Ivan is ordered by the general of the secret police to interrogate him. Although Ivan initially complies, he later insists on Knorr's innocence. When Knorr is brutally beaten and murdered in a re-creation of Ivan's father's fate, the futile and repetitive aspects of his quest for vengeance and retribution come home to Ivan, catalysing a shift from enactment to narration. Such a shift is evident in Ivan's tribute to Knorr when he is posthumously rehabilitated and given an honourable burial after the purge of Stalinism.

> Andor Knorr, one of your murderers has come to your grave to say goodbye to you. . . . In saying goodbye to you, I am saying goodbye to myself. I stood by and watched my father be tortured and executed and I did nothing and then I watched them do the same thing to you and I did nothing.

The speech may be seen as an act of mourning and reparation in that it shows conscious recognition and remorse for his own destructive role in Knorr's death with its echoes of his helpless acquiescence in the face of his father's death. Subsequently, Ivan participates in the anti-Soviet rebellion of 1956, and again we see him hoisting Hungarian flags onto Russian tanks with fellow demonstrators, in scenes that intermingle real and fictional footage. When the Prague spring rebellion is crushed by the Soviets, Ivan is sentenced to five years in prison, on the basis of evidence provided by the documentary filmmaker whom he interrogated at the beginning of his work with the secret police. The ubiquitous presence of this documentary filmmaker, who shifts his filmic perspective according to the prevailing political currents of the time, brings home the idea that in film both factual and fictional images are constructed. The placing of fictional characters in actual newsreel footage, the combination of real and imaginary characters, not only anchors individuals in the historical circumstances that spawned them, but also reminds us that even supposedly objective newsreels and photographs are themselves constantly being shaped for narrative purposes. In *Sunshine*, representations of historical events, whether fictional or documentary, are repeatedly shown to be subject to mystifications. And while film may provide a mode for detecting the nature of these constructions or mystifications, it may also promote illusions or simulations that subvert or substitute for real events. For example, as part of his work with the secret police, Ivan confronts the filmmaker who made propaganda films for the Nazis with his footage of mass graves of women and children, supposedly murdered by the Bolsheviks. He confronts the filmmaker with his own footage, saying, 'You went to the Russian front 17 times. . . . Don't lie to me, it's on film', only to be told by the filmmaker that he was ordered to shoot film 'like I was at the Russian front', but that in fact it was made on a stage set, 17 kilometres outside of Budapest. In similar fashion, the head of the secret police tells Ivan that the evidence implicating Knorr in a Zionist plot is irrefutable because it exists on film. 'We have films of Knorr speaking with Israeli agents,' says the communist general. When Ivan confronts Knorr and advises him to confess, telling him 'We have it on film', Knorr replies, 'Really? And who played my part?'

Ivan's incarceration symbolizes the relinquishment of the various substitutions and illusions he has used to reinstate his lost world and relationships, and a confrontation with the empty circle of trauma. After his release, he wakes in terror from a dream, saying, 'I have no face.' The dream attests to the state of fragmentation and objectlessness, often noted in the repetitive dreams of Holocaust survivors (Laub and Auerhahn 1989, 1993). Based on psychoanalytic investigations, Laub (1996) has distinguished between the intensely ambivalent object ties that are often the bequest of individual and intrafamilial traumas and the states of total objectlessness and inner devastation that are the legacy of massive state sponsored atrocities. Ivan's dream also expresses his fear of the elimination of his sense of self as a witnessing presence. Ultimately, Ivan's capacity to reconstruct a narrative that not only attests to the reality of the trauma, but also re-establishes linkages with the lost pre-traumatic past, comes through his relationship with his grandmother, Valerie. His emotional connection with Valerie allows him to reach beyond the fragmenting barriers of Holocaust memories and experiences to find a new and integrated identity, constructed in part through finding a resonating responsive other within the self.

The predominant images in the latter part of the film involve intimate scenes between Ivan and Valerie, who share one room in their former apartment, now subdivided among a number of families. The shrunken interior in these scenes serves not only as a poignant reminder of the shrunken, decimated family, but also as an arena of psychic and familial regeneration. The images of Valerie and Ivan sharing a bed evoke the original incestuous pairing of Valerie and Ignatz. This final symbolic Sonnenschein coupling spawns a transitional space for the creation of shared illusions, which forms the matrix of all wishing and symbolization (Milner 1952; Winnicott 1951). When Ivan is in prison, it is Valerie who offers him this sustaining illusion, 'My darling, it is they who are in prison not us.' After his release, she tells him, 'You must try to find joy in your life. . . . I've always tried to photograph what is beautiful in life but it hasn't always been easy.' He tells her that he has lost the pocket watch that his grandfather had given him, the loss of this family artifact a symbol for all the losses of his life, and she replies, 'much more important things have disappeared, love, people, what is a pocket watch?' She instructs him on the sustaining power of daily pleasures, stating, 'I've enjoyed waking every morning', and points out how beautiful it is that 'The light keeps changing.' This statement reminds us of the paradoxical capacity of cinema to evoke and preserve visual pleasure even in the representation of unspeakable trauma. Valerie's photographs and indeed the film itself become the vehicle for preserving beauty and humanity in the face of destruction and dehumanization.

Surrounded by images, photographs and artifacts from the past, Valerie and Ivan seek to reconstitute their lost world and objects by resuscitating family traditions and representations. They embark on a quest to find the black recipe book for the 'Taste of Sunshine', hidden in the house many years previously by Ivan's grandfather, Emmanuel Sonnenschein, for fear that it would be lost or stolen. When Valerie becomes ill and is taken to the hospital, Ivan learns, much to his surprise, that she has given her name as Sonnenschein rather than Sors. After Valerie's death, Ivan escalates his search for the recipe book, only to have it lost forever when it is inadvertently tossed into a garbage truck as he finally cleans out the family apartment. This scene is reminiscent of Rosebud in Welles's *Citizen Kane* (1941), with the loss of fetishized objects signifying the loss of a beneficent longed-for maternal presence. But this loss is counterbalanced by his discovery of a letter from Emmanuel Sonnenschein to his sons, urging them to hold fast to their religious traditions, not 'for God' but because 'religion is a well built boat that sustains one in a life of permanent uncertainty.' As he reads this letter, he imagines it being read aloud by his forebears, first his great-grandfather Emmanuel, then his grandfather, Ignatz, and finally, his father, Adam, their visualized presence signifying his rediscovery of them as sustaining introjects. Subsequently, Ivan changes his name back to Sonnenschein, a gesture that on the surface signifies his acceptance of his Jewish identity, and his reconnection with Jewish traditions that bind and heal. This gesture is also driven by his need to reconfigure the strands of the pre–Holocaust, Holocaust and post–Holocaust family experiences into a unified narrative in which the intricate patterning of linkages between historical trauma and individual subjectivity across the generations is revealed and explored. But most importantly, Ivan's resumption of his family name signifies the freeing of impulses and fantasies from the confining circle of traumatic re-enactments, enabling his life to go forward, as reflected in his final tribute to his grandmother:

> For the first time I walked down the street without feeling like I was in hiding. My great-grandfather Emmanuel Sonnenschein must have been the last Sonnenschein to feel like this. . . . I remembered the recipe book that we had lost and suddenly realized that the family secret was not to be found on its pages. It was preserved by my grandmother, the only one in our family who had the gift of breathing freely.

This final statement encapsulates the essential paradox in the film's portrayal of familial and individual identity. Ivan, like his forebears, finds his identity only in the negation of that identity, integration only through the duality inherent in embracing both his Jewish heritage and his Hungarian roots, with their embranglement of religious and secular, Judaism and Christianity, communism and capitalism. Indeed, the grandmother that Ivan comes to emulate is one who alternately embraced aspects of communism and capitalism, Judaism and Christianity, freedom and commitment, without slavish allegiance to any system or institution. Indeed, she affirmed that they were fated to become communists because 'it was the communists who liberated us', while at the same time asserting that she never embraced communism as did her grandson. In similar fashion, Valerie was the first Sonnenschein to reclaim her Jewish name, but she does so shortly after expressing her scepticism to Ivan about the existence of God as constructed by her forefathers. The identity that Ivan consolidates at the end of the film, like that of his grandmother, is thus a postmodern one, riddled with contradictions and oppositions, inherent in his dual gestures of changing his name back to Sonnenschein at the same time that he throws away the family formula of the same name. He inadvertently loses or negates one aspect of his past, the formula that permitted his family's ascendancy and assimilation into Hungarian society as Jews, while at the same time preserving the primary signifier of that past, the family name. The preservation of identity in the face of the negation of identity, the unity of identity discovered through the multiplicity of identities – that is perhaps the universal paradox embodied in the Sonnenschein saga.

Acknowledgements

The author gratefully acknowledges the contributions of Drs Harriet Wrye, Catherine Portuges, Lissa Weinstein, and Eliot Jurist, all of whom read this paper with mind and heart and whose comments helped bring it to fruition.

References

Alter, R. (1986) 'Mother and son lost in a continent', review of A. Appelfeld *To the Land of the Cattails. New York Times*, 2 November.

Brown, N. T. (2000) 'The Holocaust in film – the enigma of indifference: Christian ideology and the portrayal of the Jew', paper presented at the 32nd Annual Scholars' Conference on the Holocaust and the Churches, 2–5 March, Kean University, Union, New Jersey.

Deak, I. (2000) 'Strangers at home', *New York Review of Books*, 20 July.

Diamond, D. and Blatt, S. J. (1994) 'Internal working models and the representational world in attachment and psychoanalytic theories', in M. B. Sperling and W. H. Berman (eds) *Attachment in Adults: Clinical and Developmental Issues*. New York: Guilford Press.

Horowitz, M. (1972) 'Modes of representation of thought', *Journal of the American Psychoanalytic Association*, 20: 793–819.

Insdorf, A. (1989) *Indelible Shadows: Film and the Holocaust*. Cambridge: Cambridge University Press.

Kestenberg, J. (1993) 'What a psychoanalyst learned from the holocaust and genocide', *International Journal of Psycho-Analysis*, 74: 1117–1129.

Knafo, D. and Feiner, K. (1996) 'Primal scene variations', *Journal of the American Psychoanalytic Association*, 44: 549–569.

Kracauer, S. (1960) *Theory of Film: The Redemption of Physical Reality*. Oxford: Oxford University Press.

Laub, D. (1996) 'The empty circle: children of survivors and the limits of reconstruction', *Journal of the American Psychoanalytic Association*, 46: 507–529.

Laub, D. and Auerhahn, N. C. (1989) 'Failed empathy: a central theme in the survivor's holocaust experience', *Psychoanalytic Psychology*, 6: 377–400.

Laub, D. and Auerhahn, N. C. (1993) 'Knowing and not knowing massive psychic trauma: forms of traumatic memory', *International Journal of Psycho-Analysis*, 74: 287–302.

Laub, D. and Podell, D. (1995) 'Art and trauma', *International Journal of Psycho-Analysis*, 76: 991–1005.

Levi, P. (1969) *Survival in Auschwitz*, trans. S. Woolf. New York: Collier.

Loewald, H. (1980) 'The waning of the Oedipus Complex', in *Papers on Psychoanalysis*. New Haven and London: Yale University Press.

Metz, C. (1982) *The Imaginary Signifier: Psychoanalysis and the Cinema*. Bloomington, IN: Indiana University Press.

Milner, M. (1952) 'The role of illusion in symbol formation', in D. Tuckett (ed.) *The*

Suppressed Madness of Sane Men: Forty-four Years of Exploring Psychoanalysis. London and New York: Routledge.

Mulvey, L. (1989) *Visual and Other Pleasures*. Bloomington, IN: Indiana University Press.

Rose, G. J. (1995) *Necessary Illusion: Art as Witness*. New York: International University Press.

Rosenblum, R. (1999) 'And till the ghastly tale is told: Sarah Kofman, Primo Levi – survivors of the Shoah and the dangers of testimony', paper presented at the International Conference, Freud at the Threshold of the 21st Century, 13–16 December, Jerusalem, Israel.

Scott, O. (2000) 'Serving the empire, one after another', *New York Times*, 9 June.

Sontag, S. (1976) 'Fascinating Fascism', in B. Nichols (ed.) *Movies and Methods, Vol. 1*. Berkeley and Los Angeles: University of California Press.

Wilgowicz, P. (1999) 'Listening psychoanalytically to the Shoah half a century on', *International Journal of Psycho-Analysis*, 80: 429–438.

Winnicott, D.W. (1951/1971) 'Transitional objects and transitional phenomena', in *Playing and Reality*. London and New York: Tavistock Publications.

Horror perspectives

8

NOTES ON THE RELEVANCE OF PSYCHOANALYTIC THEORY TO EURO-HORROR CINEMA

Steven Jay Schneider

Is the Euro-horror film particularly susceptible to psychoanalytic theorizing and interpretation, and if so, why? Before even beginning to tackle such a monstrous question, one needs to get clear on just which 'Euro-horror' – and just which 'psychoanalytic theory' – one is talking about. Equally important, one needs to specify the sense of 'susceptible' here. There are, after all, a variety of ways, neither mutually exclusive nor necessarily connected, in which psychoanalysis can be brought to bear on discussions of the horror genre.

I

'Euro-horror' is a term used primarily by reviewers and fans (and fans who are reviewers) to refer to post-1970 horror cinema coming out of France, Spain, Italy and, to a lesser extent, Germany. With the recent opening up of academic film studies to such previously undesirable and neglected cinematic categories as 'trash', 'psychotronic', 'exploitation' and 'cult', however, film scholars in North America and Great Britain (including Ian Conrich, Michael Grant, Mikita Brottman, Joan Hawkins, Leon Hunt and Peter Hutchings) have started to give the term a wider currency.[1] Critical attention to and interest in Euro-horror continues to grow today, just as it does with respect to the horror film output in so many other countries.[2] This refreshing change has as much to do with the increased availability of the films in question to English-speaking scholars – primarily via paracinema mail-order companies and internet websites – as with any unfounded critical bias towards British and North American productions.

While formal and systematic research along these lines has yet to be conducted, judging from a casual survey of the term's employment it would appear that 'Euro-horror' is more often associated with the stylistic and visual excesses and idiosyncrasies of certain cult auteurs than with the generic horror output of any particular national or regional European cinema; Eastern Europe, despite claiming such auteurs of dark fantasy and horror as Juraz Herz, Wojciech Has, Jan Svankmajer and Lucian Pintilie, seems somewhat outside the Euro-horror loop. The implication here is that we are dealing less with a descriptive (geographic) designation than with an evaluative term of endearment, or, in some cases, of disdain. Moreover, it is one that threatens to collapse a number of traditional and deeply entrenched binary oppositions that remain operative in academic film studies discourse, such as that between 'art' and 'trash' cinema, that between quality and exploitation, and that between experimental and conventional filmic practices.[3]

Among the most popular and prolific Euro-horror directors are Lucio Fulci, Dario Argento, Aristide Massaccesi (aka Joe D'Amato), Lamberto Bava and Michele Soavi in Italy; Jacinto Molina (aka Paul Naschy), Jorge Grau, Argentinian-born León Klimovsky, Amando de Ossorio and José Ramón Larraz in Spain; and Jess Franco (b. Madrid), Walerian Borowczyk (b. Poland) and Jean Rollin in France. A number of seminal Italian and Spanish horror directors – including Mario Bava, Riccardo Freda, Antonio Margheriti and Sergio Martino – whose most influential films were made prior to the mid-Seventies, are usually not positioned squarely within the Euro-horror camp, even though their narrative and stylistic trademarks frequently appear, either as theft or homage, in myriad uncontroversial examples of Euro-horror cinema.[4] Also omitted from Euro-horror consideration are those continental filmmakers who may have contributed one or more key films to the horror genre,[5] but whose work spans a variety of genres, and who are not generally considered horror directors *per se*, or even at heart. Interestingly, however, subgeneric distinctions do *not* seem particularly important for Euro-horror classification. Thus, one finds gore, *giallo*, stalker, slasher, splatter, cannibalism, zombie, serial killer, body horror, snuff and lesbian vampire films included for discussion, regardless of these films' countless and immediately recognizable differences at the levels of convention, narrative, iconography, atmosphere and setting.

For distributors, promoters and, of course, fans, the Euro-horror tag is something of a badge of honour, implying membership in a fairly exclusive club of horror films that manage to be simultaneously artistic *and* generic, innovative *and* derivative, highbrow *and* lowbrow. The cultural value and prominence of Euro-horror has risen dramatically in recent years with the advent of DVD technology and what Raiford Guins, discussing the promotion and consumption of Italian horror cinema in the United States, identifies as processes of 'remediation'. According to Guins,

> companies such as Anchor Bay have begun to market their products, especially 'affective products' that are nearly impossible to distinguish from Criterion titles available on DVD. The best possible original prints are sought for digital remastering onto DVD. 'Extras,' digital transfers, widescreen/letterbox, subtitles, original soundtracks, and attractive packaging easily close the gap between the high-brow cinema attributed to Criterion's restoration process and the low-brow aesthetics once associated with tattered videocassette covers, dark prints, poor dubbing, and cut-up releases. . . . The companies promoting the likes of Argento, Bava, and even Fulci on DVD, selling a title as part of a 'collection,' place their directors on the market as auteurs in order to invoke value statements that valorize the director's work as an art-object, an 'authored original,' and a masterpiece of Italian horror cinema.
>
> (Guins 2003, p. 20)

For concerned parents, teachers and policy makers, on the other hand, Euro-horror is often treated – and therefore targeted – as among the most dangerous of cinematic products, the lowest of the low, in large part because the violence depicted in such films is frequently sexualized with a degree of explicitness not found in most American (certainly most Hollywood) products. It is precisely because Euro-horror is a term with shifting, ambiguous, even contradictory meanings, one which cuts across various subgenres of cinematic horror while still managing to exclude any number of candidate films on grounds that are, if not arbitrary, at the very least difficult to identify or justify, that any comprehensive theoretical (including psychoanalytical) inquiry into its narratives, conventions and imagery needs to address in far greater depth than can been done in this chapter the complex issue of selection.

At this still-early stage in Euro-horror analysis, the scholar's main task should be to identify key directors, actors, films and audiences, looking at whether or not, and (if so) the extent to which psychoanalysis sheds privileged theoretical and/or interpretive light. It must be kept in mind, however, that parallel questions can, and at some point certainly should, be asked about, for example, the horror output of Central and Eastern European nations, and about the work of directors from Italy, France, Spain and Germany whose films, for whatever reason, rarely seem to qualify as 'Euro' (as opposed to simply 'European') horror.

II

Especially since the late 1970s, there has been a tremendous diversity of psychoanalytic approaches to the horror film. These approaches differ and often conflict in substantial ways. In addition, the objections levied in recent years by analytic philosophers, film aestheticians, sociologists and cultural theorists, cognitive and feminist film theorists, and empirical psychologists, many of whom position themselves well outside the circle of Freud and his followers, constitute a serious threat, or challenge, to psychoanalytical horror film theory. This is because such objections could be fatal to psychoanalysis if proven correct (admittedly a big if!). Clearly then, and following James Donald (1991), it is crucial for us to 'be clear about *which* psychoanalysis it is that we are talking about, and so about which claims are and are not being made for psychoanalysis' (1991, p. 2) when it comes to horror cinema.

When it comes to *Euro*-horror cinema, moreover, it behoves us to acknowledge the enormous debt this tradition owes to Gothic literature, as well as the past susceptibility of the Gothic to psychoanalytic, especially Freudian, theorizing. The films of Bava, Argento, Naschy and Rollin, each in their own indiosyncratic ways, manage to suggest through such elements as *mise-en-scène*, atmosphere, colour scheme and set design the existence of repressed desires, long-buried secrets and ominous dark powers lurking in the shadows. If this sounds more than a little Freudian in spirit, that is no accident. William Patrick Day hardly overstates things when he writes that 'no discussion of the Gothic can avoid discussing Freud; one of the most obvious ways of thinking about the genre is to read it in terms of Freud's system. . . . We cannot pretend that the striking parallels between Freud's thought and the Gothic fantasy do not exist' (1985, p. 177).

Day seeks to account for the obvious correspondences between Freudian psychoanalysis and Gothic literature at the level of theme (e.g. the drama of selfhood played out within the family; the struggle to contain and control sexual energy; the conflict between masculine and feminine modes of identity) as well as of narrative (e.g. the subversion of linear plot structures; the substitution of mechanisms such as transformation, condensation and projection for clearly defined patterns of cause-and-effect; the prioritization of subjective experience and the dynamics of 'inner life'). He first rejects the orthodox and uncritical psychoanalytic view according to which these correspondences were *inevitable* because the Gothic simply anticipated truths soon to be discovered by Freud. He also rejects the pragmatic and hermeneutic view that these correspondences were *fortuitous* because, regardless of whether Freud was right or wrong, the Gothic simply lent itself to allegorization in psychoanalytic terms.

Instead, Day argues that the two systems – one imaginative-literary, the other intellectual-scientific – have a 'common, or at least related, origin':

> The Gothic is not a crude anticipation of Freudianism, nor its unacknowledged father. Rather, the two are cousins, responses to the problems of selfhood and identity, sexuality and pleasure, fear and anxiety as they manifest themselves in the nineteenth and early twentieth centuries. The Gothic arises

out of the immediate needs of the reading public to escape from conventional life and articulate and define the turbulence of their psychic existence. We may see Freud as the intellectual counterpart of this process. [The Gothic] acclimatized the culture to the types of ideas Freud was to present as truth by presenting them as fiction.

(Day 1985, p. 179)

Notice how questions concerning the logical or referential status of orthodox Freudian psychoanalysis are bracketed here. Instead, we get an account which takes the narrative and thematic affinities holding between this theoretical paradigm and traditional Gothic literature to be historically and culturally conditioned, even determined. Such affinities are neither immutable nor traceable, at least in the first instance, to the intentions of individual authors – not those of the Gothic novelists, and certainly not Freud's own. This latter is the case, despite the 'Gothic' tone of some of Freud's case-histories. Rather, the affinities in question are to be understood primarily in formal and generic terms, the two systems developing, changing and subdividing in what may well be read as a strange but significant sort of tandem.

A parallel can be drawn here, and perhaps an intellectual debt is owed, to the work of Stanley Cavell. In his collection of essays, *Disowning Knowledge in Six Plays of Shakespeare* (1987), and even earlier in *The Claim of Reason* (1979), Cavell makes a convincing case for the affinities between Shakespearian tragedy and what philosophy calls 'scepticism':

Shakespeare could not be who he is – the burden of the name of the greatest writer in the language, the creature of the greatest ordering of English – unless his writing is engaging the depth of the philosophical preoccupations of his culture. . . . My intuition is that the advent of skepticism as manifested in Descartes's *Meditations* is already in full existence in Shakespeare, from the time of the great tragedies in the first years of the seventeenth century, in the generation preceding that of Descartes.

(Cavell 1987, pp. 2–3)

Elsewhere, Cavell writes that 'tragedy is the working out of a response to skepticism – as I now like to put the matter, that tragedy is an interpretation of what skepticism itself is an interpretation of' (1987, pp. 5–6). If Freud and the Gothic both provided responses (of a sort) to 'the problems of selfhood and identity, sexuality and pleasure, fear and anxiety' as these were manifested particularly in Europe in the nineteenth and early twentieth centuries, Shakespearian tragedy and Cartesian scepticism both concern 'the sense of the individual human being not only as now doubtful in his possessions, as though unconvinced that anything really belongs to him, but doubtful at the same time whether there is a place to which he really belongs' (Cavell 1987, p. 10).

123

Whether Freudianism, or any other species of psychoanalytic thought, can successfully shed light on Euro-horror cinema's textual processes and the nature and mechanics of its effects on viewers, while presenting itself as one among a number of rival candidates for the job, remains an open question. It is one which depends at least in part on the truth value of the various claims and arguments made in support of psychoanalysis more generally – if not as medical-therapeutic practice, then as theory of human development – though precisely *how* such truth or falsity is to be determined is yet another open question. But even if, for the sake of discussion, psychoanalysis at this more general level is somehow proven *false*, its value as a tool for shedding light on specific Euro-horror films, cycles and subgenres – particularly those with readily identifiable Gothic linkages – can hardly be denied. Such films and groups of films may be profitably interpreted as thematizing, narrativizing and embodying ideas and constructs similar to those found in orthodox psychoanalytic theory and its revisions.

Having said all this, it may well be the case that the particularities and peculiarities of Euro-horror cinema warrant a bringing to bear of psychoanalytic concepts, theses and principles coming from outside, even well outside, Freud's own purview. As Michael Grant notes in his paper for the 'Psychoanalysis and Euro-horror' panel at the *First European Psychoanalytic Film Festival* (see Chapter 11), Lucio Fulci's 1981 Italian zombie-gore classic *The Beyond* (1981) seems an obvious choice for explication via Lacan's notion of the 'Real'. Interestingly, however, Grant himself, in an earlier essay, denies the impulse to utilize Lacanian/Zizekian psychoanalytic theory with respect to Fulci's picture on the grounds that such practice, 'despite its attractions, finally will not do. It obscures too much of what is unique to a given film, and by so doing distorts what is unique to the work in question' (Grant 2000). (One wonders whether this statement cannot be turned around, why it might not be the case that a given film – here, *The Beyond* – is especially well-suited for interpretation in the terms of this particular theoretical model.) And Julian Hoxter (1998) has looked at how, in the *gialli* mystery thrillers of Dario Argento, the 'complex, shifting connection between individuals and the world of objects which they inhabit' (Hoxter 1998, p. 99) exemplifies certain key principles of Kleinian object-relations theory. As early as 1914, Otto Rank himself referred to Stellan Rye and Paul Wegener's German *Doppelgänger* picture, *The Student of Prague* (1913), in order to explain the prominence of the 'double' in literature and film. His thesis was that this figure represents 'the normally unconscious thought of the approaching destruction of the self' (Rank 1914, p. 77); that it signifies, in other words, a return to consciousness – in disguised, wish-fulfilling form – of the repressed fear of death (Schneider 2001). Why not go further, and seek to apply the insights of such key psychoanalytic theorists as Abraham, Ferenczi and Jones to the Euro-horror film? The benefits of such efforts could potentially extend to the academic discipline of cinema studies as a whole.

Let me conclude this very brief inquiry by returning to the third qualification I listed at the start. In what sense of 'susceptible' might the Euro-horror film be considered especially susceptible to psychoanalytic theorizing and interpretation? Following Noël Carroll (2003), we can say that, since many (perhaps most, quite possibly all) Euro-horror films presuppose, either implicitly or explicitly, psychoanalytic concepts and imagery, interpretation in these terms is well justified on historicist grounds. Note that such a hermeneutical employment of psychoanalytic thought does not require that such thought be *true*, or even valid. It just requires that it capture, on some level, what is manifest (in some cases, latent) in the films themselves. Carroll goes on to argue that

> this sort of defense . . . places limitations on the specificity of the psycho-analytic framework one may mobilize with respect to a given horror film. . . . Many of the psychoanalytic ideas available to filmmakers and their audiences are extremely general, rather vague, and even inchoate. These the interpreter must approach gingerly. In such cases, one's deployment of psychoanalytic concepts should be correspondingly general.
>
> (Carroll 2003)

This is a highly debatable series of claims which should not be taken as given on *a priori* grounds. One needs to look at particular horror films, directors and cycles on a case-by-case basis in order to determine the extent to which certain psychoanalytic ideas may have seeped into the narratives and imagery. And for those who *do* believe in the truth of some species of psychoanalysis, a *theoretical* defence of its applicability to the Euro-horror film may be available as well, if the practitioner can establish that such films have a defining characteristic – an essence, if you will – that is explicable, or that is best explained, only with reference to the species of psychoanalysis in question.

I would just add that, because they effectively constitute different *levels* of interpretation, the two uses of psychoanalysis identified here – historicist and theoretical – are capable of being combined in all sorts of interesting, even surprising, ways. Thus, a film such as Argento's *The Stendhal Syndrome* (1996) may well *thematize* (intentionally or not) Kleinian object-relations theory, even while submitting to analysis in terms of Rank's theory of the double. The possibilities are there, we need only to begin exploring them.

Notes

1   See Grant (2000), Hawkins (2000) and Hunt (2000). Previously, and to his credit, Kim Newman (1988) devoted a chapter to Italian horror in his study *Nightmare Movies*.
2   These include Japan, Australia, Mexico, Turkey, the Czech Republic, Hong Kong,

Indonesia, Scandinavia, South Korea, Thailand, New Zealand, India and the Philippines. See Schneider (2002), Schneider and Williams (2003) and Black (1998).

3   Cf. Hawkins: 'Paracinema consumption can be understood . . . as American art cinema consumption has often been understood, as a reaction against the hegemonic and normatizing practices of mainstream, dominant Hollywood consumption' (2000, p. 7). The trouble with Hawkins's argument is that, even while problematizing the opposition between art cinema and the so-called 'trash' film, she effectively recasts it in terms of an ideological and equally misleading dichotomy between Hollywood and non-Hollywood filmmaking practices (whether alternative, experimental, 'underground' or simply foreign). As recent scholarship has endeavoured to show, however, the relationship between Hollywood and its various 'others' is every bit as complex, evolving and mutually influential as that between trash (cult, psychotronic, etc.) filmmaking and the cinematic avant-garde. See Mendik and Schneider (2002).

4   For a useful set of essays on Italian Gothic (pre-'Euro') horror cinema, see the special 'In Focus' section of the online journal *Images: A Journal of Film and Popular Culture* 5, 1997: http://www.imagesjournal.com/issue05/infocus.htm

5   E.g. Georges Franju's *Eyes without a Face* (1959), Roger Vadim's *Blood and Roses* (1960), Harry Kümel's *Daughters of Darkness* (1970), Eloy de la Iglesia's *Cannibal Man* (1972), Pupi Avati's *Zeder* (1983) and Dick Maas's *The Lift* (1983).

References

Black, A. (ed.) (1998) *Necronomicon: The Journal of Horror and Erotic Cinema, Book Two*. London: Creation Books.

Carroll, N. (2003) 'Psychoanalysis and the horror film', in S. J. Schneider (ed.) *Freud's Worst Nightmares: Psychoanalysis and the Horror Film*, Cambridge: Cambridge University Press.

Cavell, S. (1979) *The Claim of Reason: Wittgenstein, Skepticism, Morality, and Tragedy*. Oxford: Oxford University Press.

Cavell, S. (1987) *Disowning Knowledge in Six Plays of Shakespeare*. Cambridge: Cambridge University Press.

Day, W. P. (1985) *In the Circles of Fear and Desire: A Study of Gothic Fantasy*. Chicago: University of Chicago Press.

Donald, J. (1991) 'On the threshold: psychoanalysis and cultural studies', in *Psychoanalysis and Cultural Theory: Thresholds*. London: Macmillan.

Grant, M. (2000) 'Fulci's Waste Land: cinema, horror, and the dreams of modernism', in G. Harper and X. Mendik (eds) *Unruly Pleasures: The Cult Film and its Critics*. Guildford: FAB Press.

Guins, R. (2003) 'Blood and black gloves on shiny discs: new media, old tastes, and the remediation of Italian horror films in the US', in S. J. Schneider and T. Williams (eds) *Horror International*. Detroit, MI: Wayne State University Press.

Hawkins, J. (2000) *Cutting Edge: Art-Horror and the Horrific Avant-garde*. Minneapolis, MN: University of Minnesota Press.

Hoxter, J. (1998) 'Anna with the devil inside: Klein, Argento, and *The Stendhal Syndrome*', in A. Black (ed.) *Necronomicon: The Journal of Horror and Erotic Cinema, Book Two*. London: Creation Books.

Hunt, L. (2000) 'A (sadistic) night at the opera: notes on the Italian horror film', in K. Gelder (ed.) *The Horror Reader*. London: Routledge.

Images: A Journal of Film and Popular Culture 5, 1997: www.imagesjournal.com/issue05/ infocus.htm

Kinoeye: A Fortnightly Journal of Film in the New Europe: www.kinoeye.org

Mendik, X. and Schneider, S. J. (2002) *Underground USA: Filmmaking Beyond the Hollywood Canon*. London: Wallflower Press.

Newman, K. (1988) *Nightmare Movies*. London: Bloomsbury.

Rank, O. (1914) *The Double: A Psychoanalytic Study*. Chapel Hill, NC: University of North Carolina Press, 1971.

Schneider, S. J. (2001) 'Manifestations of the literary double in modern horror cinema', *Film and Philosophy* special issue, pp. 51–62.

Schneider, S. J. (ed.) (2003) *Fear without Frontiers: Horror Cinema across the Globe*. Guildford: FAB Press.

Schneider, S. J. and Williams, T. (eds) (2003) *Horror International*. Detroit, MI: Wayne State University Press.

9

DARIO ARGENTO'S *PHENOMENA* (1985)

A psychoanalytic perspective on the 'horror film' genre and adolescent development

Donald Campbell

The virtual other and the actual other

From the beginning, the development of our sense of self is primarily an intersubjective process. Psychoanalysts study the dynamics in the infant–mother dyad through the medium of the patient's transference and analyst's counter-transference during psychoanalysis. Discussion of the contributions that Sigmund Freud, Anna Freud, Melanie Klein and Donald Winnicott have made to psycho-analytic views about early mother–infant communication are beyond the scope of this chapter. However, I will briefly mention Bion's (1962) observations of projective identification as the infant's first mode of communication and the medium through which the mother becomes aware of and thinks about her child's emotional and mental state, as they are pertinent to my focus. According to Bion, the mother contains the child's projections of frustration and anxiety in her 'reverie' and uses these projections (represented by Bion as K) to understand her child. When the child is able to introject its mother's understanding, the child has an experience of being known in a particular way by an other. The child who is not too persecuted or envious will be able to introject modifications of its originally projected painful affects and anxiety-ridden perceptions, made tolerable by mother's responses influenced by her understanding, as well as introject and identify mother's capacity to think.

Through the medium of direct observation of mothers and infants, research in child development has confirmed psychoanalytic views and made new discoveries. I will briefly refer to hypotheses which are germane to the subject of this chapter, beginning with Braten's (1988) contention that the prerequisite for intersubjectivity is the inherently dyadic organization of the individual. Braten proposes that there are circuits within the newborn's central nervous system that specify the immediate co-presence of a complementary participant, which he refers to as a 'virtual other', whose potential is fulfilled by an actual other. The 'virtual other' is a 'felt prospective' waiting to be realized by an actual other. The infant and mother thereby create a dialogic circle by virtue of the mother's becoming the first actual other. Other researchers (Brazelton *et al.* 1974; Stern 1974; Trevarthen 1979; Murray 1991) have observed the infant's capacity to actively engage the mother, to cue a response from the parent from as early as two months, which suggests that the infant has the ability to attract or stimulate into life the object it is seeking which, in turn, is the object who will nurture the infant's development. This process is non-verbal and prior to self-awareness.

Stern has observed a similar process in which the mother's intuitive sense leads her to match some aspect of her child's behaviour with her own feeling state. This is the beginning of 'affective attunement' (Stern 1985, p. 142), an intersubjective process that expresses the quality of feeling a shared affect without imitation. Imitation can focus only upon external behaviour. Stern identifies affect attunement as a response to internal states and, thereby, shifts the attention to what lies behind behaviour, to the sharing of feelings. The 'virtual other', in this respect, the child's internal world of affects, requires the mother, the 'actual other', to actualize feeling states by sharing them. The sharing of affective states is the most pervasive and clinically germane feature of intersubjective relatedness. It is initiated by a mother's intuition and conveys, without words, that she is feeling something very like what her child is feeling (ibid., p. 140). Tracking and attunement 'permit one human being to "be with" another in the sense of sharing likely inner experiences' (ibid., p. 157). For the 9-month-old child, it probably feels like magic, a manifestation of its omnipotence, or being the object of mother's telepathy.

As we grow older, other relationships function as actual others that we use to bring a virtual other within us into being. A similar process occurs when the viewer moves from perception to feeling in art. Susan Langer (1967) quotes Mrs Canbell Fischer as saying, 'My grasp of the essence of sadness . . . comes not from moments in which I have been sad, but from moments when [through art] I have seen sadness before me released from the entanglements with contingency' (p. 88). Art provides a refuge from the inevitable contingencies and the particular and irreversible entanglements in the real world. The illusory form and behaviour of the horror-film monster enables the viewer in the 'safety' of the cinema to transform perception into an actual feeling, a feeling which is no less real even though it is elicited by the unreal. This experience may be cathartic, or a trial by fantasy, before we can express the actual feeling in the real world.

The '*uncanny*'

Freud's 1919 paper 'The "uncanny"', has been referred to by film scholars (see Schneider 1999) to explain the nature of the monster's impact on the viewer's psyche, namely that 'the uncanny is in reality nothing new or alien, but something which is familiar and old-established in the mind and which has become alienated from it only through the process of repression' (Freud 1919, p. 241). The uncanny, in Freud's view, represented a return of repressed infantile fears about birth and death, castration anxieties, traumas, fantasies, etc., as well as their 'solutions'; the 'surmounted beliefs' based on magical or omnipotent thinking, such as belief in the ability of the dead to return to life, or belief in the existence of doubles.

The monster is unlikely to generate a feeling of the uncanny unless the viewer is able to suspend disbelief and experience what Freud refers to as a 'conflict of judgement', that is a belief in the possibility of the monster. Following Lakoff (1993), Schneider (1999) emphasizes that the horror film's narrative serves 'to reconfirm surmounted beliefs [which] are "embodied" not in language, but by horror film monsters. In other words, the medium of our metaphor is primarily visual, not verbal'.

The monster, unlike other uncanny objects, is experienced as an object of horror because it elicits a visceral response of revulsion and disgust. Disgust is the most visceral of emotions and functions as a defence against anxieties associated with helplessness, loss of body boundaries, ego disintegration, separation from and loss of bodily creations (urine and faeces), as well as a reaction formation aimed at denying genital pleasure. These pre-genital and genital anxieties are revived during adolescence.

Other developmental experiences, such as affective attunement, provide the basis for beliefs that later, in adolescence and adulthood, are surmounted and give rise to benign, even reassuring, uncanny moments.

Adolescent development

Turning now to adolescence, I want to emphasize a progressive and regressive oscillation in adolescence that creates so much confusion and anxiety in teenagers and their parents. On the one hand, there is a progressive push, fuelled by the hormonal and physiological changes initiated by puberty, which gives the young girl the capacity to bear her father's child, the young boy the ability to impregnate his mother, and both of them the musculature with which to kill their parental rival. This radical change in the child's body thrusts its sexuality and musculature to the centre of the psychic stage and creates a conflict with earlier self-images. On the other hand, there is a regressive pull to earlier infantile fears and anxieties about survival and omnipotent fantasies of triumph over loss, death and castration.

Before puberty the body was passive to the extent that it could not enact sexual and murderous fantasies. Puberty introduces a radical new insistence that the body becomes active. Physiological changes introduce a new capacity to act out fantasies. This dynamic creates dangerous conflicts between pre-pubertal wishes, to be suckled by mother and protected by father, and adolescent sexual and murderous wishes toward the same objects.

The monster in 'body horror' films

'Body horror' is the horror film sub-genre that is most relevant to my focus on the adolescents' anxieties associated with the change of their childhood body into an adult body. The term 'body horror' first came to prominence in 1989 in Philip Brophy's article 'Horrality: the textuality of contemporary horror films'. The monster in the body horror film is not an alien, an animal, or a fantastical creature external to us, but a human being with a body like ours. Wolfman and the Werewolf were humans bitten by werewolves and transformed into were-wolves at every full moon. After Dr Jekyll had taken his drug in order to separate good and evil in human personality, he became Mr Hyde. In the Vampire movie, which became a sub-genre in its own right, vampires were originally human beings who were bitten by vampires and given vampire blood to drink before they expired. Monsters that emerged from normal human beings were the progenitors of what is now regarded as body horror.

Body horror plays on the fear, disgust, shame and apprehension about one's own appearance and bodily functions (usually internal ones), their mystery and our inability to control them. Some adolescents experience their body as under-going a metamorphosis during puberty with accompanying anxieties about loss of the familiar, about narcissistic wounds, and worries about what to do with their new bodies. This is represented, for instance, in Croenenberg's *The Fly* (1986). Brian DePalma's *Carrie* (1976) depicts female adolescents' fears about menstruation and male reactions of disgust.

Phenomena

An example of body horror in European cinema is Dario Argento's *Phenomena* (1985, titled *Creepers* in the cut version for distribution in the USA). I will briefly highlight certain aspects of the monster in *Phenomena* in order, firstly, to address a developmental conflict about the body in adolescence and, secondly, to discuss a psychological solution that is derived from a very early period of development.

The film begins with a sweeping high crane shot across a green mountainous countryside, as two adults herd a group of adolescent tourists on to a bus. As the bus drives off we see an adolescent girl, who has been left behind, forgotten by her peers and the supervising adults, running after the bus calling for it to stop – to no avail. We hear the wind begin to howl. The young girl has been left alone in a landscape, empty except for a chalet, devoid of any sign of life, at the end of a road. We are watching a classic horror film beginning.

We enter the house from the girl's perspective as she calls out, 'Is anyone home? I'm a foreigner and I'm lost!' We hear and see two chains being wrenched from a wall. Suddenly the chains are thrown over her head and tightened around her neck. The girl shrieks in terror, manages to break free, her hand is stabbed by a pair of scissors into the doorframe, but she runs out of the house into the woods. We now watch her flight from the pursuer's eyes. She is cornered, stabbed in the chest with the scissors, and her head breaks through a pane of glass behind her. Her decapitated head is thrown into a raging river. We never see the murderer. The wind howls.

We are on familiar adolescent horror film ground. The child is lost, a stranger in the foreign territory of adolescence, abandoned by peers and forgotten by her substitute parents. Murderous impulses cannot be restrained. The phallus cannot be escaped and is deadly.

Every film can be seen as the depiction of a problem. In *Phenomena* typical adolescent anxieties about sexuality, body image and madness are played out as the film progresses. Similarly, every film can be viewed as representing the director's solution. As we can see in the opening sequence, the problem facing the girl is one of survival in the face of abandonment and isolation. Argento demonstrates from the very beginning that murderous sexuality is the primary problem. Can union with a partner in intercourse become the medium through which the adolescent overcomes loss and alienation? In fact, Argento retreats from sexual intercourse as a solution to loss and alienation to something more primitive and mysterious.

In the next scene Inge, a trained monkey, our primitive ancestor, is viewed very much like a human child, called 'my nurse and friend' by Dr MacGregor, a kindly, wheelchair-bound entomologist (a scientist who studies insects), and is being admonished as a 'naughty girl' for carrying a knife. Argento has introduced a 'whodunnit'.

Eight and a half months later Jennifer Corvino, another foreign adolescent girl, arrives in the Swiss Transylvania from the New World (USA). As she is being driven to a female boarding school, a bee flies into the car and scares the accompanying teacher. 'Don't kill it', exclaims Jennifer. The insect calms and settles gently on the girl, who says, 'Insects never hurt me. I love them. I love all insects.' It is clear that she has a special telepathic relationship with insects.

Jennifer's father, an idealized film star adored by other adolescent girls, is away for a year and 'can't even be reached by phone'. Jennifer's mother is not mentioned. Her roommate's mother has left her some baby food. Early in the film, parents have abandoned and infantilized their adolescent daughters.

After an admonition by a strict teacher to behave, Jennifer's roommate leaves the school to meet her boyfriend. She is chased and impaled through the mouth by the same weapon we saw in the first murder. Meanwhile, Inge, the monkey, rescues Jennifer from two amorous teenage boys. Inge, whom Jennifer calls her 'saviour', takes her to the home of the renowned insect scientist, who notices she sexually excites the insects: 'He likes you. The sound you hear, that's its mating call. You're exciting it. He is secreting a gland to attract a mate. He's doing his best to excite you.' 'We just met', says Jennifer. 'It isn't the mating season. I've never seen anything like it', replies Dr MacGregor. Later, he remarks that insects and the human soul are each linked by their multifarious mystery. 'I was alone, in the dark, I needed help. It was as though the firefly heard me and answered my call', says Jennifer. Dr MacGregor replies, 'The things I've discovered, my fellow scientists consider absurd. Extrasensory perception. Paranormal powers. Some species can communicate over vast distances by telepathy. It's perfectly normal for insects to be slightly telepathic.' 'Normal for insects, but am I normal?' asks Jennifer. She sees this power as part of her split personality. The staff at the school and her peers think she is mad, or possessed. The school doctor tells her there is a new personality in her trying to emerge. It could be the first step to schizophrenia. The madness of the adolescent is linked to difference and special sensitivity.

In a later scene, a detective who has been investigating the murders inquires about a woman, who currently works at the school, but who had previously worked in a mental hospital. He is told at the hospital that 'the further down you go, the more monstrous the patients'. We learn that his suspect has a small son who doesn't want to see his reflection. 'He stays in his room', his mother says, 'with his crazy thoughts. He changed my life. Drives me mad.' The link between adolescent anxieties about body image, sexuality and madness is confirmed when we learn that the mother had worked in the mental hospital fifteen years ago where a psychotic inmate sexually assaulted her. Heterosexual intercourse is presented as violent, the father is insane, and the fruit of the coupling is an adolescent son with 'crazy thoughts' who drives his mother mad.

Jennifer tries to escape from the room the bad mother has locked her in by crawling down a long hole into a dungeon beneath the house. There she discovers the detective chained to the wall and tortured. She falls into a large vat of primordial soup in which bones and skulls in various stages of decomposition are floating: a graphic representation of an anal universe (Chasseguet-Smirgel 1985) where all differences are abolished. This is the universe of faeces, where all particles are the same and interchangeable, which has here replaced the genital universe. 'The abolition of differences prevents psychic suffering at all levels: feelings of inadequacy, castration, loss, absence and death no longer exist' (p. 6). This is a prelude to the introduction of the monster.

The detective attacks the woman and the girl escapes. She follows the sound of a child crying until she sees its back as it faces into the corner of the room.

The camera is tracking from the girl's perspective. We share the girl's sympathy for the vulnerable, frightened little creature who says, 'Go away. You scare me. I don't want you here.' The girl replies, 'Don't worry about the mirrors any more. It's all over.' Then she sees a hideously deformed face, screams in terror, and runs away pursued by a monstrous adolescent.

In the middle of a lake, insects again swarm to Jennifer's rescue and attack the monster's face. He claws at his face, falls into the water and the boat explodes. He is trapped in a circle of fire and perishes. Jennifer arises, in white, out of the water. The father figure finally arrives. As he rushes down to her, he is suddenly decapitated. We then see that the mother of the monstrous boy is the perpetrator who turns to kill the girl. 'He was diseased, but he was my son . . . and you have . . . why didn't I kill you before? I killed the Inspector and your professor friend to protect him.' Just as she is about to kill the girl, the monster's mother is repeatedly slashed across the face and killed by the monkey. The film ends with the girl stroking and nuzzling the monkey.

The monster

The world Argento created is dominated by the depiction of familiar, uncanny anxieties aroused by puberty and the adolescent phase of development. It is not uncommon for adolescents to feel estranged, isolated and lost in the world around them. At the film's beginning, an adolescent is abandoned by her peers and responsible adults. Speaking for many adolescents, she calls out for help, saying, 'I'm a foreigner and I'm lost.' It is not uncommon for adolescents to view sexuality as bad, dirty and violent. Jennifer's roommate is killed after an illicit meeting with her boyfriend, confirming some adolescents' worst fears that sexuality will be punished by murder. The monster in *Phenomena* targets young adolescent girls. The revival of infantile sexual fantasies and incestuous wishes within the new context of a sexually active and potent body leaves some adolescents feeling they are mad – a child in an adult's body. The characters descend into a psychotic nightmare. In Argento's film, a single-parent family with a pathological bond between mother and son replaces the absent parents of the heroine. The mother who had kept her son chained and infantilized kills the men who attempted to rescue the girl. Heterosexual intercourse is presented as violent and damaging of the foetus. Compassion, sympathy and the wish to help are overcome by horror and disgust. The momentarily triumphant world of the mother and her monster son is presented as an anal universe. The Inspector, who represents law and order, is chained helplessly to a wall watching a vat of decomposing bodies where age and gender are indistinguishable.

The most horrific scene in the film, for me, was not one of the violent murders or the vat of bones and skulls, but a narcissistically vulnerable moment. It was preceded by shots of covered mirrors. We are being prepared for something that is too horrific to look at. Most importantly, the monstrous adolescent is protected from seeing its own image. The mother's shame in her son is evident. Shame is a psychically annihilating event. It is not uncommon when we feel shame to reflexively cover our face with our hand, or wish the earth would open beneath our feet and swallow us up. Erikson (1950) views these reactions of shame as expressions of rage turned against the self. 'He who is ashamed would like to force the world not to look at him, not to notice his exposure. He would like to destroy the eyes of the world. Instead he must wish for his own invisibility' (p. 227). However, when the shame shield (Campbell 1994) is breached, invisibility is not an option, and relief is sought by resorting to actions which project the confusion, passivity, disgust and annihilation into others.

As the camera follows Jennifer into a bare room, we see the back of a small creature that hides its face and does not want to be seen by her. He tells her to go away. She feels pity for a small frightened creature. Argento has built up a psychological profile of a monster; its background and internal world of desperate isolation and its wishes which are never to be seen. Jennifer's shock and horror are in seeing a deformed face.

We are known first by our face, that highly cathected part of our body that is the most visible and vulnerable medium of our narcissism, whatever our age. However, the face becomes a focus of acute attention during adolescence. It is

Plate 13 Phenomena (Dario Argento 1985)
Source: bfi Collections

135

not uncommon for adolescents to displace anxieties about their bodies onto their faces. Hours will be spent in front of the mirror fretting, studying and primping to make the face acceptable. A deformed face is a narcissistic catastrophe, a source of shame and disgust. Jennifer and the audience recoil from the deformed face of the adolescent monster in *Phenomena* – an uncanny image that revives our worst fears about being an ugly, disgusting, shameful object. Unwittingly, Jennifer has breached the shame shield and the shameful monster can no longer hide. The annihilating experience of 'being seen' triggers the monster's aggression, now no longer directed at himself, cowering in shame, but launched at the intruder – Jennifer.

Intuition, attunement and telepathy

I want to turn to a second example of the uncanny in *Phenomena*: Jennifer's capacity to communicate with animals. Argento's solution to a world of anality, castrated and absent fathers, psychopathological mothers, and murderous and physically deformed adolescents is to endow his heroine with a primitive mental sexuality which does not involve the body or relationships with humans, but where, instead, sexual power for the virginal adolescent girl is derived from telepathy with insects. Dr MacGregor had observed how Jennifer excited the insect, which was doing its best to attract her as it would a mate. We can only speculate that a young adolescent girl might react to the failure to perceive her mother as a 'felt prospective' by looking for it elsewhere. The solution to the developmental failure of the absent 'felt prospective' of a mother is to replace it with a 'felt prospective' based on animal instinct and represented by the insects and the monkey.

Freud (1918) noted the way children who are disappointed in their parents substitute animals for them. This substitution is grounded in the recognition that human beings, like animals, possess an instinctual endowment 'the nucleus of the unconscious, a primitive kind of mental activity, which would later be dethroned and overlaid by human reason' (p. 120). *Phenomena* takes the viewer back to a period in every childhood when we could see no difference between our own nature and that of animals (ibid., p. 140). Mythology also supports the fantasy that children and animals have a special rapport, a facility for communication that has been lost by adults.

Jennifer, who is cut off from her parents and alienated from her peers, survives by relying upon affective attunement; a primitive pre-verbal mode of relating that is initiated by intuition, that is, knowledge that is obtained by neither reason nor perception (Collins 1994). Telepathy, the communication of thoughts and feelings that cannot be understood in terms of known scientific laws (ibid.), is the application of intuition to the realm of relationships. In *Phenomena*, telepathy, a kind of affective attunement to insects and a monkey, is superior to reasoned understanding and adult modes of relating. Although Argento's heroine survives in the end, she does so at the cost of her adolescent development, not by resolving her Oedipal conflicts and establishing her own non-incestuous relationships with humans, but by employing primitive, irrational modes of communicating with animals. This is not the destructive use of telekinetic power exercised by Carrie, in the film of the same name, but telepathy used in a more benign and protective way. We recognize this as a reference to our own infantile experience of pre-verbal encounters with the actual other, whose intuitive response provided us with an experience of affective attunement. Without the presence of an actual other – which contains residues of early, intuition-based affective attunement, that is, a good-enough mother and/or father – the adolescent's virtual other of a sexually creative, independent and interrelated person cannot be realized.

References

Bion, W. R. (1962) *Learning from Experience*. London: Maresfield Reprints, 1984.

Braten, S. (1988) 'Dialogic mind: the infant and the adult and in proto conversation', in M. Carvallo (ed.) *Nature, Cognition and Systems*. Dordrecht: D. Reidel.

Brazelton, T. B., Koslowski, B. and Main, M. (1974) 'The origins of reciprocity: the early mother–infant interaction', in M. Lewis and L. A. Rosenblum (eds) *The Effects of the Infant on its Caregiver*. New York: Wiley.

Brophy, P. (1989) 'Horrality: the textuality of contemporary horror films', *Screen*, 27(1): 2–13.

Campbell, D. (1994) 'Breaching the shame shield: thoughts on the assessment of adolescent child sexual abusers', *Journal of Child Psychotherapists*, 20(3): 309–326.

Chasseguet-Smirgel, J. (1985) *Creativity and Perversion*. London: Free Association Books.

Collins Shorter English Dictionary (1994) Glasgow: HarperCollins.

Erikson, E. (1950) *Childhood and Society*, 2nd edn. St Albans: Triad/Paladin, 1977.

Freud, S. (1917) 'A difficulty in the path of psycho-analysis', in *Standard Edition 17*. London: Hogarth Press, 1959.

Freud, S. (1918) 'From the history of an infantile neurosis', in *Standard Edition 17*. London: Hogarth Press, 1959.

Freud, S. (1919) 'The "uncanny"', in *Standard Edition 17*. London: Hogarth Press, 1959.

Lakoff, G. (1993) 'The contemporary theory of metaphor', in A. Ortony (ed.) *Metaphor and Thought*, 2nd edn. Cambridge: Cambridge University Press.

Langer, S. (1967) *Mind: An Essay on Human Feeling, Vol. 1*. Baltimore, MD: Johns Hopkins University Press.

Murray, L. (1991) 'Intersubjectivity, object relations theory, and empirical evidence from mother–infant interactions', *Infant Mental Health Journal*, 12: 219–232.

Schneider, S. (1999) 'Monsters as (uncanny) metaphors: Freud, Lakoff, and the representation of monstrosity in cinematic horror', *Other Voices*, 1: 3.

Stern, D. (1974) 'Mother and infant at play: the dyadic interaction involving facial, vocal and gaze behaviors', in M. Lewis and L. A. Rosenblum (eds) *The Effects of the Infant on its Caregiver*. New York: Wiley.

Stern, D. (1985) *The Interpersonal World of the Infant*. New York: Basic Books.

Trevarthen, C. (1979) 'Communication and cooperation in early infancy: a description of primary intersubjectivity', in M. M. Bullowa (ed.) *Before Speech: The Beginning of Interpersonal Communication*. New York: Cambridge University Press.

10

FREEDOM THROUGH RE-INTROJECTION

A Kleinian perspective on Dominik Moll's *Harry: He's Here to Help* (2000)

Candy Aubry

Melanie Klein's descriptions of primitive defences have been brought to life in *Harry: He's Here to Help* (2000), a remarkable French film written by Dominik Moll and Gilles Marchand and directed by Dominik Moll. It is a mystery thriller in the Hitchcockian tradition but with what seems to be a very ambiguous moral message. However, if you care to take a closer look, which actually means taking a step back and assuming an analytical stance, you will find that this film is practically a study of the use of primitive defences. Move too close and you get swallowed up without realizing what is happening to you, but move too far away and you won't have a clue what's going on. In a very subtle, yet at the same time terrifying way, we are shown how the defence mechanisms of splitting and projective identification can drain the personality of much instinctual energy, restricting sexual and aggressive drives and, with them, many creative elements. It shows how one may be ready to compromise and accept this situation, rather than face the sometimes overwhelming anxiety involved in recuperating these elements which are felt to be much too threatening by the ego. Despite the very down to earth, realistic beginning of the film where external reality dominates, we slowly enter, without realizing it at first, into a more surreal world, the inner world of Michel, the main character in the film. Slowly and eerily, fantasy becomes reality but the audience, like Michel, is at first naïve, unaware of what is happening.

Michel is a French teacher. He has an attractive, understanding wife, Claire, and they are the parents of three young girls. They are worn out by the small but innumerable problems of everyday life. Michel is a 'nice guy', a man of compromise who tries to accommodate everyone in order to avoid conflict. He is a young man with much patience – or is he? What is the price he has paid for his 'normal/neurotic' appearance? Suddenly, Harry appears on the scene. Harry is travelling with his fiancée Plum (*bébé*), and they invite themselves for a visit. In fact Michel has no recollection at all of Harry, but Harry seems to know and remember a great number of things about Michel. He recounts that Michel was reputed to be a great lover and he also tells of how Michel used to write for the school newsletter. Harry remembers every story and poem. He even knows one of the poems off by heart and he recites this to Michel and his wife one evening. The poem is about a long knife covered by a 'skin of darkness'. Michel had forgotten the poem, forgotten those seemingly exciting and productive times, but suddenly his wife, and we in the audience, discover a new and surprising side to Michel. It is a side previously unknown and so different to what we do know, that it is slightly disconcerting.

Now the rest of the film's manifest content can be seen as a thriller involving a psychopathic Harry, with a homosexual fixation on Michel, who decides to go on a killing spree in order to 'help' or control Michel. However, a psychoanalytic interpretation reveals the allegorical nature of the film. From the beginning, Harry can be seen as an unconscious force. Indeed he even has another name: Dick. He is Tom, Dick and Harry, 'everyone' and 'no one' at the same time. When Harry explains that, in order to maintain his virility, he always swallows a raw egg after making love, it may also be that he does so in order to regenerate himself, in order to exist and take on the 'appearance' of Harry. In fact, it may be that he exists only through others; he has come to life, taken on a human form and there is no stopping him now. Michel would like to continue as before, often repeating 'it doesn't concern me' or 'it's none of my business', but it is too late.

Wilfred Bion, in his paper 'The imaginary twin' (1967), speaks of 'personification of split-off parts' and Harry may be seen to represent all the destructive, split-off parts of Michel which have come back to claim their territory with a vengeance. The fact that it involves splitting and not repression is important to highlight. Michel has not just 'forgotten' Harry. In high school, Harry had lost a tooth in a scramble with Michel in a football match, the tooth ending up in Michel's forehead. Everyone remembers it, except Michel. It does not come back to him. He really has no idea. His replies to Harry consist of 'that's absurd' or 'I don't understand a word of what you're saying'. His poem and stories ring a bell though, even if they seem to have been written by someone else. Only once split-off parts are recognized, even if just a little (in the form of Harry), can repressed content, the poem and the short stories, appear. However, the relationship between the defence mechanisms of splitting and repression may be even more complex. Melanie Klein examined this relationship and concluded that if splitting and projective identification have been particularly

140

Plate 14 Harry: He's Here to Help (Dominik Moll 2000)
Source: bfi Collections

violent in the early stages, if there has been difficulty in establishing the depressive
position, subsequent repression may reproduce the violence of these first
processes. 'In other words, the extent to which the various parts of the mind
remain "porous" in relation to one another is determined largely by the strength
or weakness of the early schizoid mechanisms' (Klein 1952, p. 204).

So Michel slowly starts to recognize parts of himself. His creativity as well as
other useful narcissistic elements seem to have been taken hostage as it were
with the rest of the split-off parts, leaving a rather masochistic, unexciting though
kindly person behind. But how to recuperate what is good without being taken
over and dominated by what is frightening and crazy? Michel has deep, unfilled
holes in his garden. These are like the 'holes' in his ego – 'holes' which need to
be filled if he is to feel 'whole'. But the fact that these holes exist, means that he
must have needed to empty them at some stage of his development, to split-off
and 'lose' through projective identification whatever was filling them for fear
that he would be invaded by it. The only problem is that a good deal of his
creativity was also lost. Melanie Klein stressed the importance of normal splitting
for healthy development. The young child loves and hates its objects at the same
time but the ego is too immature at this stage to be able to tolerate ambivalence.
Klein (1958) wrote that the infant resorts to splitting of objects in order to keep
love and hate apart so as not to be overwhelmed by anxiety. This splitting is

141

associated with projective identification right from the start and may lead to a weakening of the ego as it too becomes victim to the same splitting process.

In the film, Michel's unconscious desires and fantasies slowly emerge and Harry acts on them. 'Uncanny' events, much as Freud described in his article of the same name (Freud 1919), begin to take place. When Harry shows his intense dislike of Michel's parents and then causes the 'accident' which kills them, this may be seen as the splitting-off of bad parts and their projection into external objects. These objects then become identified with the projected parts and become persecutory objects which must be eliminated. He disposes of Michel's brother in much the same way. Now, Michel stopped writing and apparently changed at some point during his adolescence. We gather that in his youth, he had been writing a collection of fantasy short stories concerning gibbons that had propellers transplanted onto their heads in order to carry out useful household tasks. However in the stories, the gibbons slowly get out of control and this appears to be where Michel's youthful writing stops. Later in the film, just after his parents' deaths, Michel has a dream where one of these bizarre creatures attacks him while he is sitting in his father's dental office. Is it his father? Does it represent a 'bizarre object' as described by Bion, which intensifies feelings of persecution? Was an earlier infantile split reactivated and further deepened in adolescence? During the turbulent times of his adolescence, did Michel try to run away from the dangers he felt growing inside him? In any case, Michel is in a state of panic in his nightmare. Despite this regressive content, this dream may show that some measure of integration has now taken place. As Jean-Michel Quinodoz states in his article 'Dreams that turn over a page' (1999), an increased capacity for symbolic representation may indicate whether the movement concerned is one of integration or of regression and it is following this dream, and much encouragement from Harry, that Michel feels the desire to write again. Even so, his first efforts at resuming his writing are without success.

The tension builds and Michel (and the audience) feel more and more confused. Reality and fantasy seem no longer to be separated. As Freud says of Jensen's *Gradiva*, 'it is not only our hero who has evidently lost his balance; we too have lost our bearings' (Freud 1907, p. 17). Now Harry feigns his own death, knowing that only if Michel feels less threatened by him, will he be able to regain his creative capacities. At that very moment Michel is able to start writing again. However, he is surprised to see Harry back a short time later. Harry's girlfriend Plum becomes the next victim. Michel, who had thought nothing of her previously, has suddenly been inexplicably attracted by her. Plum is a superficial but touching caricature of a 'babe', following Harry around dutifully, satisfying his every need. At one stage she dares to express her desire to have children, when she repeats what Claire (Michel's wife) has been telling her about motherhood; but Harry makes it quite clear that Plum will never have children. She is doomed to remain a 'woman-babe-child', a sexual object. Plum in fact seems to represent another split-off and previously unrecognized part of Michel, his sexuality which is now slowly awakening. It is when, unquestioningly, he helps Harry (who has just murdered her) to drag her body down the stairs, that we know that Michel and Harry are psychically one and the same, sharing similar fantasies, narcissistic prolongations of each other.

The question now becomes: is Michel's house, the home he has built for himself all these years, strong enough to withstand the assimilation, the filling-in of those empty holes? Will re-introjection of these split-off parts of his personality lead to overwhelming persecutory anxiety and confusion, or will his ego be able to withstand this coming together? Herbert Rosenfeld (1987) states that there is a danger that abrupt attempts at assimilation of split-off parts of the personality may not only cause acute anxiety but even disintegration. This is Michel's fear. Even though Michel is not overtly psychotic, re-introjection of these split-off, fragmented parts is a violent process. This is what makes this film so interesting and instructive. It shows all the violent and danger-ridden aspects of these mechanisms which are part of normal early development. The psychotic individual resorts almost exclusively to these primitive defences throughout his existence. Although, quantitatively speaking, the more neurotic individual makes much less use of such defence mechanisms, qualitatively the associated fears and anxiety may be felt in much the same way.

At the culminating point of the film, everything comes together, so to speak. Michel and Harry seem to be locked together for one brief moment and Michel must make a snap decision about the way he will go. Which part of his personality will dominate? Will he let Harry do everything as he proposes, let him take over once and for all, give himself up to the omnipotent, narcissistic part of his personality? Will he recognize Harry's madness for what it is or will he be dragged into Harry's mad world, to be trapped in a *folie à deux*? Can he take the good without the bad or will he be lost forever? In the end, Michel looks his split-off partner in the face, recognizes Harry as being part of himself, but does not allow him to dominate him. He makes his choice. He is handed a knife (and one recalls here the knife of his poem, the knife that had been put away): but this time Michel decides that the time is ripe to use it, on Harry.

Is Michel in a state of denial and omnipotence? If we consider all that has taken place as being based in reality, we would come to this conclusion. But if we interpret all these events as having taken place in Michel's unconscious world, we can say that he has integrated the different facets of his personality and so feels stronger for it. Harry and Plum have filled in his empty spaces, become part of him, buried but not gone. Reduction of splitting has led to modification of his internal objects. He can now use the good, creative elements they have brought him, without risking domination by them. His internal world no longer frightens him. Finally, Michel is able to express the useful, creative and ego-enriching elements that Harry and Plum have brought him, symbolized by his keeping the 'containing' new car Harry had bought for his family, but most importantly by his being able to write again. Michel's new piece of writing is a story which involves eggs, again something Harry was closely associated with. Eggs may also symbolize birth, a rebirth in Michel's case, much as the flowers his daughters give him the day after the final murder symbolize rebirth in the form of the coming spring. Michel is now able to share his literary productions with his wife, who appreciates them. He does not feel anxiety or guilt about what has happened. Many incredible and frightening things have taken place, but in the final scene when all the family is driving back home from the holiday, one is surprised by a feeling of relief – just like one feels when waking up from a bad dream.

Acknowledgements

I would like to thank Jean-Michel Aubry for his stimulating comments in our post-film discussion and Danielle Quinodoz for her helpful suggestions and encouragement. This chapter was previously published in 2002 in *British Journal of Psychotherapy*, 19 (2): 225–259.

References

Bion, W. R. (1957) 'Differentiation of the psychotic from the non-psychotic personality', *International Journal of Psychoanalysis*, 38: 266–275; reprinted in *Second Thoughts: Selected Papers on Psycho-Analysis*. London: Heinemann, 1967.

Bion, W. R. (1967) 'The imaginary twin', in *Second Thoughts: Selected Papers on Psycho-Analysis*. London: Heinemann.

Freud, S. (1907) 'Delusions and dreams in Jensen's *Gradiva*', in *Standard Edition 9*. London: Hogarth Press, 1959.

Freud, S. (1919). 'The "uncanny"', in *Standard Edition 17*. London: Hogarth Press, 1959.

Klein, M. (1952) 'Some theoretical conclusions regarding the emotional life of the infant', in *Developments in Psycho-Analysis*. London: Hogarth Press.

Klein, M. (1958) 'On the development of mental functioning', *International Journal of Psycho-Analysis*, 39: 84–90.

Quinodoz, J-M. (1999) '"Dreams that turn over a page": integration dreams with paradoxical regressive content', *International Journal of Psycho-Analysis*, 80: 225–238.

Rosenfeld, H. (1987) *Impasse and Interpretation*. London: Tavistock.

11

CINEMA, HORROR AND THE ABOMINATIONS OF HELL

Carl–Theodor Dreyer's *Vampyr* (1931) and
Lucio Fulci's *The Beyond* (1981)

Michael Grant

I want to begin by touching on certain aspects of imaginative experience, in order to suggest something at least of what aesthetic appreciation consists in. My purpose in doing this here is to raise a question – by indirection rather than by explicit argument – as to the relevance of psychoanalytic interpretation to that appreciation. It should be noted at once that there have been many and varied approaches to cinema making use of psychoanalytic theories of one kind or another. A recent tendency, associated especially with the writing of Slavoj Zizek, has been to read film in terms of the Lacanian notion of the Real. As Zizek has presented the idea, for example in *Enjoy Your Symptom!* (2001) with respect to the films that Roberto Rossellini made with Ingrid Bergman, he has given to it a persuasiveness and cogency that otherwise it might have lacked. Nonetheless, it will be my suggestion that such an approach, despite its attractions, finally will not do. It obscures too much of what is unique to a given film, and by so doing distorts what is unique to the work in question. For Zizek, the films that Rossellini made with Bergman always 'contain some picture of "authentic" or substantial life and it seems as if the heroine's salvation depends on her ability to immerge [*sic*] into this substantial "authenticity"' (Zizek 2001, p. 54). The strategy of the films is to denounce the 'lure' of this imaginary salvation, and to effect a transition from the seeming reality of it to the Real, to what in reality is more than reality – the traumatic Thing that resists symbolization (in Rossellini's *Stromboli* [1949], for example, what on the island is 'more than the island' is the volcano). This approach does not in fact resist symbolization: it encourages it. Interpretations proliferate, and the film, held at a distance in order that it may be subsumed beneath a pre-existing theoretical template, ends up reduced and reified. My purpose, in contradistinction, will be to propose that, just as there are certain verbal expressions of which it is right to say 'I *know* what this means but I can't *say* what it means', so there are certain films of which something similar may also properly be said. There comes a point in the appreciation of such a film at which one finds oneself almost forced to say: 'This is what I see. Reasons, explanations, interpretations, have come to an end'.

I shall be looking, very briefly, at two films: the first is a classic, Carl-Theodor Dreyer's *Vampyr* (France, 1931), while the second is less well known, and far from a classic, Lucio Fulci's *The Beyond* (Italy, 1981). I will try to clarify my approach by setting them against the background of a specific tradition of writing – that of the post-symbolist strand of modernism.

My starting point is the thought on aesthetics of R. G. Collingwood, and in particular his claim in *The Principles of Art* (1958) that art is expression. His account of the idea follows from a distinction he draws between what he calls 'betraying' an emotion and 'expressing' one. A person betrays his fear if 'he turns pale and stammers'; he betrays his anger 'if he turns red and bellows; and so forth' (p. 121). The betrayal of emotion makes clear the fact that one is in a certain emotional state. With respect to art, however, Collingwood wishes to contrast the notion of betrayal with what he calls expression. As Aaron Ridley (1998) has made clear in his study of Collingwood's aesthetics, expression, as understood in the context of art, 'consists, not merely in making it clear that one is in a certain state, as the betrayal of emotion does, but in making clear just *what* that state is' (p. 26).

The person engaged in artistic expression initially knows next to nothing of what he feels. Collingwood writes:

> All he is conscious of is a perturbation or excitement, which he feels going on within him, but of whose nature he is ignorant. While in this state, all he can say about his emotion is 'I feel . . . I don't know what I feel.' From this helpless and oppressed condition he extricates himself by doing something which we call expressing himself.
>
> (Collingwood 1958, p. 109)

As Ridley points out, expression is the activity of getting clear about one's own experience, an activity which brings about the transformation of the experience even as it makes it clear what that experience is. In Ridley's words, '[o]ne's experience is thus fully and completely distinctive only once expression is itself complete' (1998, p. 27). As Collingwood puts it, '[u]ntil a man has expressed his emotion, he does not yet know what emotion it is' (1958, p. 111). In other words, emotion is not revealed for what it is by being expressed: it is through being expressed that it becomes what it is.

This implies that there can be no distinction between the emotion expressed and the expression of it. Not only that, but also one must express one's emotion in something – in some medium or other, words, music, paint, film, etc. The act of expression can't be separated from the medium in which the expression takes place. And there is a further consequence of this view. Collingwood is clear that expression is an 'exploration' of one's own experience (1958, p. 111). But, if expression is inseparable from a medium, it is clear that that exploration must also be an exploration of one's medium of expression. Ridley takes up this aspect of things by considering Collingwood's appreciation of Cézanne, who explored his response to Mont Saint-Victoire, in fact his obsession with it, by painting it again and again. Cézanne explored his obsession through his paint. But equally he explored his paint through his obsession. The response to the mountain is at the same time and in the same gesture a discovery concerning the possibilities of the medium in which that response is embodied.

Expression, then, differs from betrayal inasmuch as expression, unlike betrayal, is a process whereby emotion comes to clarification. In fact, one might go further and say that expression, as Collingwood envisages it, is not only a process of clarification, it is a process that might more properly be called *constitutive* of emotion. However, there is more to Collingwood's argument. He says:

> If you want to express the terror that something causes, you must not give it an epithet like 'dreadful'. For that describes the emotion instead of expressing it. . . . Some people have thought that a poet who wishes to express a great variety of subtly differentiated emotions might be hampered by the lack of a vocabulary rich in words referring to the distinctions between them. . . . This is the opposite of the truth. The poet needs no such words at all. . . . To describe a thing is to call it a thing of such and such a kind: to bring it under a conception, to classify it. Expression, on the other hand, individualizes.
>
> (Collingwood 1958, p. 112)

Description clarifies by generalizing. Expression, on the other hand, clarifies by distinguishing not merely between different kinds of thing but between things that might be described in the same way. The artist, for Collingwood, does not want 'a thing of certain kind, he wants a certain thing' (1958, p. 115). Description only yields 'a thing of a certain kind', while expression gives the thing itself. As Ridley puts it, 'what a particular work of art expresses is something unique, to be found there and nowhere else' (1998, p. 29).

★★★

The view of art I have just set out has, of course, its roots in Romanticism. From the beginning of the nineteenth century, with the onset of Romanticism, art began to make the matter of its own status central to what constituted it, one result of which was to incorporate the problematic and ambiguous into what makes it what it is. This concern with the problematic was itself to develop into a significant feature of modernism, and it is to be found in certain horror films also. That is to say, on occasion, horror films have addressed themselves to the procedures and forms whereby they create what they create, and it is not too extravagant to suggest in this regard that films like *Vampyr* and *The Beyond* (among a number of others) exhibit an order of self-interrogation that overlaps with what we find in the literature of modernism.

Self-interrogation is undoubtedly central to the project of Dreyer's *Vampyr*. Aporia and contradiction are fundamental to it, and Dreyer accords them a particularly vivid and focused realization. For instance, Gray's first walk to the mill is both a narrative event and at the same time a disruption of the logical sequence of that narrative event. We are first presented with a disruption of the intelligibility of the relations between body and reflection, as Gray sees a figure, in reverse motion, reflected in the river, digging a grave. There is then a further fracturing of normal physical relations, when we see a man's shadow separate itself from his body. At the same time, the usual structure of narrative and temporal order is broken by a sudden, unmotivated irruption of music occurring when Gray enters the mill, an irruption which immediately calls forth what look like cut-out figures, dancing or circling around each other. These different elements of cinematic device, combined with the sudden intrusion of the commanding voice of the vampire, compromise the meaning of the narrative at this point, rendering the presentation of events suspect.

The action of the film is thus situated ambiguously, in a world which is that neither of life nor of death. What happens in the film occurs elsewhere, in a place self-consciously created out of cinematic effects, and, as a result, we cannot really be sure of what it is we are seeing. David Bordwell has argued that such a systematic dismantling of secure relations between the elements within the film extends to *Vampyr* as a whole (1981, p. 103). As he puts it, the film aims to create a displacement of the presuppositions necessary to a stable spatio-temporal continuum.

This is one way of construing the fact that the narrative order of the film in its totality is not to be trusted. The status of what we are seeing has become undecidable, and as a result the temporal progression of the events we see has also become uncertain. The only order of time that we can trust is the time it takes for the film to be seen, the time it takes for the reels of film to pass through the projector and to cast an image on the screen and to bring up sound through the speakers. It is in this sense that *Vampyr* can be said to resemble music. The action that is represented and the process of representing that action have been collapsed endlessly into one another, so that the time it takes the events we see to elapse and the time it takes to show us those events are almost, but never quite, one and the same. What *Vampyr* narrates, we might say, is the occurrence of the events that compose it, in the very instant that it is narrating the events themselves.

At the conclusion of *Vampyr*, the mechanism driving the mill wheels that are drowning the doctor (the vampire's human assistant) in flour finally stops, under its own volition and without visible cause. The doctor has been assimilated to the whiteness of the flour, a whiteness which is finally inseparable from a whiteness that has come to dominate the balance of light and shadow across the whole film, a fact made evident in the penultimate sequence, when Gray and Gisèle move across the water into the light of the dawn sun. As they step out of their boat onto the river-bank, they walk into, and are transfigured by, the intensifying rays of light streaming through the forest. Suffusing the mist rising around the branches, the light comes to acquire almost as palpable a material presence as the objects it illuminates. And at this juncture, we cut back to the mill. The whiteness of the flour has by this time so filled the projected image that there appears no discernible difference between it and the whiteness of the screen behind the image, and it is in this same moment of assimilation of the image to its support that the movement of the mechanism comes to a halt.

The seeming coincidence of the image and the screen behind it is doubled by the fact that the movement of the mill gears and that of the projector showing the film also coincide. The two movements collapse into a single duration, as the teeth of the gears and the sprockets of the projector gears mirror one another,

Plate 15 Vampyr (Carl-Theodor Dreyer 1931)
Source: bfi Collections

in a concurrence that effectively links an action internal to the film with an action external to it. It is as though the film were being completed in a time that had already been superseded, inasmuch as it has been this same action, the action of the mechanisms of the projector, that began the film and that has sustained it throughout the time of its showing. The result, in this case, is a tension. *Vampyr* exists as a movement by means of which whatever is imaged is abolished; and yet whatever is abolished is sustained, since the being of the thing is taken up into the being of the image. The world of the film is peopled by beings who are at once present and yet somehow shadowy, almost inhuman, monstrous. It is a world in which death may be said to have doubled the impulse to life.

★★★

If we are to accord this way of thinking due weight and seriousness, then we must recognize that art of this kind has come upon states of mind and modes of experience that are accessible only by virtue of a unique employment of image and narrative, similar to that of the post-symbolist poetry of T. S. Eliot or W. B. Yeats. What this kind of experience gives onto is the true horror, the horror of the uncanny and the fantastic. It is the return of being in negation, the impossibility of death, the universality of existence even in its annihilation. It appears to us in the obsessions and insomnias of the night, and it is fear *of* being, not fear *for* being, the fear of death. It is the experience of living death. And we find it explored in Lucio Fulci's *The Beyond*.

Released by Fulvia Film (Rome) in 1981, the film takes up the motif of the gateway to hell from *The Sentinel* (Michael Winner 1976) and living dead imagery based on Romero's first two zombie films. Here are some of the major points of the narrative, which opens in Louisiana, 1927. A posse, bearing torches, rifles and chains, is rowing across a lake towards an isolated hotel. Inside the hotel, Schweik, an artist, is completing an indistinct landscape, littered with grey shapes, perhaps corpses. The men burst into the hotel and seize him, the leader of the group accusing him of being a warlock. They beat him mercilessly across the face with a heavy chain. They then take him to the hotel's cellar, crucify him, and throw acid over his head, watching him as he dissolves in agony. At the same time, a young woman, Emily, is reading from the Book of Eibon, which contains ancient prophecies concerning the seven sacred gateways into hell. Schweik is then walled up.

In 1981, Liza Merrill arrives from New York to claim the hotel, which she has inherited. On the way, Liza meets Emily, who now is blind. Emily takes Liza to the house where she lives, and warns her to leave immediately. Instead Liza decides on the hotel's renovation. At the same time, Martha, the hotel's Mrs Danvers-like housekeeper, guides Joe, a local plumber, towards the far end of the hotel's cellar, which is flooding, to find out where the water is coming from. He knocks down the wall entombing Schweik's body, and is killed by a hand that reaches out and seizes him.

Mary Ann, Joe's wife, goes to the hospital mortuary to prepare her husband for his funeral, when she stumbles and falls, lying unconscious at the foot of a cupboard, on top of which stands a large bottle of acid. The bottle falls forward, spilling its contents over her head, which dissolves into a sea of bloody foam. John McCabe, a doctor, investigates Emily. He goes to her house, only to find it in ruins. Here he discovers the Book of Eibon and reads in it that the hotel stands on one of the seven gates of hell. In the hotel, Martha is cleaning the bathroom of Schweik's former room. She puts her hand into a bath of foul black water, and frees the plug. As the water drains away, Joe arises from the water, and drives Martha back, impaling her head on a large nail sticking out of the wall.

Schweik appears before Emily, summoning her back to hell. She refuses to obey. Her guide-dog tears out her throat. Liza is set on by the dead in her hotel, but escapes with McCabe to the hospital, pursued by 'living' corpses from the morgue. They escape down to the basement, only to find that they are back in the cellar of the hotel. They pass through the gap in the cellar wall, and enter a landscape that seems everywhere the same. It is the landscape of the painting that Schweik completed at the time of his destruction, and it is the site of hell.

★★★

Plate 16 The Beyond (Lucio Fulci 1981)

As this summary should indicate, the plot is anything but concisely organized. Elements are pulled in from many sources, and strung together in a series of set-pieces, involving various degrees of violence and bodily mutilation. Of these, the opening sequences are the most striking, as Schweik is crucified by the posse and dissolved in acid. The score, by Fabio Frizzi, dominates the soundtrack, carrying over to the reading by Emily from the Book of Eibon. The same musical motif recurs throughout, especially at moments of violent death, such as Mary Ann's and Martha's. The music here is at least as effective as the narrative in providing a cohesive force for the film. Its repetitious insistence draws the disparate narrative events together, emphasizing pace and rhythm at the expense of motivation or psychological insight. Visuals and music cohere in a unified sound-image. This is brought home at the end of the film, when Schweik's painting has come to fill the screen, accompanied by the throbbing musical score. It is precisely at this point that Liza and McCabe are recognized as having become part of Schweik's landscape, which he completed as the film began, a painting which does not simply depict hell – it *is* hell. The film's end is established at a point prior to its beginning, and the organization of its temporal development identified with that of a painting internal to it. In this way, a disruption of temporal order takes place in *The Beyond*, and it does so at the moment when image and what is imaged become one, a unity achieved as the film concentrates at the end on Schweik's painting. What occurs here displaces the dominance of narrative, and reveals the film's fixity and subordination to a time impotent to go anywhere except interminably back to its beginning.

Seen in this light, the film is nothing other than a catalogue of notations of its own aesthetic, and it exhibits them everywhere, in the blind yet seeing eyes of Emily, in the eyes of Liza and McCabe as they are abandoned in hell, the hotel itself, the undead and, as I have argued, most significantly in Schweik's painting. Liza and McCabe become elements of its plastic composition, in a transformation that defines the aesthetic undertaking of the whole film. Characters constantly die into the beyond constituted by their images, a doubling we first see in the death of Schweik himself, who returns from the dead, still in the atrocious condition in which he died. He is not resurrected into the sunlight; he remains in the tomb, and of the tomb, and is evil, lost.

Similarly with the hotel: putrescence and rot pervade it, and the dead dwell there. As with the 'old houses' in Dario Argento's *Suspiria* (1976) and *Inferno* (1980), the hotel exists suspended in the empty place between life and death, and ultimately no character is possessed of the power to escape it. The degradation of the world represented in Fulci's film is in effect a degradation marking the reversal by which reality is removed, and replaced by the shadow of the image. All darkens into the shadow of the beyond, and this peculiar death of the shadow serves in Fulci's hands to undo the narrative from within, inverting it into what is at once an image of death and a dead image. This view of the film is supported by the longest Italian version of the film's title, which translated reads as: '. . . And you shall live in terror! The beyond'. It is a title that points towards the notion of a future that is conditional on the past – a terror *beyond*, beyond the grave, beyond the end and before the beginning, in which you shall live.

The Beyond is in many ways a failure, as its detractors have been quick to note, remarking on its haphazard and derivative narrative, and its often crude effects. However, its concluding sequence acknowledges it to be a failure in a different, more far-reaching sense. Liza and McCabe are lost in a place where to go forward is to go back, and where every beginning is simply a repeated end. This is what characterizes the abomination of Fulci's hell. As the voice of Eibon has it, in the penultimate shot of the film: 'And you shall face the sea of darkness and all therein that may be explored'. At the end, Liza and McCabe dissolve into the nothingness of the image and the image prevails over them.

What I have been attempting here is to show something of how Fulci creates the unique thing that his film is. One obvious strategy would have been to interpret *The Beyond* in terms of the Lacanian theory of the Real, a theory based in large part on the Hegelian concept of the word as the murderer of the thing. The idea is that the use of language emerges against the background of an essential abyss of non-meaning, of the empty nothingness that is organic life. When we begin – as human subjects – to use language and reach towards self-consciousness, we negate this nothingness. We do so by entering into a pre-existing structure of language, which, in contrast to the nothingness it negates, is inorganic and external. Human subjectivity is therefore always already subjected to an external authority – an authority that is always alien to us. As Richard Allen and Malcolm Turvey (2001) have written:

> This subjection is at once essential to concealing the abyss of nothingness that is organic life and, at the same time, is only made possible and sustained by the existence of that concealed abyss and the 'pressure' exerted by it.
>
> (Allen and Turvey 2001, p. 29)

This abyss of nothingness is what Lacan calls 'the Real'. It is a traumatic core at the heart of human society and culture and is always threatening to return. Its return will disrupt the inert structure of human civilization and meaning that its concealment serves to make possible. From this perspective, one might argue that a major purpose of art is to bring about the return, the disruptive intrusion, of the Real. Inasmuch as representation is a function of the lack or abyss without which it would not exist, a lack withdrawn or concealed beneath it, the overriding aim of art must be to make that lack effectively present. The result is to be a process of representation subverted from within.

That there is an overlap between the Lacanian account of the Real and the position for which I have been arguing is clear. Both Lacan's theory of language and the tradition of writing to which I have alluded – namely, the post-symbolist strand of modernism – are based on concepts of language deriving from, or similar to, those of Hegel. It has to be said, however, that the overlap lends no support to a general explanation or theory of human behaviour or psychic functioning. My projection in this chapter of certain procedures of symbolist poetry onto features discernible in *The Beyond* has been no more than a way of clarifying an elucidation or appreciation of certain aspects of the film in question. I have adduced no grounds for appealing to any general theory of psychic structure in order to justify an interpretation of the film, or to vindicate an explanation of its aesthetic effect. What I have attempted is to allow *The Beyond* to speak out of its own specificity – in terms of the relations of presence and absence that it irreducibly confronts us with. It is this that has been the point of my reference to the post-symbolist strand of modernism. The post-symbolist poem is nothing other than the enactment – the foregrounding – of the unique act of its own coming into being. In this connection, I would suggest, Collingwood's ideas on art are of immediate pertinence, as are those of Stanley Cavell (1969), who has written of aspects of the post-symbolist poetry of Wallace Stevens and Hart Crane in the following terms: 'One may be able to say nothing except that a feeling has been voiced by a kindred spirit. [Poems of this kind] may be left as touchstones of intimacy' (p. 81).

In conclusion, I would like to return to *Vampyr*, in order to suggest that the consciousness induced by it is exterior to itself, and attenuated, incapable of mastery over its own negativity. In *Vampyr*, in the classic scene of Gray's dream, Gray sees himself being buried alive, while he is nonetheless dreaming elsewhere. It is as though my consciousness were present to me, but without me, lacking me. There are parallels in this to the state of consciousness that a symbolist poem like Eliot's *The Waste Land* aims to induce. The central consciousness of the poem is that of Tiresias, an old man with wrinkled breasts, who has walked among the lowest of the dead, a prophet gazing, like Orpheus, into the night at what the night is concealing.

So with *Vampyr*: the characters and figures called up are similarly spectral, their identities shifting and uncertain. Their existence is an existence coterminous with the existence of the sounds and images that create the film, and to participate in that existence, as a spectator of the film, is to participate in something neuter, as Tiresias is neuter, and the vampire, Marguerite Chopin. Gray's experience is like that of the narrator of Poe's 'The Premature Burial', who, though beyond death, is unable to die. Gray is caught up beyond himself, as we are with him. He is solicited by images from which he cannot escape, condemned to the empty interval of dying, of the impossibility of dying. In *Vampyr*, as in *The Beyond*, the dead are conscious of being dead, and so unable to die. They induce us to approach them, but in doing so we find ourselves as other, where what we hear is the echo of our own step, a step towards silence, towards the void.

References

Allen, R. and Turvey, M. (eds) (2001) *Wittgenstein, Theory and the Arts*. New York and London: Routledge.

Bordwell, D. (1981) *The Films of Carl-Theodor Dreyer*. Berkeley and Los Angeles: University of California Press.

Cavell, S. (1969) *Must We Mean What We Say? A Book of Essays*. New York: Scribner.

Collingwood, R. G. (1958) *The Principles of Art*. Oxford: Oxford University Press.

Ridley, A. (1998) *R. G. Collingwood*. London: Phoenix.

Zizek, S. (2001) *Enjoy Your Symptom!* New York and London: Routledge.

Documenting internal worlds

12

NARRATIVES AND DOCUMENTARIES

An encounter with Michael Apted and his films

Michael Apted and Helen Taylor Robinson

Helen Taylor Robinson (HTR)   Michael Apted's career of nearly forty years as a film director has earned him British Academy Awards for his work in television, a British Academy Award, the International EMI and the International Documentary Award for his remarkable documentary series *Seven Up* (1964) through to *Forty-two Up* (1998), a study of the developing lives of a small group of children followed through to adulthood. It is a series which Michael replicated as executive producer with children in the USA and also children in Russia. It has been a most influential and significant film. Michael's feature film *The Coal Miner's Daughter* (1980), the story of country-and-western singer Loretta Lynn, won the Best Actress Award for his star, Sissy Spacek, and received seven Academy Award nominations. His film *Gorillas in the Mist* (1988) received a further five Academy Award nominations. Michael's documentary film, *Moving the Mountain* (1994), an account of the Tiananmen Square massacre in China, took the Grand Prize at the Heartland Film Festival, together with an International Documentary Award. In 1999 Michael Apted won the Career Achievement Award from the International Documentary Association for his work in the documentary field.

Michael has worked with many great figures in British and American television and cinema. He has made documentary films that examine the creative process both in science and the arts. He is probably most recently familiar to you as the director of the James Bond movie, *The World is not Enough* (1999), as well as his latest film *Enigma* (2001), a story set in Britain during the Second World War at Bletchley Park where the enigma codes of the Germans were broken, with consequences for the outcome of the war for the Allies.

Michael Apted's career cannot be summed up in these brief words, as he has made over twenty major full-length films in twenty years, of which I have made no mention. Rather, we are privileged to look today with him at some of the images he has created in his direction of real and imaginary lives, and the way fiction and non–fiction, feature and documentary, and their interrelations have been used by him.

Michael Apted (MA)   I suppose the biggest adventure, challenge of this event is to see if there is any common ground between what the professional psycho-analysts in the audience do, and what I do. I suppose we are both interested in authenticity, in the truthfulness of the characters we deal with, whether it is in a documentary film or a character that is being created by a writer and an actor. We all have our little tricks, our agendas, our processes, and what I would like to do is describe my process to you. When I joined Granada in the Sixties I remember two pieces of advice that were given to me. One is that there is no right way to do anything, to direct a film or a movie. You have to figure it out for yourself, you have to find who you are and then how best to communicate who you are; there are no lessons, there is no template, no book about it, you just have to figure it out; and you can only figure it out, I was told, not by learning, but by doing it.

The other thing that I was told was that you have to own the material. Now, I never write my own movies, and so I get my authorship 'buzz' out of doing documentaries. But whatever I am doing – and this advice was given to me in my early days doing drama, when I was directing *Coronation Street* for Granada (I will never forget it!) – is you have to take a grip of the material, own it, make it your own, put your own personality, whatever that might be, in it.

My thesis here, then, is that *I have learnt this through doing documentaries and I have applied the lessons of documentaries to all my narrative work and all my fictional work.* My career has been a sort of two-pronged attack on that – I have managed to keep documentaries going while making movies.

Let us start where I began, which is with this '*Up*' series of films (*Seven Up* through to *Forty-two Up* and beyond). It started in 1964 as an examination of England in that year. England was going through a lot of cultural changes, the Rock'n'Roll fashion, the Swinging Sixties, and whatever. We wanted to look at England and see whether England was in fact changing or whether this cultural movement was just cosmetic. So, rather than drag in a load of psychologists, politicians, educationalists, whatever you want, we had the idea of bringing in some 7-year-old children and asking them what they thought about England, what they thought about themselves, what they thought about money, race, sex and all that. It was only ever intended to be one film, one snapshot of England at that time. Anyway, the film was incredibly successful and out of it grew this whole series of films. We decided seven years later to go back and visit these characters, which was pretty chilling – the 14-year-old spotted interviewee is not the most eloquent of creatures, it tends to be more or less monosyllabic, yes and no – but nonetheless, when we put it together we could see that we had the beginnings of a very powerful idea. And then we went on and I think that it really came good at about *Twenty-eight Up* (1985), and I had an epiphany then when I realized that I was not actually making the film I was making. I took the film to America, I was persuaded to take it to film festivals there. I did not want to take it as I did not think that anyone could understand it there, because so much of it was about social class, with lots of reference to public schools, private schools, comprehensives, and I thought Americans are not going to figure this out at all. Frankly, at the time, we all thought that we were making a political film about the state of the class system. The class system was alive and well (even though Rock'n'Rollers could own the world) and your average person, who was not born into opportunity, had much less of a chance of getting what he wanted out of life. Anyway, in the end I took *Twenty-eight Up* to America and they all got it!

It then occurred to me that maybe I had not been making a political film all this time, but that I had been making a humanistic document, I had been making a film about things that we all go through, all over the world: growing up, having children, having jobs, and all of that. And then I realized what I had really been doing, which I suppose encouraged me to keep going. We have now got up to 42 and we will keep going, as long as I am above ground and enough of them (the featured documentary children/adults) will do it.

I am now going to show you clips from the *Up* series which really lays my territory on the ground, as it were. This is the kind of bookend of my career, the first thing I ever did. Initially I was only a modest researcher on *Seven Up*, but it stayed with me my whole working life and probably will be the thing that is the most lasting of anything that I have done. Here we will see one of the characters called Neil, from Liverpool, and this is a little excerpt from *Forty-two Up* (1998) which shows the way that we integrated the different generations of his life from 7 years old to 42 years old.

Clips from the *Seven Up* series (1964, 1970, 1977, 1985, 1991, 1998)

Neil (N), age 7   Well, we pretend we've got a sword and we make the noises of the sword fighting and we go: aaaaaagh. . . .

Background voice (BV)   Neil grew up in a Liverpool suburb.

N, age 7   In the winter if you live in the country, well, it was just all wet and there wouldn't be anything for miles around and you get soaked if you try to go out, and there is no shelter anywhere except in your own house. But in the town you can go out on wet wintry days because you can always find somewhere to shelter, 'cos there's lots of places.

BV   At 14 Neil was at a local comprehensive school.

N, age 14   I think it's a very good idea to have competition. Otherwise you might start to relax and not try hard enough. Being in set one is very very hard to keep up with the others. I never have the time to relax at all.

BV   Neil had dreams of going to Oxford but he did not get in. Instead he went to Aberdeen University but dropped out after a term. At 21 he was working on a building site and living in a squat.

N, age 21   I came to London and I contacted an agency for squatters and they were able to give me the address of somebody who was able to help people who were looking for accommodation in the London area.

Background voice/Michael Apted (MA)   You kicked against the stability.

N, age 21   I don't think I ever had any stability, to be quite honest. I can't think of any time in my life when I ever did. I don't think I have been kicking against anything, I think I have been kicking in mid-air the whole of my life.

BV/MA   At 28 Neil was homeless, wandering around the west coast of Scotland.

N, age 28   If the state didn't give us any money it would probably just mean crime and I'm glad I don't have to steal to keep myself alive. If the money runs out, well, then for a few days there's nowhere to go to and that's all you can do. I simply have to find the warmest shed I can find.

BV/MA   How do people regard you here?

N, age 28   Well, I'm still known as an eccentric, as I have been since, umm, back to the age of 16 or so. I am not claiming that I feel as though I am in some sort of nirvana, but I'm claiming that if I was living in a bed-sit in suburbia, I'd be so miserable I'd feel like cutting my throat.

BV/MA   At 35 we found Neil living on a council estate in the most northerly part of Britain, the Shetland Islands.

N, age 35   The nice thing about here is that you can cut yourself off when you want, because there are people living around but they are pretty quiet people. It's an environment which sustains me, it's one in which I can survive. I still feel my real place is in the world where people are doing what the majority of people do, and the reason I don't feel safe is because I'm getting more and more used to this lifestyle which eventually I shall have to give up.

BV/MA   And what would you like to be doing, say, in seven years?

N, age 35   I can think of all kinds of things that I'd like to be doing, the real question is what am I likely to be doing?

BV/MA   What are you likely to be doing?

N, age 35   That's a horrible question. I tend to think that the most likely answer is that I will be wandering homeless around the streets of London, but with a bit of luck that won't happen.

[*Sound of car engines and then diplomatic voice of Neil in background speaking about the Borough of Hackney.*]

MA/BV   At 42 Neil is a Liberal Democrat member of Hackney Council, he was elected two years ago.

So there you go, that's your politicians for you! This is a story with, at least so far, a very positive conclusion. This illustrates what I like to call the two-way street of what I learn from one area and what I put into another (how documentary work helps me with feature film work): constructing this amount of material into a character, into Neil, who of course is his own character. Yet somehow taking six generations of material, which I have, and trying to make a coherent, if short, synthesis of his life, is something I have had to learn, it has taught me how to put characters in films, and vice versa as well. The structure of a character, the structure of a film, to try and create sympathy for a character before you get into the more tricky areas, I think I have learned through making narrative films with characters created by writers and whatever, and vice versa. The unexpectedness of life is something I try and inject in my movies, into the narrative of my movies, my imagined characters, if you like. But here in the '*Up*' series we have gigantic amounts of material and the most difficult part of the film is to try and put it together so that it presents, honourably and honestly, who these people are at the seven-year interval I visit them. I don't see them much between the seven years, but I like to see if I can catch who they are in that seven years. I must say that though I have lost three of the original fourteen participants, none of them have ever moaned about how they are presented – so I take that as a compliment.

I will never forget what Bernardo Bertolucci said about working with actors: that *working with actors is in a sense making a documentary about that actor, the way that the actor becomes the character, the rehearsal* – I don't know whether Bernardo likes to rehearse with actors, but I do – and the shooting process is, in a sense, that process. As the actor becomes more and more attuned to the character, he brings what he is to the character and takes what he wants from the character, and it is a sort of documentary experience. When I rehearse films I try and keep it as loose and as 'documentary' as I can. Often this means that people who are going to play policemen, or doctors, or nurses go out and do that for a short time.

I have always been encouraged to give an actor as much information about the life and time and the world that his character lives in. It is a double-edged sword because when they do that they then begin to have their own ideas about their character which I cannot ignore. If they say, 'well, the character wouldn't say this', I have to pay attention to that. As the actor begins to approach his character, he begins to adopt the voice and so he may want the voice of the character in the imagined piece changed to fit his own speech patterns. Often you get into very tricky situations when actors want rewrites. But I think that if you are going to involve an actor, as Bertolucci says, in becoming the character, you also have to extract from the character the rhythms, the mannerisms, the behaviour that that person has.

So, one of the other things that I like to do is to mix up actors and non-actors, to use both. I find that that adds a real dynamic, a real tension into the process. As long as you cast people – I'll call them people 'from the street' as opposed to trained actors – for who they are and what they can do, and don't ask them to overreach themselves or overreach you, I think that it can bring an enormous authenticity, not just to a scene, but to the other actors' work because they cannot play tricks, as the people in front of them are offering their own personality, they are delivering who they are.

I am going to now show you a piece from *The Coal Miner's Daughter*, which is the intriguing story of the country music singer Loretta Lynn, who grew up in the very poorest part of the Appalachians. She was married at 13, she was a grandmother at 29, and nonetheless she still managed to find a great strength out of her roots to become one of the great country music singers of the twentieth century. What I had learned from England – and I had done twenty years of work in documentaries and drama and television and film in England – was that if you were going to go on location, as I was going to go with this to the Appalachians, it was not just a question of shooting the landscape; there is also the human landscape to deal with, to get the right tone, the right voice, the right accent in the film. This particular film was a very dangerous piece of material: it was odd that an Englishman was doing this, and this was largely because the Americans were not interested in doing it – the Americans saw these people as white trash, whereas I did not know anything about them, going in from my background. So I just went in, as an outsider, to do the best I could. It was a very arduous job filming this, and I again, as I said, wanted to create the human landscape of the thing, so I only used three trained actors in the whole movie – Sissy Spacek who played Loretta, Tommy Lee Jones who played her husband, and Beverly De'Angela who played another country music singer, Patsy Cline.

In this clip from *The Coal Miner's Daughter* you can see the effect that you get when you put a non-actor up with an actor; I think it gives a certain authenticity.

Clip from *The Coal Miner's Daughter* (1980)

The scene is a pie sale at a local school where Doolittle (Tommy Lee Jones) makes his first serious play for Loretta (Sissy Spacek). If you get the pie you get the girl!

Clearly none of those children had ever acted before and I thought it gave a real 'voice' to that scene. I think I learnt how to deal with non-actors from dealing with documentary subjects. The skill that you need is to put them at ease, get them to relax, if it is possible, and to be 'in' the moment, create the moment for them, and let them loose in it. This is what I did with the young people in *The Coal Miner's Daughter* and that is my main objective when I do a documentary: to try and make the subject feel as comfortable as possible. It is the same sort of lesson as in documentary, that is, to really spot what the gift of that person is, to spot what you really need from them, and to use it.

So the question is: why do both? Why do documentaries? Why do feature films? Not only is it just a two-way street, but it is terrific fun! For the documentary I make, I have five people in a van, and we go out and do all our stuff, and we are spending very little money, and there is no great pressure on it, and it is exciting because you have to keep 'light on your feet', and you have to figure out what's going to work, what isn't going to work, what's a productive avenue, what's not. Then when you have all the material together, you start to write it, you start to put it together, you begin to see what you have.

With a movie (feature film) you have crews of hundreds. On the James Bond set I had a crew of over a thousand people working on the film, and that is a whole different process. I believe you can work towards getting a complexity, an economy, a more emotional range, maybe, in a narrative film, and the process is so different. Again, the job is to have a text, to examine the text, and to bring the text to life by whatever devices, whatever tricks, you have. But then, in that case, you already start with something, you are not *creating* a script as you are in a documentary. In a documentary, of course, what you are doing is nosing around in people's lives and getting away from all the unreality of Hollywood, or the British film industry, or whatever. It is exciting to go out into the world and get away from all that and to really figure out what people think, dream, want to deal with in their lives.

Also, it gives you – at least it has given me – a calling card. I now get asked to do films which have a kind of documentary tone to them. For example, it was decided to make a film of *Gorillas in the Mist*, the book by Dian Fossey, the woman who had spent eighteen years in the Varunga Mountains in Rwanda, Zaire and Uganda, observing and protecting the mountain gorilla of which there were only three or four hundred left on the planet. They were looking for a director who could handle both narrative and documentary, because the heart of the movie, which is a kind of bizarre idea, is this relationship between a wild animal and a Hollywood actress, in this case Sigourney Weaver. They wanted a director who could deal with the documentary footage of wildlife material incorporated into the fictional stuff that we created. Undoubtedly, it was Dian Fossey's life (she had been murdered about eighteen months before, so she was not with us, but there were people around who were with her, who knew her); yet, nevertheless we had to compress her life, we had to tell the story of her life in two hours. So it required all the narrative skills to do that, plus the documentary skills of using wildlife material in order to tell the story.

Here is a clip from *Gorillas in the Mist* to show you how we integrated wildlife footage, narrative footage and fake footage – and small cash prizes to spot the fake!!

Clip from *Gorillas in the Mist* (1988)

Dian Fossey (Sigourney Weaver) is making her first real contact with the mountain gorillas. She is improvising a way to communicate by copying what the gorillas are doing to her.

That was pretty hairy stuff! The way we made the film was simply that we went up for eight weeks with Sigourney Weaver and three wildlife units, and parked her up there and just watched what happened. We were not allowed to handle the gorillas – I don't think I would have wanted to, they weigh five hundred pounds – but I was not even able to suggest that they might want to go this way or that; we were not allowed to do anything but observe them. Sometimes when you went up there you did not even find the gorillas, you could just hear them farting and belching, because the terrain was so rough! If we consider the shot of the silverback running down at her, for example [just shown]: we took that shot and built that into a scene. After eight weeks we had five or six moments like that and they then became the scenes in the film of her relationship with the gorillas. There is not much fake stuff in that, just a couple of close-ups. We then had to complete the sequences by building toy gorillas – Rick Baker did that, an extremely distinguished animotronic wizard – and we shot that material in Kenya, which has a similar kind of topography to Rwanda where we shot those initial images.

Anyway, *Gorillas in the Mist* shows you how you can mix documentaries and narrative – the attitudes, the style, everything, and in fact, as I said, we had to create a script out of what really did happen up there, there was no point in me reading out 'a gorilla does this', 'a gorilla does that', because I could not create that. I just had to wait and see what happened. Film is dependent on reality!

Now the next thing is: this is all very well, but it can also get you into trouble, ethical trouble, when you start mixing things up, mixing documentaries and fiction. For how do people know what they are looking at?

I bring an example of this 'mixing', just to show you how it can be done and to consider whether it is obnoxious or helpful. I made a film called *Moving the Mountain* which looked at Tiananmen Square [the events of the Tiananmen

Square massacre, China, 4 June 1989]. I had always wanted to make a film taking a massive public event, but done, or doing it, in a very private, intimate way. A Chinese student, Lee Liu, had written a book called *Moving the Mountain* about his experiences before, during and after Tiananmen Square, and I met with him and there was some discussion as to whether we should do this as a feature film. However, it seemed impossible to go to an American studio and spend hundreds of millions of dollars re-creating Tiananmen Square, so what we decided was to do it as a documentary. I found five other students who had also lived through that experience, all of whom had been major players in Tiananmen Square, and made this documentary about their childhood: how they had got to Tiananmen Square, what happened in Tiananmen Square, how they got out of Tiananmen Square, where they went to and the effect it had on them. I made this film for the fifth anniversary of the event itself. But I was slightly lumbered because the material I had was a lot of archival stuff: all the American networks and the BBC and CNN had been recording continuously throughout the period – they had not necessarily been broadcasting everything, but they had been recording so much, and there was thus a ton of archival material on Tiananmen Square. I also had all of the interviews that I did with the Chinese students themselves, one of whom was still in China, and we smuggled ourselves and some film in to interview him. The other four students had relocated in America. So I had the interviews, I had the archival, and yet to me it seemed to be very much a *character-driven* documentary; I really wanted to understand and know and dramatize the major events in these people's lives which explained why kids, of 19, 20, 21, became major players in a huge political drama.

I therefore decided to reconstruct some stuff, to use dramatics skills, casting skills, and taking, as my foundation, the interviews I had done with them, to dramatize from those interviews some events that had taken place in their childhood.

Let me show you a piece of the main character, Lee Liu, who had written the book *Moving the Mountain*, to show you how, by using narrative and feature film methods, I fleshed up the story he was telling me about an event that happened four or five years before he went to Tiananmen Square. This clip is a mixture of interview, reconstructed archival and television footage.

Clip from *Moving the Mountain* (1994)

The scene describes a terrible earthquake that Lee Liu witnessed as a child. Thousands of people were killed, including one of his young friends. It was Lee Liu's first brush with death and forever changed his view of the world.

That was a mixture of documentary and drama. It's tricky stuff and I do not know the ethics of it. I worried about it a lot, but then I thought: well, I cannot imagine that my audience is going to think that a documentary crew was following Lee Liu around in his childhood and adolescence, so I think that they will have the leap of faith to suppose that this is material that has been found elsewhere. Nonetheless, this sort of clip does open up issues of the morality of mixing the message, as it were.

In the early 1990s I was given a very unusual opportunity, which was that I was offered a documentary and a movie about the same subject matter, that is to say I was allowed to deal with the subject both as a documentarian and as a movie-maker. In some senses for me this brought into vivid highlight my whole career with all its challenges, raising all the questions regarding what you can do with a documentary, what you can do with a piece of written narrative.

I will show some detailed contrasts between the two. The movie itself was called *Thunderheart* (1992) and the documentary was called *Incident at Oglala* (1992). They deal with the history of the American Indian movement, particularly in the mid-Seventies on the Pine Ridge Reservation in South Dakota. During that time, around the late Sixties, early Seventies, various ethnic groups were standing up and getting a political voice. The Native Americans formed the American Indian Movement which was trying to develop a strong independent political stance because American Indians have been 'ghettoized' in America and live in appalling conditions – and, in all the hundreds of years that the place has been colonized, nobody has yet figured out a way to deal with it. In the Seventies this American Indian Movement started to express itself, usually violently – it marched on Washington, took buildings, and there was this very famous incident at Wounded Knee in South Dakota when, again, there was a lot of gun-fire between the Nixon government and the American Indian Movement. What the American government was doing – really through the FBI – and what my films analyse, is the way that, on the Reservation, through the lessons of Vietnam, they were dividing the two strands of Native American: the Traditionals and the Half-Breeds. The Half-Breeds tended to be very sympathetic towards the government and the Traditionals tended to be very sympathetic towards the American Indian Movement. As in Vietnam, the FBI moved in and gave a lot of money and a lot of arms to the Half-Breeds in order to fight the Traditionals, and they created an atmosphere on the Reservation of violence, fear and dread which lasted many years. This ended in 1975 with a horrendous shoot-out, where two FBI officers were brutally shot at point-blank range and the government finally succeeded, through the courts, to close down the American Indian Movement.

That was the kind of volatile period that I was dealing with. Of course, I knew nothing about it going in, and I was asked to make the documentary first, which was a dangerous assignment because, although the events had happened fifteen years before, there was still tremendous conflict between the Traditional Native Americans and the Half-Breed Native Americans, and there were a lot of old wounds and resentments. I had to go in and open them up to make this documentary. So I did that and then I started making the movie which was a sort of dramatization of that.

My documentary was based on the final shoot-out and the case of one of the men who was sent to prison – who is still in prison as he was rail-roaded, we thought – and so the burden of the film is an attempt to get him another trial, which we failed to do.

The movie is the story of a white FBI agent who goes in to deal with these sort of problems, discovers his Native American roots, and changes sides. So already you can see Hollywood looming down: that the film has to be about a white guy, that it has to have a leading American actor in it (in this case Val Kilmer), and it is the normal pressure you are under. If you are going to spend fifteen or twenty million dollars of someone's money, you want to make sure that people get to see it. But those are the sort of pressures you are always under when doing a movie.

It is pretty remarkable that a studio would make this movie, since the burden of the movie is that the FBI were actually murdering people on the Reservation. It is remarkable that they would even go down that road, but they did. And yet there is a price to be paid. When I was doing the movie I had obviously already finished the documentary and it was very much in my mind.

Let me give two examples of the way that I used the documentary to construct the movie. One of the issues was casting. When I was making the film there was the role of an important American Indian Movement leader and, much as I tried, I went through every actor I could find and I could not find anybody who had that kind of weight, that gravitas, that dynamism that I was looking for – someone who could lead their people. I then remembered having talked to some of these men while making the documentary and so I went back to one and asked him whether he would be in the movie, and he said 'why not?'

First, then, a clip from the documentary *Incident at Oglala* of this actual American Indian Movement leader, John Trudell, who is here talking to me.

Clip from documentary *Incident at Oglala* (1992)

He describes how, in his mind, the US government punished him for his political views by turning a blind eye when his house was burned down and his wife and children died in it.

That is John Trudell the politician. I have this character in the documentary and I thought, if he would be prepared to do it, if he had the patience and I had the skill, why not get him also to do this in the movie?

So here is a scene of him playing the same role in the movie, *Thunderheart*, alongside Val Kilmer and an interesting elder, who again is a real elder. When I went on the Reservation I decided I wouldn't import any actors, I would use the best elder I could find and do the best he and I could do with it.

So, now John Trudell *as actor* in the movie *Thunderheart*.

Clip from *Thunderheart* (1992)

An FBI agent (Val Kilmer) visits a local elder only to find the fugitive he has been looking for (John Trudell) is hiding out there.

That is an example of the character. Now, let me just show you an incident, in this case an example of an incident described by an actual Native American woman, about the sort of treatment they were getting on the Reservation from the mixed-breed police. This is a clip of Debbie Whitebloom telling her story to me in the documentary *Incident at Oglala*.

Clip from documentary *Incident at Oglala*

It tells of a drive-by shooting one Sunday lunchtime, when her house was riddled with bullets and one of Debbie's children was injured.

So we turned that incident into the following scene in the movie *Thunderheart*.

Clip from *Thunderheart*

A similar scene where an FBI agent (Val Kilmer) is interrogating an activist (Sheila Tousey) and is interrupted by a drive-by shoot-up. Her child is shot and injured.

So obviously the grandmother there was not an actor either, and she did not want to be an actor after that – I tell you! In fact, she didn't even want to show up for Day Two!

It was an interesting illustration in my life about the relative powers of the two mediums, the visceral power of the documentary and the narrative complexity of a movie. I think I got myself slightly in a muddle because I became a prisoner of the truth when I was making the movie; I was so involved in the politics of the American Indian Movement and the various ramifications of it all, that I probably made the movie too complicated. So it is not necessarily a good thing to have a lot of documentary attitude towards doing a movie – you can run into trouble.

I always get amused when people talk about the purity of a documentary, and I have a lot of well-meaning shouting matches with colleagues, because the idea that a documentary is pure, and that a movie is not, is to me ridiculous. When I made this documentary, I had an agenda: I was after the FBI. I invited the FBI to be in the film and to state their case, but they wouldn't – but it was clear to me from the start that I went in to make as passionate a film as I could about what I considered the mistreatment of the American Indians. I loaded the documentary as much as I could to make that case, I was unashamed about it.

Whenever people bring that up, I have a feeling that the movie is a far more considered and a fairer view of that period of history than the documentary is. I was looking for one thing in the documentary and another thing with the movie.

I want to show you a couple of examples in two of my more commercial films of how my documentary 'soul', my little documentary 'heart', beats.

Even when I was asked to do the James Bond film, the first thing I did was haul everybody onto the Caucasus, to Azerbaijan, which was where this mythical story was set, in order to have a look at the reality of where they brought the oil and the gas out of the Caspian Sea. I think everybody on the set thought I was barking mad, because there was no way that we were going to do much filming there, it was too volatile, too dangerous. But by having that real landscape,

Plate 17 The World is not Enough (Michael Apted 1999)

171

and by going out there and by actually filming a little bit, it got me a couple of really astonishing images.

The first clip is a remarkable landscape of the oilfields left derelict by the Russians' departure in 1991. The second is of a city that the Russians built on the Caspian Sea to enable them to extract the gas and the oil out of it – images again so startling that I don't think I had ever seen anything like them until I went out there.

Two clips from *The World is not Enough* (1999)

James Bond (Pierce Brosnan) is driving to meet his Russian antagonist (Robbie Coltrane). The route takes him over a complex of roads and bridges that the Russians built in the middle of the Caspian Sea.

Lastly, in my commercial filmmaking mould, just a little piece of *Enigma*.

Again I shot myself in the foot, this time trying to figure out how to decode everything. These people who worked on breaking the enigma codes during the Second World War made it possible for the English to read the German traffic codes. Their work was so brilliant, that if we could understand it, it would not be so brilliant, if you see what I mean. And yet I put these poor actors through trying to understand what it was to decode, I really gave us all a headache!

Here's a little clip from *Enigma* then, to show the verisimilitude that I try and get in movies. All these codes, all these things being written down, this is completely accurate, and I think that it adds an authenticity, a truthfulness to the scene.

Clip from *Enigma* (2001)

Our hero (Dougray Scott) and his colleagues at Bletchley Park are working against the clock to decipher the U-boat codes before the U-boats attack an American convoy in the North Atlantic.

I will just conclude by going back to the film that is probably closest to my heart – and possibly also to this *First European Psychoanalytic Film Festival* – and that is back to *Forty-two Up*. Normally, when I do these films, I just do portraits of each of the characters and then I juxtapose them. However, I broke style in *Forty-two Up* because the question that I was always being asked, and which was driving me crazy, is: what effect does being in a film have on these people? So I decided to ask them this very question and to then inter-cut them all at 42, answering that question. Here to conclude my clip presentation therefore is this little section of *Forty-two Up* – what's it like being in a documentary?

172

Clip from *Forty-two Up* (1998)

(All those being interviewed here are 42 years old.)

MA   What effect does it have on you being in these films do you think?

Female 1   It's funny, because before the films start you think: what on earth have I done in seven years that I could possibly say? What can I talk about that I have done? And you panic and you think, I should have done something, I should have done something dramatic. I was hoping I would win the lottery last night so that I could come on and say that. But life's not like that.

Male 1   We were talking about my ambitions as a scientist, I mean my ambition as a scientist is to be more famous for doing science than for being in this film, but unfortunately, Michael, it's not gonna happen!

Male 2   I've met some of the most interesting people I know and I am still in contact with, and this includes people in different parts of the world. One or two particularly close friendships have been forged through the programme, although I have to say I was very suspicious when the initial contact was made.

Female 2   I mean, I don't think I'd ever have kept a record of my life in the way that we have with this programme. So yes, I enjoy doing it, but it's not something that takes a great precedence.

Male 3   If you came and asked me if you could do this to my children, I certainly wouldn't be enthusiastic. I think it's something that I wouldn't want to wish on someone particularly.

Male 4   I think for the first forty odd years it's restricted me because I was always shy to start with and, knowing that people were going to be looking at me and watching me, rather than do something that's gonna look stupid, I've always pulled myself back.

Female 3   There's a lot of baggage that gets stirred up every seven years for me, that I find very hard to deal with, and I can put it away for the seven years and then it comes round again and the whole lot comes tumbling out again and I have to deal with it all over again.

Male 5   It hasn't sort of changed my choices in life – I haven't thought well, I have to be doing this by then, or how will this seem to others, and so on. It's just a kind of periodic little intrusion.

Male 6   It's the only time, when you're a cabbie, instead of you picking up the celebrity and saying, 'Hallo, you're so and so', say for example 'Paul Gascoigne, aren't you?', and they'll say, 'Oh I know you, right?', and then they turn the tables on you.

MA   And do you like that?

Male 6   It's not a question of liking it. I'm used to it!

Male 7   It has to be said that I bitterly regret that the headmaster of the school where I was when I was 7 pushed me forward for this series, because every seven years a little pill of poison is injected into . . . [*interrupted*]

Male 8   Being honest, I think despite all things that I might have said over the years – I know, and they're coming again – I think that there is a certain amount of excitement there too, and I lie, I'm old enough to admit it now, I suppose. No, it probably is a bit of good fun.

Female 4   Some of us don't see family one year from the next, seven years on, and I think that is how we all feel about each other, that we're linked, and that can never go.

MA   So there you have it. As I said, this is a kind of skim through some things and I don't know what's of interest, what will bear through or what won't, but that is the presentation of documentary versus narrative.

HTR   Thank you Michael. It's not appropriate to have a chair who's crying, is it?!

MA   It wasn't that bad, was it?!

HTR   We have very little time to do justice to such a generous account of one man's complex working life using the medium of film. Michael Apted has covered so much, we have been given so much. It's now the turn of the audience to respond, in this encounter with Michael Apted's work.

The audience

A1   I would like to ask you to address a question that is very much on my mind, which is about the relationship that develops between you and the protagonists of your documentaries, in particular in the *Seven Up* series or in the American Indian film. Do you feel that there is some kind of pattern of closeness, distance, identification? Are people happy with what you do? Unhappy? Do you like them? Dislike them? How does it influence the films?

MA   It's an interesting question because in a sense my documentaries fall into two categories. In this one, the *Seven Up* series, I have a very long-term relationship with them and so, frankly, I have to behave myself because I want them to come back next time! So any promises I make to them about what I do, what I don't do, I have to hold. I have known these people and this film for over thirty-five years now and it is a bit like a family. I lost all sense of objectivity – if that ever exists – a long time ago. I care about them, I'm involved in their lives, I see them in between time, if they come to America they come and stay

– so any idea of objectivity with these particular subjects I abandoned a long time ago. And I also have to deal with the very emotional issue of whether I will outlive some of them because it's getting to that time as well. So I think that with these subjects, these people and this film, I am very close and very unobjective about it, and all I can do when I put the films together is just figure out what has been important to them in the last seven years and go for that. I like them all; like family, I like some more than others, some like me less than some others like me. Some don't like me, some find me a pain in the ass! So it is a very personal thing.

I think that with other documentaries, for example *Moving the Mountain* or *Incident at Oglala*, which are very one-off things, it is a bit more complicated in so far as you don't have to go back, you can take advantage of people, you can lie to people about what you want to do, you can deceive them. I tend to think that I encourage a relationship with my subjects, that that is the way that I get the best sort of material, but then, I suppose, what is the best sort of material? If it is a very political documentary, like the Native American one, then I am trying to lead them, guiding them into saying something that is provocative or will help my agenda, because, as I said earlier, with some of these movies I do have a clear agenda, I am not out to be objective, I feel I have a passion about an issue and I want to spell that out and make my case as strongly as I can.

When I am dealing with character-driven documentaries, rather than issue-driven ones, I think that my relationship is always something that is of the most importance. For example, when I shoot a documentary I never look down the camera, I only ever use two or three cameramen to shoot with me, because my whole dynamic on the set of the documentary is my relationship with the person I am going to interview. I always do the interview myself, so I need cameramen who know what I want without being told what I want. I think that I always want to like them, I want them to like me, I feel, that is, as with actors: I like collaborating with actors, I am sensitive to actors, I enjoy actors, I admire actors, I respect what they do, I don't treat them like cattle, I let them know everything that is going on, I don't try and trick them, and I think that is the way I get the best work out of them, to make them partners. Similarly, I think with documentaries, unless it is a particular business, then it is that sense of partnership that I think I look for.

A2   The main thing that struck me when I was looking at the documentary films, as opposed to the Hollywood films, was the difference in the cinematic language – you talk about only using three cameras on the documentary stuff. I am referring in particular to that North American Indian one, where technically you have the same subject matter and you re-create it entirely differently in the Hollywood version. As a viewer, you can feel the difference: within the first few seconds of watching it, immediately you react differently. I was interested as to what language you 'speak' when you are in Hollywood and how you feel about that language: do you have a cinematic style that you step into as if you are speaking '*Hollywoodese*' as opposed to '*Granadaese*', or something?

MA   This is a tough one! I tend not to think I have a style, I don't know about that. I tend to adapt the style to the subject matter. But clearly you are right, there is some – I like the word – 'visceral' attack about doing a documentary. Whereas doing a movie, for better or worse, is for me a much more complicated thing, you have many more weapons to use, and one of those weapons is cinematography – atmosphere and mood – which you can create.

I do both and I get tired of both. I do documentaries and I get tired that people don't say what I want them to say, frankly, and I think to myself that if I had a writer and an actor I could say what these people have been burbling on about for half an hour, in five seconds! And then when I do movies I get fed up with that because I think, 'This is so fake, is anybody ever going to believe this?' So I get impatient with both and I tend not to have a cinematic style, I don't think. I hire different cameramen for different projects, so I don't have someone that I always work with whose eye and style I am employing all the time. I cast the crew, the cinematographer, the designer, the casting director sometimes, depending on what the material is. I am not unaware – and that is the power of the documentary – that there is a certain directness in the visual style of it, simply because it has to be that way, you don't have the time and it is inappropriate to start re-creating stuff in a documentary with the documentary subject, and most of my documentaries are interview based.

With the price you pay for the texture of a movie, as you say, there may be a loss of that immediacy. Personally, I love movies where I don't notice the cinematography, although it is in the back of my brain that someone is creating a tone and an atmosphere. Once I start looking at it and thinking 'This is a great shot', or 'My god, this is beautifully lit', in some ways as a member of the audience I am being taken out of the movie. On the other hand, you don't want a movie to look indifferent, to look neutral or flat. So it's very tricky, but in some ways I am employing the documentary style in the movies by trying to make each element of the movie fit the subject, I am looking at the truth of the subject I am dealing with and I am trying to fit everything in its own way into that.

A3   I am very interested in these references which you make to the truth, 'prisoner of the truth', and it seems to me that it is not so much 'mixed messages' as 'mixed media', really, to get through one message. It seemed to me that what shines throughout is a certain consistency to a certain kind of truth which has to do with subjectivity but also authenticity, and I wondered what you thought about that, what does one mean by the 'truth' – this term that is so relevant to both cinema and psychoanalysis?

MA I would be interested in what you lot think – for me it is unanswerable. When I am doing a piece of work, I am faced with people. At the moment, for example, I am doing a piece about marriage – taking nine couples who are all getting married at the same time from different parts of America, different social, sexual orientations and so on, and I am going to follow them for ten years. They stood in front of me and yet I don't know whether they are telling me the truth.

Maybe you have the same thing when you are with a patient and you don't know whether they are telling you the truth – in fact I do not even know whether I am telling *you* the truth now! All I say to myself is that it's the best I can do, I create an atmosphere, an environment, I get to know these people a little bit. I try on the other hand also to trip them up a little bit, because I don't want them to be prepared for it – I don't want them to know what I am going to ask, although they sort of know – so I want to catch them unaware so that it is not all pre-programmed. Again, it is even more complicated when you are re-creating something in a narrative situation – 'does this make any sense at all?', I ask myself! The bewildering thing about making a movie is that you never know until you put it all together: is the whole equal to the sum of the parts? If you're lucky, it is, and you have a good movie. Sometimes, more often than not, it isn't. You look at the scenes, you look at the rushes, you look at all that and it seems authentic and truthful; and then you put the whole thing together and it doesn't make any sense at all! It's a mystery, I don't know whether it is a mystery in your psychoanalytic world too, but what is 'truth'?

All I can say is that as a documentarian I do the best I can do. I feel I can push people; on this *Forty-two Up* I feel I can ask them extremely frank questions – on the other hand, they can create the agenda. If they say to me 'I don't wanna talk about money', as Tony does because he is always ripping off the old tax-man and all that, or if they say 'I don't want to talk about sex', then I have to respect that. Nonetheless, I always feel that I can ask very intimate questions of them because I know them so well.

The better word I have for 'truth', especially in movies, is 'authentic'. I take a lot of trouble if it is available to me to find the real thing, and in a sense act in some way as a copyist. I remember when I made an adaptation of *Gorky Park* (1983), it drove me barmy because we weren't allowed into Russia to film it (this was in the early Eighties, pre-Gorbachev) and I went in to research and someone blabbed off and we all got thrown out! Simply not to know what a Russian apartment looked like, or what Russians ate for breakfast, and all that, was a nightmare. I realized how much I depended on that simple, unprepossessing modest research about how people live, and when it is cut off from me I feel very much at sea, and that is why very little of my work is to do with special effects or fantasy or whatever, because I flourish off trying to make things authentic, always being interested in that.

So I simply cannot answer that question and you, as a psychoanalyst, could probably answer it better than I could anyway! Whether this is common ground, or whether we have a different attitude towards the truth, as filmmakers, as psychoanalysts, I don't know. I suppose that is really the burden of this whole festival!

A4　I was very interested in your descriptions of yourself as observer and communicator through both media that you described, and I think that in that sense I see a great similarity to the work of psychoanalysts, or psychotherapists, in that we observe in a close and intimate way and we communicate. One of the differences is that we have a way of noticing what happens to our communication in a very close way, from one session to the next, monitoring ourselves and what we do next. Of course we use only words and body language, yet what I am struck about in your work is that you are prepared to observe and communicate and then let everybody see and make whatever they want of it, and you have no control over it.

MA　You're right, you live with your one-on-ones; I mean, I do the piece of work, I have to live with these things, but not only do I put it out there and say 'there it is', but also I never think about it afterwards. I find I am so neurotic about what I am doing at the moment that I don't go back and look at stuff, it is only on occasions like this one that I do. In my mind – and I know this is a horrible way of putting it – it is as if it were disposable: you do it, you put it up there, it exists. In the present world of video shops and DVD and Internet and all that, the work stays around for a long, long time – it didn't use to. It used to be on the television, when I started, and if you missed it, you missed it, and that was the end of that! But I don't really carry it with me consciously.

A5　The other difference between psychoanalysis and filmmaking is the medium of the visual which is so fascinating. I wondered if you wouldn't mind extending your generosity and telling us what exactly it is about the visual image that attracts you to it?

MA　The visual image, it's so powerful and it is the sort of thing that I found most difficult about my career, my background. I came from a very literary background, I mean I would much rather read a book than go to an art gallery, so my roots were literary, rather than visual – which is very much an English thing, I think. I fell in love with the movies, I had a moment down in Oxford Street, when I was 17, and saw *Wild Strawberries* (1957), Ingmar Bergman. Up to then, going to the movies had really been about following girls, nothing more than that! And then I suddenly saw this, and here was a whole new world to me, the idea that literary ideas, visual ideas, could all be expressed with as much poetry and skill as any book, any picture, or whatever. So that is when I really fell in love with movies and found that is what I wanted my life to be. I had no possible remote chance of ever doing it, I had no background connections to

178

the industry at all. But I got lucky and left university at the right time and got taken up by Granada Television, so that was my gigantic piece of luck. With *Wild Strawberries* I just began to see the power in it, and particularly the famous dream sequence – it changed my life, it was an epiphany, whether I was poised for it, who knows. But it has been a struggle for me that, moving and starting working visually in television in the very small box, trained at the feet of young Norman and whatever, and all that [*Norman is the cameraman filming Michael Apted during this event for a programme on him in the USA*]. And then moving out into the movie world and into the bigger and bigger screen and trying to figure out for myself a visual language. I have to say it is a struggle and you learn a lot from someone like Bernardo Bertolucci, the way he moves the camera. I worked with his distinguished cinematographer, Vittorio Storaro, doing a movie called *Agatha* (1979) with Dustin Hoffman and Vanessa Redgrave. All the time it has been a learning process, and still is, because I don't think that a visual art, an eye, is at the heart of me. I think there is something else there that drives me along, that informs my work. I am not unhappy about the way my movies look, I think that my Bond movie looked as good as anybody else's – which is no small achievement, as it were! – but to me that is a big learning process, a big struggle. That is really it, *they are called 'movies', and I love to move the camera and I know that a piece of behaviour or an image can speak a thousand words*. If you can look for behaviour and if you can somehow work at that with actors, through improvisation, through research, or just through the great gifts of an actor – or at least to spot it when they do it – to realize when something is offered up to you, even if it is unconsciously being offered up to you, and to nail it and say 'that is great', to recognize it – that is a lot of the skill of the job. But it is a struggle and, as I said, I am not unhappy with the way my films look, but I am sure that it is a part of my work that still needs a lot of attention.

A6 With your heart and intelligence I wish desperately that it is you and not Blair and Bush who are doing the jobs they have undertaken! The other thing is to do with your exploration, particularly the young Neil in *Seven Up*, of the theme of loneliness. For these people for whom you are a continuous figure in their lives, can you get to the essential loneliness, that loneliness that some of us really know something about, not only in our patients but in ourselves, when one has absolutely nobody in the world? And you are always there for them.

MA Absolutely. I cannot think that I even begin to approach the kind of closeness that you would if Neil was a patient of yours, I cannot imagine that I can even begin to get that out. We are there for him, we look after him, we see him whenever we can, but he is a mercurial character.

Going back to the visual point, these images of him in the Shetland Islands, at least to communicate loneliness, is very very powerful – and the way he walks, and his behaviour and that strange shamble that he has – since I communicate to a general audience, I think the power of those images is very potent and expresses loneliness without that kind of intimacy that you as a psychoanalyst would have. I have a certain experience of myself being in therapy, and I sometimes feel like a therapist when I am doing these interviews, but as you say, you know, I don't go back. I do one session and then I move on.

So it's kind of phony to even put ourselves on the same plateau here, but I think that I have other tools which can express at least outwardly some of the inner feelings that people express verbally to you psychoanalysts, which I can express visually.

HTR   But, in conclusion, you couldn't see what you saw in the presentation of Neil, the shambling gait, the way he was, without having your own eye, your own sense of something. You couldn't look for that, even if you had the camera, without having the feeling about a human being that clearly you do have, and that comes through in all your work.

Michael Brearley   I'm on the Organizing Committee of this festival and I just wanted to talk very briefly of a different kind of 'seven up', which is that almost fifty years ago two small boys set off from opposite ends of the District Line, one from Upminster and one from Ealing Broadway, nervously, one September, and arrived at the same class of the 'City of London School' which was called Old Grammar: one was him and one was me! [*laughter from the audience*] We've had, since then, our various mutual 'seven ups', or thereabouts, and it's thanks to that that Michael has had the generosity to come all the way from Los Angeles. He is moving house on Monday into the bargain, would you believe it, and I just wanted to say, both collectively and personally, thank you very much indeed for coming.

MA   Thank you, *I* shall start to cry now, so thank you very much!

13

THE CINEMATIC DREAM-WORK OF INGMAR BERGMAN'S *WILD STRAWBERRIES* (1957)

Elizabeth Cowie

When film is not a document, it is a dream. . . . No form of art goes beyond ordinary consciousness as film does, straight to our emotions, deep in the twilight room of the soul.

(Ingmar Bergman, 1960, p. 73)

If the cinema is not made to translate dreams or all that which, in conscious life, resembles dreams, then the cinema does not exist.

(Antonin Artaud, 1927, p. 81)

At bottom, dreams are nothing other than a particular form of thinking, made possible by the conditions of the state of sleep. It is the dream-work which creates that form, and it alone is the essence of dreaming – the explanation of its peculiar nature.

(Sigmund Freud, 1900, p. 506)

Cinema as a 'dream-machine' is a familiar notion, implying a realm of fantasy, of wish-fulfilment. It is not, however, the wishful scenarios of film as forms of daydreaming which audiences take as their own which I am concerned with in this chapter, rather I want to consider cinema as a dreaming-machine and to do this by examining the use of dream sequences within films, in particular, Ingmar Bergman's *Wild Strawberries*.[1] It is the focus which emerges in the course of Freud's thinking on the processes of the unconscious rather than its contents that I want to draw upon here. I will be addressing here two ostensibly opposed aspects of dreaming and cinema. On the one hand there is the sense-making of dreams in film, as symbolic, as allegory, and as – in psychoanalytical terms – the return of the repressed in the unconscious. The portrayal of dreams in films as a device to reveal unconscious wishes has been used in cinema since the early silent period, for example in *His Phantom Sweetheart* (Ince 1915), which withheld from the viewer the information that the protagonist pursuing the beautiful woman he encounters at the theatre was in fact dreaming – a device also used by Fritz Lang in *The Woman in the Window* (1944). On the other hand, there is a cinema of dreams as radically nonsensical, as visual and auditory experiences which cannot be translated into the communicating of a message, and it was this possibility in film which engaged the interest of the surrealists such as Antonin Artaud and Luis Buñuel, as well as later filmmakers like Ingmar Bergman. In each case, however, the figuring of dreams and dreaming within a film raises questions both about cinema's dreamings and the status of narration within a film.

An analogy between cinema and dreaming has long been drawn, films appearing to us as dream-like, while our dreams are experienced – at least to our waking minds – like movies. At the cinema, however, we are not asleep, indeed we are subject to considerable auditory and visual stimuli, as well as mental challenges in making sense of the characters and plot. Nevertheless our cognitive state is not that of our normal waking life for, although we retain all our motor abilities, we are immobile, silent and in so far as we are attuned to only those stimuli arising from the film performance we become oblivious to other events around us, while the exigencies of reality, and the demand to test for reality, are placed in abeyance. There are a number of mental states which involve the mind being neither conventionally conscious nor unconscious, such as meditation, hypnosis and hallucination. None of these are fully understood; however each is assumed to be in some sense a state in which the person is out of touch with reality, while in the latter two the person is also subject to false or illusory sensory information. Cinema, on the contrary, presents us with real sensory, perceptual, information but which is nevertheless fictional. Christian Metz has produced the most complete and subtle consideration of this relation.

> Its signifier (images accompanied by sound and movement) inherently confers on it a certain affinity with the dream, for it coincides directly with one of the major features of the dream signifier, 'imaged' expression, the consideration of representability, to use Freud's term. It is true that the image can organise itself – and that it usually does so, in the cinema as elsewhere, caught as it is in the constraints of communication and the pressures of culture – in figures as 'bound', as secondary as those of language (and which classical semiology based on linguistics, is in a good position to grasp). But it is also true, as Jean-François Lyotard has rightly insisted [in *Discours, figure*], that the image resists being swallowed up whole in these logical assemblages and that something within it has the tendency to escape. In every 'language', the

characteristics inherent in the physical medium of the signifier, I have noted at another level in *Language and Cinema*, have a certain influence on the type of logic which will inform the texts (this is the problem of 'specificities' considered on the level of formal configurations). The unconscious neither thinks nor discourses; it figures itself forth in images; conversely, every image remains vulnerable to the attraction, varying in strength according to the case, of the primary process and its characteristic modalities of concatenation.

(Metz 1974, p. 124)

Metz also suggests, however, that cinema can be 'the delusion of a man awake' (1974, p. 109). This view of the film as deceiving and as illusory – the 'imaginary signifier' – has been important to ideological critiques of cinema, for example in the work of Jean-Louis Baudry. The problems in the use of Lacan's account of the 'mirror stage' by Metz and others to support such an account have now been widely recognized, most notably by Joan Copjec (1994).[2] The paradox of cinema's perceptually real fictions cannot be resolved in a politics of representation, and I am not adopting here such a view of film's dreamings.

For Freud dreams are wish-fulfilments. It has been shown that dreaming is a normal part of sleep, identified primarily with the period in sleep characterized by rapid eye movement (REM), which is instigated by chemical changes in the brain stem (pons), during which a further activation in the brain stimulates the accessing of stored perceptual images which form our dreams (in Reiser 2000, citing Hobson 1988, p. 252). Our wishes don't cause us to dream, it seems, but they may nevertheless cause our dreams. Both memory and emotion are known to be active in the brain during dreaming, and we may surmise that if dreaming serves to enable memory processing, the organizing of the 'day's residues' in memory, then we might assume that something of the affect engaged is also a memory being processed. Certainly, we are strongly affected by our dreams, even when we cannot – even incompletely – remember them, whether as nightmares or as joyful. Moreover, in so far as, awake, we are wishful subjects with intentions and goals whose outcomes we will anticipate or imagine with hope, then it seems likely that our mental activity in dreaming will also include such hopings, such intentions, such wishing.

'The royal road to the unconscious' is how Freud characterized the interpretation of dreams. That dreams are meaningful and readable is an idea which is both very ancient and found in almost all cultures; however, Freud not only posited dreamers themselves as the source or author of the meaning of their dreaming, but also proposed that dreams, while readable, are not messages to anyone, and certainly not the dreamer. Dreams are not ordinarily remembered, and thus typically are not present to us in our waking moments, and when they are remembered they appear to lack a proper narrative, to involve inconsistent and arbitrary images and actions, peopled by unconnected characters, so that they appear meaningless. As Metz notes:

> The dream story is a 'pure' story, a story without an act of narration, emerging in turmoil or shadow, a story that no narrative agency has *formed* (deformed), a story from nowhere, which nobody tells to nobody. And nevertheless, there is, clearly or confusedly woven by the images themselves, a succession, whether organised or chaotic, of places, actions, moments, characters.
>
> (Metz 1974, p. 125)

Dreams are a visual presentation and enactment – a performance and not a narration – of a wish, of a desire, which is not only sexual and ambitious but also unconscious. The nonsensical character of dreams arises, Freud argues, as a result of the action by the ego which seeks to prevent the articulation of wishes which have been repressed. Dreaming for Freud is thus the presenting of what must not be known in consciousness, it is a mental work of not-knowing. This is the 'dream-work', which is the psychical process which forms the dream out of the raw materials of the bodily stimuli and day's residues, together with the dream-thoughts and wishes in which the dream originates. It is a work of *distortion* which enables the latent content to evade censorship through a process of transformation. Freud identifies four aspects to this process: distortion arises through, the work of condensation on the one hand, and displacement on the other; at the same time the material is subject to considerations of representability, that is, only what is capable of being represented in images and sounds (Freud 1900, p. 507),[3] or capable of being reworked, is selected. In addition the material undergoes a process of revision by which it is intelligibly organized. This revision occurs continually during dreaming – though it is especially apparent when nearing waking – but also when recounting a dream, and it is the latter which is most specifically associated with this, as Freud terms it, 'secondary revision',[4] producing the manifest dream, in contrast to the latent content of dream thoughts and wishes.[5] For Freud the essence of the dream is neither the manifest content nor the latent content (Freud 1900, pp. 579–580, note 1, added in 1914), instead he emphasizes that 'at bottom, dreams are nothing other than a particular form of thinking, made possible by the conditions of the state of sleep. It is the dream-work which creates that form, and it alone is the essence of dreaming – the explanation of its peculiar nature' (ibid., pp. 506–507, note 2, added in 1925). However, this dream-work 'does not think, calculate or judge in any way at all; it restricts itself to giving things a new form' (ibid., p. 507).

The process of distortion which is the dream-work is a performance, a work of theatre, Samuel Weber has argued, citing Lacan's suggestion that the third element of the dream-work, the 'considerations of representability', be translated in French as 'considerations of staging'.

> Why? Because everything that is represented in a dream must conceal as much as it reveals, and moreover – and it is this that is ultimately decisive – must

conceal that it is concealing. Freud's formula for this is that the dream is not just a wish fulfillment, nor even a distorted ('*entstellte*') wish fulfillment, but a distorted wish fulfillment that dissimulates its own distortions. . . . The dream can only circulate, be remembered, and gain access to conscious memory, by disguising its own disguise and presenting itself as perfectly transparent. It is like a mirror on a door that suggests that the door *behind* it is open, while in fact what it shows is only a reflection of what is in front of it.

(Weber 2000, pp. 39–40)[6]

Conventionally the hidden is taken to be the more true, and the repressed is assumed to be the truth of the subject and the dreamer, it is what he or she 'really wants'. On the contrary, however, what constitutes the subject's unconscious is not the repressed but the repressing, not the secret but the secreting. The particular hiding and disguising is the truth of the subject, for it is in this process that the repressed returns. In understanding our dreams we discover not so much our desires as our fears, anxieties and obsessions. In his account of the lady and the theatre tickets, Freud says that 'We found that the dream-thoughts related to her anger at having married so early and to her dissatisfaction with her husband'. The staging of these thoughts is a visit to the theatre, which her newly engaged friend had also wished to attend but did not because she could get only cheap, that is poor, seats – three for 1 florin 50 kreuzers. The latter feature was shown through a series of associations to be related to the woman's regret at having married very early, while the theatre visit itself enabled the satisfaction of a scopophilic wish – to see the forbidden, since only once married might young women attend the theatre freely.[7] Freud observes that once the woman accepted her – unconscious – feelings of dissatisfaction with her husband, her symptoms disappeared; however we might also see the dream as staging her dissatisfaction as such, for which her husband is merely a prop. After all what she dreams is her failure to get what her friend has, which is viewed as something better in a husband. Thus she dreams of being at fault – she was in too much haste to secure a husband – and of being short-changed; Freud summarizes her dream-thoughts as 'if I had only waited. My money (or dowry) could have bought *three* men just as good' (Freud 1915–1916, p. 220). The dream-work is acting here not only on her thoughts about her husband, but about herself as failing to have the good-enough husband, herself as short-changed. And this is also satisfying. We dream not only in order to enjoy – even through such a distorted expression – our wishes, but also to enjoy through a staging of a not-enjoying, a not-having, our wish. Of course in doing so the wish itself is also articulated, as Freud shows in his analysis of 'A child is being beaten' (1919).

While our dreams may not be messages, they can tell us something in so far as they are a discourse of censoring, of hiding, requiring interpretation. We may think of dreaming therefore as an encoding, implying a work of interpretation within dreaming itself, which is the role Freud identifies in the work of secondary revision. Such an encoding may be thought in two slightly different ways, on the one hand as the employment of a fixed system of encoding, similar to a natural language, involving symbols which have a constant relation between two elements, the symbol and the symbolized, and which is essentially based on analogy. Freud indicates that the unconscious comparisons underlying symbolism 'are not freshly made on each occasion; they lie ready to hand and are complete, once and for all' (Freud 1915–1916, p. 165). This view is developed by Ernest Jones in 'The theory of symbolism' (1916), and of course by Carl Jung. In the human sciences in general a wide range of studies have centred on processes of symbolization and the production and use by humans of collective symbols. On the other hand the encoding of our dreams is individual, for while Freud emphasizes that the dream-work is not a creative process, that is, it does not invent, it merely selects and works upon, the material arising from the dream thoughts, day's residues, and sensory perceptions while asleep, nevertheless it creates the transformations, condensations and displacements which 'encode'. Of course, in aesthetic studies in the arts, we are familiar with treating such working-upon as itself creative – namely the production of metaphors and symbolic systems. The interpretation of this encoding, Freud showed, must be based on the dreamer's associations, but these are, manifestly, not available to the literary, film, or art critic.

The conceptualization of interpretation within psychoanalysis is itself poised between two alternatives, Jean Laplanche has argued. Freud, he suggests, remained a 'prisoner of the antithesis of *factual reality* and a purely subjective interpretation close to *fantasy*,' (Laplanche 1999, p. 165, emphasis is in original) in which psychoanalysis is either the discovery through analysis of what is to be understood as the 'true' event, or it is the construction by the analyst of an interpretation of the reality – which is not directly knowable – on the basis of the analysand's memories, dreams, and associations 'with the aid of precon-ceptions without which he would simply see nothing at all.' (Laplanche 1999, p. 140).

For Laplanche, Freud 'lacks a necessary third category, that of the *message* whose meaning is immanent, in particular taking the form of the mostly non-verbal sexual messages conveyed by the adult to the small child' (ibid., emphasis is in original). The development of the human individual is to be understood as an attempt to translate these enigmatic, traumatizing messages. 'Analysis is first and foremost a method of deconstruction (ana-lysis) with the aim of clearing the way for a new construction, which is the task of the analysand' (ibid.). It is not a factual truth (that has been or can be externally verified) which is important, but the particular yet also contingent translation of the enigmatic, traumatizing messages communicated by the analysand. Laplanche here reintroduces the analysand as interpreter, and not simply as receiver of the interpretation, in a process of detranslation and retranslation in relation to such messages. It is this view of interpretation which is central to my discussion of dreams and of dreaming in film.

Making sense of the non-sense of dreaming

Dream-work is undertaken not only in sleep, while dreaming – and is in this sense unconscious – but also in the process of remembering a dream, in its reconstruction as images, sounds, events, persons, etc. and thus its production as the manifest dream. As secondary revision, interpretation is both an aspect of the dream-work during sleep, and also a self-conscious process by which the dreamer, once awake, addresses his or her manifest dream. Secondary revision, as the imposition, or attempted imposition, of a continuous, totalizing narrative, has the role not only of story-teller but also of interpreter in making sense, that is, causal connections and rational relations, between elements, scenes and figures.[8] Freud, in 'Totem and taboo', writes:

> There is an intellectual function in us which demands unity, connection and intelligibility from any material, whether of perception or thought, that comes within its grasp; and if, as a result of special circumstances, it is unable to establish a true connection, it does not hesitate to fabricate a false one.
>
> (Freud 1913, p. 95)

Freud sees such a fabrication of causal relation in response to the demand for intelligibility as arising in both delusional disorders, including paranoia, and also in dreams in the dissembling role of the dream-work.

This sense-making involves producing an understanding of what the dream (or phenomena in reality) means *for oneself*, and not simply as a sequence of events, persons, images. In this process we produce *associations*, trying to find connections between our dream and ourselves in reality. *Free* associations to our dreams or other remembered and recounted material became the basis for Freud of the psychoanalytic method he developed. In free association analysands are asked not for what they think their dream might mean, but for whatever thoughts arise in the context of thinking about, but not necessarily connected to, the dream or day's events they have recounted. While the latter are a stimulus, the associations which arise are not controlled by any considerations of selection, that is, by any sense of appropriateness and are in this sense 'free'. While free of any direction from the analyst or analysand, these associations are nevertheless bound by unconscious processes and by transference. Through these associations a chain of connections leading to the dream or other unconscious thoughts can be discerned. Here, there is a linear relation posited, from the originating unconscious and dream-thoughts, to their disguised realization as phenomenal *visual* experience – in the dream through the dream-work – to their articulation through secondary revision as the manifest dream or recounted day's events.

The dream is 'dreamt' again as a hermeneutic requiring not the recovery of meaning hidden in the dream, but the discovery of the meaning of the dreaming, of the selection and juxtaposition of elements, the transpositions – the work of the displacements and condensations. The dream-work is not a distortion of a message or meaning fully formed prior to and discoverable behind and before its deformation, but a process or encounter involving a production in which a symbolizing representation emerges. Analysis or interpretation is then not a decoding of the displacements and condensations but a production of meaning in the process of engaging in the transference in the work of censorship-symbolizing being undertaken in the 'dream-work'. It is a work of detranslation in Laplanche's sense, which is undertaken in relation to the emotional attachment or affect engaged in these processes, giving rise to a new 'translation'. The role of this is not to achieve a (more) accurate version, but rather to produce an 'account' which works (better), that is, psychically, for the subject.

A film, as a phenomenal experience which is dream-like, is nevertheless not caused by the viewer's unconscious, as Freud suggest our dreams are. But in watching a film, and in thinking about it afterwards, we similarly become engaged in producing a 'manifest' film which we construct from our memory. We engage in a cognitive process of sense-making of this film-remembered and in finding connections or associations between elements in the film as a result of our emotional and affective response to it. That the dream-work processes of condensation and displacement are undertaken by the audience can be seen not only when we have misremembered and thus *distorted* 'what really happened' in the film, but also in the alternative understandings produced by viewers of events, actions and characters where motivations are not unambiguously stated by the film. As viewers we are engaged in a work of *transference*, where we relate – if only just at times and for brief moments – to the story's fiction 'as if' it were real, and we relate to actions and characters 'as if' they were figures in our own psychical history. Moreover, we relate to the images and sounds 'as if' produced in relation to considerations of representability found in dreams, thereby figuring unconscious thoughts.[9] At the same time these are formal, aesthetic devices – metonymies and metaphors for example[10] – employed within the film which we are thus invited to interpret in a process of organized evaluation based perhaps, for example, on expectations of story, character and events as forming a theme.

In psychoanalysis this process of interpretation is also an encounter with an interlocutor, the analyst, to whom the patients address their speech and their dreams, whom they expect to hear them, and thus for whom they are performing themselves and their dreamings. The time is not that of the night before of the dream recounted, but of the recounting of the dream in the present time of address to the analyst, and the present time of the analyst's hearing. In the cinema, as audience, however, we are both dreamers and dream-interpreters, analysands and analysts.

The impossibility of meaning in the non-sense of dreaming

> We must find a film with purely visual sensations the dramatic force of which springs from a shock on the eyes, drawn, one might say, from the very substance of the eye, and not from psychological circumlocutions of a discursive nature which are nothing but visual interpretations of a text.
>
> (Antonin Artaud 1927, p. 20)[11]

> I brought dreams directly into my films, trying as hard as I could to avoid any analysis.
>
> (Luis Buñuel 1982, p. 92)

While Freud warned against an excessive respect for a 'mysterious unconscious' (1923b, p. 112) he also notes that 'there is at least one spot in every dream at which it is unplumbable – a navel, as it were, that is its point of contact with the unknown' (Freud 1900, p. 111, note 1). Meaning is not however hard to get at, it is mined not in the depths of the dream but rather lies on the surface, out in the open, in the analysand's own recounting of, and relation to, the dream. It is something else which is inaccessible. In the analogy of the Moebius strip which Lacan employed, both the manifest and the latent dream-text and meaning are on the 'surface'; what is occulted is something else, a third element, namely the impossible real of the subject, his or her desire and organizing fantasy, which is hidden in the twist of the Moebius strip. Lacan comments: 'the navel of the dreams, he [Freud] writes, to designate their ultimately unknown centre – which is simply, like the same anatomical navel that represents it, that gap of which I have already spoken' (Lacan 1973, p. 23). It is the unconscious which shows 'us the gap through which neurosis recreates a harmony with a real – a real that may well not be determined' (ibid., p. 22).

Wilfred Bion's (1963) characterization of mental functioning as taking two forms according to whether it involves what he termed Alpha or Beta elements has been drawn upon by Hanna Segal to develop an account of dreaming. She writes:

> Beta elements are raw perceptions and emotions suitable only for projective identification – raw elements of experience to be gotten rid of. Beta elements are transformed into alpha elements by the alpha function. Those are elements which can be stored in memory, which can be repressed and elaborated further. They are suitable for symbolisation and formation of dream thoughts. It is the beta elements which can become bizarre objects or concrete symbols, in my sense of the word, that I think are elements of the psychotic-type dream, and alpha elements, which are the material for the neurotic and normal dream.
>
> (Segal 1992, p. 243–4)

Segal connects the failure of alpha functioning to the failure of the mother to act as a container for the child's anxiety, giving rise to a failure in the function of dreaming as alpha processing, instead becoming 'concrete dreaming', in which symbolization is limited and there is an invasion of reality, 'as though there was no differentiation between their mind and the outside world'. Thus there was 'no internal mental sphere in which the dream could be contained'. There was an accompanying inability to 'dream-work', replaced by a compulsion to act out the dream, for example in dreams of being late, predicted to the minute. Here, for Segal, the symbolizing processes of distortion – metaphor and metonymy – are absent and instead there is a concrete or literal replacement which is felt to have material or 'real' consequences, in the loss of the analyst as container.

This process of 'concrete dreaming' points to an unassimilable, uninterpretable figuration, reminiscent of that which both Artaud and Buñuel look to find, or create, in the cinema.

The dream-work of *Wild Strawberries*

> I've no verbal memory at all. I can only recall images. . . . For me
> the film is tangible, concrete.
>
> (Ingmar Bergman 1973, p. 138)

If cinema is a dream-machine, rather than merely ready-made dreams or fantasies, how might film engage us in its dream-work? As audience we are involved in two different kinds of sensibility in relation to film. One is a making sense of the film, of our sense of the sense or the meaning of the dreams *for the dreamer*, that is, for the place of origin of the dreaming. This is the character Isak Borg, who is the dreamer and chief protagonist of the film, as well as Ingmar Bergman, as author of the film. The other sensibility we are involved in is making sense of our sensible experience of the film, how we are moved or affected by the film. Thus, alongside our unfolding understanding of the narrative and characters, we may respond to the material of the film through associations which exceed or are irrelevant to the film's narration. The sounds and images, I have suggested, become available as raw material for a dream-work.[12]

Wild Strawberries has three strands of action. The film centres on Isak Borg, a distinguished and elderly physician and professor emeritus, and his story of remembrances on his journey by car to Lund to receive a special jubilee doctorate as recognition of his fifty years of achievement. He is accompanied by his daughter-in-law Marianne, whose marriage has inherited the same circuit of repression and guilt as Borg is shown in the course of the film to experience, and her marital problems form a second story which functions not only as a mirror but also a counterpoint to Isak's story of lost love and unhappy marriage, for it is his son Evald's fear of having a child who might be as unloved as he had been which is the basis of their marital breakdown. Their story is resolved as Evald, unwilling to lose Marianne, accepts her pregnancy and desire for motherhood, invoking a possible new generation and the hope that it will be unburdened by the past. The third strand involves a young woman, Sara, and her two male friends who are travelling to Italy and hitch a lift with Isak and Marianne. The young people's story mirrors Isak's, for both this modern Sara, and the earlier Sara whom Borg loses to his older, more seductive, brother Sigfrid, are played by Bibi Andersson, while the triangle of Isak, his older brother Sigfrid and Sara is repeated with Anders, whom Sara is 'crazy about', and Viktor, also in love with Sara, who is her father's appointed chaperone (though Sara declares, 'I'll probably have to seduce Viktor to get him out of the way'). They point to a future in which Isak will not partake, at the same time acting as a rhetorical and theatrical counterpoint.

Wild Strawberries is highly self-conscious in its creation of references, metaphors, parallels and substitutions, that is, it foregrounds these and asks its audience to read the film in terms of such interrelations.[13] It is a work of art, not, it might seem, a dream-work. Bergman mimics the dream-work's use and reworking of material from immediate experience so that we can read the later dreams in relation to the events and conversations we have seen and heard.

Plate 18 Wild Strawberries (Ingmar Bergman 1957)
Source: bfi Collections

Bergman is explicit, too, about the film's relation to his own life, saying, 'I made it as a run-down of my earlier life, a searching, final test', but denies it is a psychoanalytic film: 'As for the psychoanalytical aspect, I had no real grip on it. It's other people who've stuck that on afterwards. For me the film is tangible, concrete.' Later, however, in explaining the references around the characters of Alman and his wife, Bergman admits that 'I suppose I must have been splashing about in psychoanalytical ideas' (1973, p. 138). The use of such references as well as the parallels, doublings and repetitions in the film requires a further level of making-sense not only, however, of these interconnections but more importantly of the limits of such mirrorings, namely the points at which a divergence between the actions, *mise-en-scène* or characters is apparent, introducing difference rather than similarity. It is here that we may discern what Freud referred to as the 'navel of the dream', its limit of interpretability, and which may enable us to experience a point of divergence between our consciously and unconsciously motivated interpretation or secondary revision.

The film opens with a pre-credits sequence of Isak Borg at his desk as he introduces himself in voice-over while the camera travels around the room, revealing the photographs of his family, and then Agda, his housekeeper, who appears at the door to announce his supper. Isak leaves with his dog saying, 'Tomorrow at Lund I will celebrate the fiftieth anniversary of my doctorate',[14] suggesting that the film is a form of direct narration of the events as well as his thoughts and dreams as they occur on the journey to Lund. The subsequent narration, however, telling us, 'I had a strange and very unpleasant dream', in the past tense, over what we may take as a flashback to his dream, raises a question about the time of narration which is never clearly answered by the film. (The very premiss of the cinematic flashback here, of seeing and hearing again, from memory, a past experience, conflicts with Freud's theory of the dream and dream-work.) The nightmare motivates Isak to change his travel plans, cancelling his plane booking and deciding to travel by car instead. Cognizant of his own considerable age, perhaps he takes the dream as a forewarning of death. Arlow (1997) interprets Borg's action as 'Unconsciously he is behaving like the servant in O'Hara's parable, *Appointment in Samara*, who had hoped to escape the Angel of Death by changing the time and place of their presumably ordained encounter' (Arlow 1997, p. 595). The film subsequently suggests, however, that Isak fears not death as such but his own living death, and it is in relation to this that the first dream must be considered. More significantly, therefore, Isak chooses a mode of travel which will enable him to traverse the time and place of his own life as he journeys to Lund. Early in this journey he revisits his family's summer home where he spent his childhood holidays, and where he experiences a strange reverie whereby 'the clarity of the present shaded into the even clearer images of memory'. Although prompted by memory, he was never in fact present at the scenes he now witnesses; they are in fact imagined, or a screen memory. At the end of this reverie he is confronted by the young Sara, who asks what he is doing there, claiming that her father owns the whole area, and then cadges a lift for herself and her two friends. Shortly afterwards Isak is forced to avoid a collision with another car, driven by Berit Alman, who is travelling with her husband Sten Alman. Unable to restart their car, the Almans join Isak and his other passengers until Marianne, now driving, can no longer bear their vicious bickering and she asks them to leave and find a phone at a nearby house.

Continuing their journey they arrive at Lake Vättern where Borg spent his boyhood and later worked. At the petrol station he is recognized by Akerman, the owner, as the much-loved former local doctor, is introduced to his pregnant wife and, when payment is refused, promises to be godfather to the child. The suggestion of a future lost is made when Isak says to himself, 'Perhaps I should have remained here'. The next scene shows the travellers lunching at the lake; with heated debates and love songs, Isak revels in his companions' conversation. Afterwards Marianne and Isak visit his mother living nearby, whom Marianne later describes as 'a very ancient woman, completely ice-cold, in some ways more frightening than death itself'. During the visit Isak's mother brings out a box of remnants from her children's childhoods, a doll, toy soldiers, a photograph, a train and a colouring book in which four of his sisters have written. Each of her ten children are represented by these mementoes and all but Isak are dead. She then asks whether she should give Sigbritt's eldest boy, shortly to be 50, Isak's father's watch, even though it has no hands. We may be reminded by this of Isak's earlier nightmare with its clock with the blank dial and his watch without hands, and infer that Isak might be similarly reminded (the camera's movement is on Isak's face here, and the return of the non-diegetic music associated with Isak, appears to confirm such an inference). During the following car journey Isak falls asleep and has, in his words, a vivid and humiliating dream. He begins to tell Marianne his dream on awakening, saying, 'I was trying to say something to myself which I don't want to hear when I'm awake. . . . That I'm dead, though I live.' At this Marianne looks towards him and says that Evald has said the very same thing. She asks if she can tell him everything. He replies, 'I'd be grateful if you would'. Her account, shown in flashback, is that she and Evald had separated because of Evald's own loveless childhood and his belief that it is 'ridiculous to populate it with new victims and it's most absurd to believe that they will have it any better than us'. As a result he has told her she must choose between him and the child. The young people return to the car and Sara gives Isak a bouquet of wild flowers in celebration of his forthcoming honouring which Marianne had told them of. The film cuts to Lund, where they are greeted by Evald and Miss Agda, and Isak receives his degree. After final encounters with the other characters, it closes with Isak in bed, daydreaming a scene of searching for and finding his parents at the lake by the summer house.

The film is riven by two counterposing currents of love and hate, tenderness and violence, centring on Isak. He is revealed as a man of unrequited love and lonely in old age who is looking back on a life of professional achievement and personal loss and emptiness. His loneliness is self-chosen while he is also wilfully blind to the emotional needs of others, as well as intolerant of their demands and desires, motivating the very considerable anger which is directed towards him within the film. Isak characterizes himself in voice-over at the opening of the film through a series of likes – his work, a game of golf, a good detective novel – and dislikes – the company of others, women's tears and the crying of children. Marianne characterizes him as an egotist, selfish and inflexible, all this hidden behind a mask of old-fashioned charm and friendliness. She tells him his son, Evald, is very much like him, but also that Evald hates him. Isak's lost love, Sara, angrily challenges him in his trial dream, telling him he should know why he's hurt by her rejection, but he doesn't, for despite 'all of your knowledge you don't really know anything'. His long-dead wife, Karin, also accuses him of neglect, indifference and false compassion.

Wild Strawberries is also, however, redolent with reconciliation and hope for futures which might be different, symbolized by the child Marianne is carrying. For Isak Borg, too, there appears to be a certain redemption. This is first apparent when, during his discussion with Marianne after his humiliating trial dream, he invites her to smoke and thus reverses his own earlier prohibition and stated dislike of women smoking. Later, after the ceremony in Lund, Isak expresses a warm appreciation of Marianne when, thanking her for her company on the journey, he tells her he likes her; moreover she, with equal warmth, replies, 'I like you too'. Isak's pleasure in the young people and their enthusiastic celebration of him at the ceremony, and later when they sing to him from the garden and Sara tells him, 'We were real proud that we knew you', give us a view of him as a warm and kindly old man which, we may think, is no longer the mask of 'old-fashioned charm and friendliness' Marianne accused him of hiding his egotism behind. Isak enacts two further reversals but which are not acknowledged by the other characters – producing an irony involving in the one case comedy, and in the other case the tragedy of misunderstanding. The comedy is his apology after the ceremony to Miss Agda, his housekeeper, for his sharp words earlier that morning, but this simply leads Miss Agda to think he's ill. Isak responds, 'Is it so unusual for me to ask forgiveness?' Miss Agda does not reply to his question, allowing us to infer that it is indeed unusual, and there follows a further, comic, exchange when Isak, in a gesture of friendship, suggests that they drop the formal mode of address and say '*du*' to each other. Miss Agda, clearly appalled, roundly refuses saying, 'People would ridicule us'.

The tragic irony, to which the audience alone is privy, arises when Isak, in an unusual display of personal interest, asks Evald about his marriage after he and Marianne briefly return from the reception so that Marianne can change her shoes. Evald replies that he has asked Marianne to remain with him not, as Isak suggests, out of loneliness but because 'I can't be without her'. This powerful admission of his love for her contrasts with Isak's relation to his wife, Karin. Isak then raises the issue of the outstanding debt which, Marianne had told him earlier, had meant that they had no time to themselves, while Evald worked himself to death. Evald quickly reassures him that he will get his money, and when Isak responds, 'I didn't mean that', as if about to offer to set aside the repayment, Evald's reiteration 'You'll get your money all right' shows he is oblivious to such a possibility, while Marianne's entrance interrupts their conversation and Isak does not pursue what he did, in fact, mean.

These interactions motivate a sense that Isak has in some way redeemed himself in that, through the course of the past twenty–four hours, he has acquired a self-knowledge and also a new concern for others in his acceptance of his responsibility for the unhappiness of others. As a result we can enjoy with Isak the film's concluding restitutive scene in which, as he lays down to sleep, Isak daydreams an encounter he has returned to many times, he tells us, although it appears to be a screen memory: he is again back at the summer house with the strawberry patch. Sara is telling him that the wild strawberries have all gone, and that he should go and find his father, but he says he has searched for his parents but cannot find either of them. She says she will help him and taking his hand she leads him down to the lake where, on the bank opposite, are his father, who is fishing, and his mother who is seated nearby, sewing, who each in turn wave at him, producing a smile of pleasure on Borg's face. For many of us this is a compelling and satisfying closure, albeit marked by a sense of tragedy, in its image of an old man as the young son refinding his parents and receiving their warm acknowledgement. At the same time, in so far as we have identified with Isak Borg, we may feel pleasure in his being no longer hateful; instead, or perhaps as well, we may feel pleasure in being released from the position of hating Isak, because he is no longer hateful.

Wild Strawberries is manifestly not a simple tale of nostalgia for a lost childhood and a lost childhood sweetheart. It is a son's story of repression played out in relation to figures who stand in for the parents, not only the father, who is absent in the film, but also the mother who is absent in the remembered/imagined past but who appears in the present. This story is not latent or obscured but on the contrary clearly out in the open, on the surface. The film is crafted around this scenario, and Bergman references the Oedipal relation not only in his naming of his characters as Isak and Sara, but more explicitly by having the young Sara mistakenly identify the biblical character Sara as Isak's wife, and then being wistfully corrected by Isak who tells her that, no, she was the wife of Abraham and Isak's mother. This is as much Bergman's story as Isak Borg's, both as son and as father. Bergman has described his character Borg as 'a tired, old egocentric, who'd cut himself off from everything around him – as I had done' (Bergman 1973, p. 133), and commented:

> The truth is that I am forever living in my childhood, wandering through darkened apartments, strolling through quiet Uppsala streets, standing in front of a summer cottage and listening to the enormous double trunk birch tree.

. . . The driving force in *Wild Strawberries* is, therefore, a desperate attempt to justify myself to mythically oversized parents who have turned away, an attempt that was doomed to failure.

(Bergman 1994, p. 22)

Isak Borg is thus a composite, an identification or condensation, of Bergman and his own father, Pastor Erik Bergman, both as a father and as a son. That this identification was transferred onto Victor Sjöström can be recognized in Bergman's comment thirty years later after seeing the film again in his private cinema in Faro in 1989.

What I had not grasped until now was that Victor Sjöström took my text, made it his own, invested it with his own experiences: his pain, his misanthropy, his brutality, sorrow, fear, loneliness, coldness, warmth, hardness and ennui. Borrowing my father's form, he occupied my soul and made it all his own – *there wasn't even a crumb left over for me!* He did this with the sovereign power and passion of a gargantuan personality. I had nothing to add, not even a sensible or irrational comment. *Wild Strawberries* was no longer my film; it was Victor Sjöström's.

(Bergman 1994, p. 24)[15]

Bergman has lent his character – and father-figure – his dreams, though we cannot know if he has also given him his fears, which for Isak are not of death simply, but of death in living, for, as he told Marianne after his trial dream, it was as if 'I was trying to say something to myself which I don't want to hear when I'm awake. . . . That I'm dead, though I live.' And what makes him dead, he learns from Sara, Alman, his wife Karin, and Marianne herself, is his inability to love. The nightmare which leads Isak to journey by car and which appears to be a dream of his death was in fact Bergman's own:

That dream about the coffin is one I've had myself, a compulsive dream of mine. Not that I was lying in the coffin myself. I made that up. But the bit where the hearse comes along and bumps into a lamp-post, and the coffin falls out and tips out the corpse. I had dreamed that many times.

(Bergman 1973, p. 146)

The story is not, however, simply autobiographical. While the similarities elide the gap between creator and created, the differences between Bergman and Borg produce an uncertainty of origin – of what is Bergman's and what is not, fracturing the subjective unity of both.

It is Borg's 'humiliating and vivid' trial dream in which this is most apparent. Alman, the unpleasant engineer and his similarly acerbic wife Berit, are played by actors chosen by Bergman for their close resemblance to Stig Ahlgren, a critic who had been scathing about Bergman, and his wife: 'Stig Ahlgren had just beheaded me for something or other, and this was my revenge' (Bergman 1973, p. 140).[16] This quite conscious, and simple, condensation is doubled by the use of the Almans as mirroring Isak's own marital conflicts. Different and subtle condensations arise in Bergman's complex use of Alman in Borg's later examination/trial dream – all of these roles being signalled by his name which is alliterative with Ahlgren as well as invoking the word *allman*, which in Swedish is 'everyman' or everyone. In the dream Alman is both examiner and prosecutor which continues the idea of Alman as persecutor while he now has the authority of the Academy and the Law, just as Ahlgren may have appeared to Bergman as possessing. Alman sets Borg a number of tests which he fails in a manner we will be familiar with from our own dreams. Bergman, however, changes Alman's role from unjust persecutor to just prosecutor. Isak, confessing he cannot comprehend the language of the writing on the blackboard, is then asked instead to state what the first duty of a doctor is and, when unable to remember, Alman tells him it is 'to ask forgiveness'. Nonsensical for the medical profession in general, it has a particular truth for Dr Isak Borg, and the examination now becomes a court of accusations in which Alman lists his first offence as 'guilty of guilt', then – after Isak's next failure when, medically examining a woman (Berit Alman), whom he declares to be dead, she suddenly rises up laughing, contradicting his diagnosis – he is charged with incompetence, along with lesser charges of 'indifference, selfishness, lack of consideration'. These are the accusations Marianne has already made, and which – as she reports to Isak during their discussion in the car which follows – his son has made, and which his dead wife will shortly make in the final scene of this dream. Alman in Isak's dream is thus the voice of truth. The critic who was satirized in being made the vicious husband Alman now reappears as the still-severe but authorized judge, while it is Borg who is the cruel husband, albeit through inability to love. Alman next conducts him back to his memory of his wife's willing debasement at the hands of a fellow-guest in the gardens of a grand banquet. This lengthy sequence affords no exoneration or redemption for Borg, though no doubt audiences both then and now will divide on the justice and truth of his wife's case against him. She says he is icy cold, the words Marianne will use very shortly afterwards to describe Borg's mother and her husband's grandmother, and accuses him of cruel indifference. In an acceptance of his guilt, Isak asks, 'And what is the penalty?' Alman, however, is merely his prosecutor and not, after all, his judge, for he replies, 'Penalty? I don't know. The usual one, I suppose', which he explains is 'of course, loneliness'. And when Borg queries him further, 'Is there no grace?', Alman replies, 'Don't ask me. I don't know anything about such things.' Alman here offers Isak the truth of his sins but no absolution through punishment. Alman is the accuser who succeeds, as perhaps Sara does not, in bringing Isak to recognize his guilt, and thus achieves the son's wish. His abdication of his power to punish and thereby give release from guilt in his 'I know nothing about such things', suggests Bergman's own struggle with religion, confirming the identification while also thereby condemning Isak, as is Bergman, to atheism's torment in so far as there is no judging other who although punishing, is also forgiving.[17]

The complexity of these symbolic condensations, the excess of their over-determination, in *Wild Strawberries* suggests the processes of dream-work as well as conscious artistry. While the viewer may be unaware of Bergman's autobiographical references, the name Alman (as 'everyman') is a connotation available through general knowledge and its use points to an author other than Borg who dreams in the film, namely Bergman, the author who created the dreams of his character. The continuous reworking of parallels and symbolism in *Wild Strawberries* through reversals, transformations and doublings which dissolve into differences produces an unintelligible interconnection, that is, its sense-making is only for the moment, for in the next it is disrupted by another, associative, connection. The imposition, or discovery, of causal logic is made problematic so that no unified subjectivity – either of the son or the father, of Isak or Ingmar, can be discovered behind the imagery. In the gap between Bergman as Isak the father, and Bergman as Isak the son, lies the navel of the dream which the film and its crafted dreams both point to and dissemble.

Consider, here, Isak's final (day)dream which expresses his wish for his parents' recognition, and which appears to fulfil it. Philip and Kirsti French comment that here 'Isak has found or re-created, his *smultronställe*' (1995, p. 37), his wild strawberry patch. Earlier they explained that this is not merely a place where the fruit, held in special regard in Sweden, is found but that traditionally each family member will lay claim to his or her own wild strawberry patch in childhood, their own special preserve. 'In addition to this literal meaning', they write, '*smultronställe* has the figurative connotation of a moment in the past to which someone looks back and which they would like to revisit or recapture' (French and French 1995, p. 23).[18] The wild strawberry in Scandinavian iconography symbolizes 'innocence and the ephemeral nature of happiness' (ibid.). Yet in Isak's dream there are no wild strawberries left, Sara tells him, implying – in terms of this symbolic structure – that the innocence is gone. There is a reversal here of the earlier daydream which opened with Sara picking the wild strawberries, but in which Isak, and his parents, were absent, for it is now the strawberries which are absent while Sara brings Isak to his mother and father. The first dream-image of Sara is a scene of her lost innocence as she discovers her sexual attraction to Sigfrid, and her basket of strawberries is spilled. In Isak's trial dream the spilled strawberries are shown before cutting to Sara, who confronts Isak with the knowledge not that he is innocent of, but which he refuses. In this last dream there are no wild strawberries, that is, there is neither innocence nor the loss of innocence, instead Isak's parents replace the strawberries, introducing an ambiguity in his innocent joy in gaining the parents. A loss is marked before the regaining; the impossibility of the fantasy is embedded in its very articulation.

The film abounds with such *mises-en-scène* which both invite and disturb understanding in terms of symbolization. The hesitation in relation to these images makes them available to a further dream-work through their appropriation by our own associations, producing a new series of transferences, condensations and displacements themselves subject to a 'secondary-revision' of sense-making in order to similarly dissemble and disguise what we have enjoyed and which our ego seeks to censor. The images of Isak's nightmare, in being at the beginning of the film, are the most difficult to organize into a story and indeed the film's subsequent events do not explain them. Instead I catch the terror and anxiety it also invokes in Isak, of the familiar become unfamiliar – uncanny – in a manner which impresses as both significant and yet meaningless. I nevertheless make a series of associations whereby, for example, the missing hands on the watchmaker's clock and Isak's own watch seem to me to be an image of time lost, that is, standing still, with no past and no future, rather than representing time ceased, as in death. The man with his eyes and mouth shut tight might be an image of closure, or enclosure, of knowledge denied, but who, as Isak touches him, collapses into oozing liquid, becoming perhaps a premonition of the body's – Isak's – forthcoming decay, but which is also for me a fear of death, a loss of self.[19] His closed eyes contrast with the open eyes appearing in the optician's glasses hanging below the handless clock which is seen in several of the shots. The horse-drawn hearse carries death explicitly onto the scene, which clearly as a result is not its latent meaning. What then does it signify? The auditory and visual violence of the carriage repeatedly battering the post on which its axle is caught as the horses try to pull free has been read as a primal scene: the hearse, as the father, thrusting forward over and over again, while the low camera shots between the wheels show Isak cowering beyond (Arlow 1997). It is also a scene of attempted castration by the father (Bach 1970), as the wheel breaks free and careers towards Isak, who narrowly escapes by jumping to one side – as if the voyeur is himself espied, and punishment ensues. The coffin reveals its occupant to be Isak himself – and we may wonder why his double seeks to grasp him from his grave – is it his killed-off self? But also, who does this double actually represent? Or, what is the dissimulation of condensation seeking to hide? Moreover this is a *mise-en-scène* not only of the seen but also of seeing, for the camera shifts us between Isak's view and an 'objective', non-character, omniscient view – the dreamer's point-of-view, in fact.

These images are not resolved here into a narration. But in so far as they remain just images, strange and penetrating and unassimilable, they constitute something like the concrete thinking Segal describes. *Wild Strawberries* fulfils Freud's epithet of the dream as rebus.

Notes

1 *Wild Strawberries* was released in 1957, UK release 1958, running time: 91 minutes. Direction and screenplay by Ingmar Bergman. Main characters: Professor Isak Borg: Victor Sjöström; Marianne Borg: Ingrid Thulin; Evald Borg: Gunnar Björnstrand; Sara: Bibi Andersson; Sten Alman: Gunnar Sjöberg; Berit Alman: Gunnel Broström. The film won the Golden Bear at the Berlin Film Festival in 1958, and Bergman was nominated and shortlisted for an Oscar for best story and screenplay in 1959. He received an Oscar for Best Foreign Language Film for *The Virgin Spring* in 1960. The screenplay, from which the film diverges at times, was published in 1960 in *Four Screenplays of Ingmar Bergman*, New York: Simon and Schuster.

2 In Cowie (1997) I have discussed the problems raised by Metz's account of the imaginary in cinema. Richard Allen (1995) provides another challenge in his wide-ranging discussion of theories of illusion, arguing instead that the spectator engages in what he characterizes as 'projective illusion'.

3 Freud refers here to 'visual and acoustic memory-traces'.

4 Freud places secondary revision firmly in the dream-work as a whole in *The Interpretation of Dreams* but subsequently observes that 'strictly speaking, this last process does not form a part of the dream-work' (1923a, p. 241). The stricture Freud is referring to here is perhaps the change from sleep to wakefulness; however as a process of distortion, secondary revision must be included in the dream-work. That is, the dream-work as a mental process is not confined to the period of sleep alone. It is this idea which I will draw on later in relation to considering the process of dream-work in the cinema.

5 Freud refers to the latent content, latent dream-thoughts and wishes interchangeably; however, he also clearly distinguishes between the thoughts and the dream-wish in his analogy of the entrepreneur of the dream – the supplier of the ideas or thoughts, and the capitalist, the supplier of the resources – psychical energy – for the enterprise. While these may be one and the same, they are not necessarily. Moreover, Freud suggests, several wishes, or capitalists, 'may combine to put up what is necessary for the entrepreneur', or 'several entrepreneurs may apply to the same capitalist' (1900, p. 561). This distinction makes more complex the way in which we may understand the dream as readable.

6 Weber also observes that the 'fact that both of the German verbs that Freud uses to describe this double duplicity are derived from the same root-word, namely *Stelle: place*, only also emphasises the theatrical nature of the masquerade' (2000, p. 42).

7 The analysis of the wish in this dream is discussed in *Introductory Lectures on Psycho-Analysis* (1915–1916), in *Standard Edition 15*, pp. 219–220, while the dream-thoughts are discussed most fully in the same volume, pp. 122–125. It is also discussed in *The Interpretation of Dreams* (1900), pp. 415, 669–670 and 673.

8 Samuel Weber comments of secondary revision that

> It is, in this sense, a *theoretical* activity as well as a *narrative* one, or rather, one in which *narration* and *interpretation* are just two sides of the same effort to impose meaningful form on resistant, conflictual material. As a tendency shared both by the unconscious, in its self-dissimulating function, and by theoretical thought, we should not be surprised to find the same struggle going on not just in the materials described by Freud, but in the very theories he is using those materials to elaborate.
>
> (Weber 2000, p. 42)

9   In psychoanalysis, however, we are familiar with ways in which we relate to one thing 'as if' it were another, most significantly in the transference, but also, for example, in Lacan's notion of the transitivist identification in the mirror phase. What is involved is not a cognitive mistake, or a voluntary act of imagination, and the 'as if' identification always involves an emotional response as well as a mental or cognitive relation.

10 In *Fundamentals of Language*, Roman Jakobson (1956) suggested that condensation might be understood as metaphor in language, and displacement as metonymy. Jacques Lacan (1966) drew on this in 'The agency of the letter in the unconscious or reason since Freud'. Jean-François Lyotard (1989) has questioned this account in 'The dream-work does not think'.

11 See Linda Williams (1981) for a discussion of dreams and the work of the surrealists.

12 My discussion here has been enriched by three interpretations of the film by practising psychoanalysts: Jacob A. Arlow (1997), Harvey R. Greenberg (1970) and Seldon Bach (1970).

13 The extra-textual references and influences on Bergman are explored extensively in the British Film Institute 'Film Classic' study of *Wild Strawberries* (French and French 1995).

14 Bergman changed Isak's words here from his original screenplay in which the film was unambiguously told in flashback by Isak. The film omits most of the text spoken or thought by Isak in the screenplay, which is rendered in the visual and music track instead. In my discussion I quote the English subtitles from the film.

15 Sjöström, the same age as the character he plays, was also a father-figure of Swedish cinema and one of the most important directors of the silent cinema period, working in both Sweden, making, for example, *Ingeborg Holm* (1913), and directing in Hollywood, notably *The Scarlet Letter* (1926) and *The Wind* (1928), both starring Lilian Gish. Sjöström was an actor-producer/director and returned to acting as his career in the late 1930s. He had worked with Bergman earlier in *To Joy* (1950), but, Bergman says, 'without any irrestistible need to do so again' (1960, p. 179). However it was also Sjöström who had helped Bergman learn his craft of filmmaking, as he reveals in his biography (ibid., pp. 68–69).

16 French and French (1995) note that Bergman seems to have later regretted this petty malice. Ahlgren is not reported as having responded to this reference, but interestingly his comment three years later, when he accused Bergman's *Through a Glass Darkly* (1961) of bringing out latent schizophrenia in the viewer, suggests he recognizes very well the nature of the power of Bergman's created worlds (French and French 1995, p. 130).

17 Bergman has described his father as just such a forgiving punisher for, after he had applied the strokes of the carpet beater 'you had to kiss Father's hand, at which forgiveness was declared and the burden of sin fell away, deliverance and grace ensued' (1960, p. 8).

18 The film's title has therefore been compared by some Swedish writers to Proust's *Madeleine*.

19 Greenberg (1970) suggests he is the father, distant and unsupportive, while the watch, later connected to the father, 'may provide another image of paternal ineffectiveness'.

References

Allen, R. (1995) *Projecting Illusion: Film Spectatorship and the Impression of Reality*. Cambridge: Cambridge University Press.

Arlow, J. A. (1997) 'The end of time: a psychoanalytic perspective on Ingmar Bergman's *Wild Strawberries*', *International Journal of Psycho-Analysis*, 78: 595–599.

Artaud, A. (1927) 'Sorcéllerie et cinéma', in *Oeuvres Complètes, Vol. 3*. Paris: Gallimard, 1961; English translation, 'Cinema and reality', in *Collected Works, Vol. 3*. London: Calder and Boyars, 1972.

Bach, S. (1970) 'Discussion of Greenberg's paper on Bergman's *Wild Strawberries*', *American Imago*, 27(1): 194–199. Reprinted in S. M. Kaminsky with J. F. Hill (eds) *Ingmar Bergman: Essays in Criticism*. London: Oxford University Press, 1975.

Bergman, I. (1960) *The Magic Lantern*. Harmondsworth: Penguin.

Bergman, I. (1973) *Bergman on Bergman*. London: Secker and Warburg.

Bergman, I. (1994) *Images*. London: Bloomsbury.

Bion, W. R. (1963) *Elements of Psycho-Analysis*. London: Heinemann.

Buñuel, L. (1982) *My Last Sigh*. New York: Vintage Books, Random House, 1984.

Copjec, J. (1994) 'The orthopsychic subject: film theory and the reception of Lacan', in *Read My Desire*. Cambridge, MA: MIT Press.

Cowie, E. (1997) *Representing the Woman: Psychoanalysis and Cinema*. London: Macmillan.

French, P. and French, K. (1995) *Wild Strawberries*, BFI Film Classic. London: British Film Institute.

Freud, S. (1900) *The Interpretation of Dreams*, in *Standard Edition 4 and 5*. London: Hogarth Press, 1953.

Freud, S. (1913) 'Totem and taboo', in *Standard Edition 13*. London: Hogarth Press, 1953.

Freud, S. (1915–1916) 'Introductory lectures on psycho-analysis', in *Standard Edition 15*. London: Hogarth Press, 1961.

Freud, S. (1919) '"A child is being beaten": a contribution to the study of the origin of sexual perversions', in *Standard Edition 17*. London: Hogarth Press, 1955.

Freud, S. (1923a) 'Two encyclopaedia articles', in *Standard Edition 18*. London: Hogarth Press, 1955.

Freud, S. (1923b) 'Remarks on the theory and practice of dream-interpretation', in *Standard Edition 19*. London: Hogarth Press, 1961.

Greenberg, H. R. (1970) 'The rags of time', *American Imago*, 27(1): 66–82. Reprinted in S. M. Kaminsky with J. F. Hill (eds) *Ingmar Bergman: Essays in Criticism*. London: Oxford University Press, 1975.

Hobson, J. A. (1988) *The Dreaming Brain*. New York: Basic Books.

Jones, E. (1916) 'The theory of symbolism', in *Papers on Psycho-Analysis*. London: Baillière, Tindall and Cox, 5th edition, 1950.

Kaminsky S. M. with Hill, J. F. (eds) (1975) *Ingmar Bergman: Essays in Criticism*. London: Oxford University Press.

Jakobson, R. (1956) *Fundamentals of Language*. The Hague: Mouton.

Lacan, J. (1966) 'The agency of the letter in the unconscious or reason since Freud', in *Ecrits*. London: Tavistock, 1977.

Lacan, J. (1973) *The Four Fundamental Concepts of Psycho-analysis.* Harmondsworth: Penguin, 1977

Laplanche, J. (1999) 'Interpretation between determinism and hermeneutics: a restatement of the problem', in *Essays on Otherness.* London: Routledge.

Lyotard, J-F. (1989) 'The dream-work does not think', in A. Benjamin (ed.) *The Lyotard Reader.* Oxford: Blackwell.

Metz, C. (1974) *Psychoanalysis and Cinema: The Imaginary Signifier.* London: Macmillan, 1982.

Reiser, M. F. (2000) 'Can psychoanalysis and cognitive-emotional neuroscience collaborate in remodelling our concept of mind-brain?', in P. Brooks and A. Woloch (eds) *Whose Freud? The Place of Psychoanalysis in Contemporary Culture.* New Haven, CT: Yale University Press.

Segal, H. (1992) 'The function of dreams', in M. R. Lansky (ed.) *Essential Papers on Dreams.* New York: New York University Press.

Weber, S. (2000) 'Psychoanalysis and theatricality', *Parallax*, 16.

Williams, L. (1981) *Figures of Desire: A Theory and Analysis of Surrealist Film.* Berkeley, CA: University of California Press.

———————— 14 ————————

FILM AS AN ABREACTION
OF TOTALITARIANISM

Vinko Brešan's *Marshal Tito's Spirit* (1999)

Ljiljana Filipović

Funny spectre

'It's such a scary movie. The film shows how *it* is still alive.' This was a comment made by one of the Croatian spectators after the projection of the movie *Marshal Tito's Spirit* (1999).

But what is that 'it'? What is the meaning of this 'it', this 'it' which is so common in our unconscious thoughts, representing for this viewer some kind of repulsion, something uncanny? For many people raised in so-called 'communist' countries, one of the associations is that 'it' is a spectre, the one from the famous Karl Marx slogan – 'A spectre is still haunting Europe, the spectre of Communism'.

Tito's death was for some the death of the father of the nation, while for others it was the long-awaited liberation from a totalitarian leader. While some were crying, others were celebrating. Tito's majestic funeral in 1980 was a preliminary to the funeral of the country itself, built, as it was, upon different republics, whose new nationalistic leaders, like liberated sons (in some aspects very much like the sons from Freud's 'Totem and taboo'), were indulging in separatist and nationalistic feelings (which in former Yugoslavia would once have been liable to sanctions). When the war in former Yugoslavia blazed up with unbelievable atrocity, Tito's name – as the name of a hated leader who had ruled over Yugoslavia – became almost too shameful to mention and, in the newly separated countries, at times, even dangerous. Those who have been making out Yugoslavia to be Second World War partisans have, in the new republics, become marginalized and considered as members of a 'red gang', while all the usual Yugoslav and communist insignia have been removed from public places.

It is not that people want to forget, but sometimes it is safer to forget, to repress the memory of something that has been blamed for all the contemporary troubles, for past injustices inflicted upon those people who fled from Yugoslavia because they feared Communism, for the alleged economic exploitation by certain republics, and so on. To forget everything which has been achieved, to rage against it, has become as politically fashionable as being a nationalist or as suddenly remembering all the family members who once were on the opposite side to the partisans or in the Yugoslav army. Yet, again, like the sons in Freud's 'Totem and taboo' who started to forbid the very things which their father was stopping by his mere presence, the nationalist leaders continued to perpetuate Tito's pattern of governing, his glamour, the undemocratic press and other such characteristics of his rule. Narcissistic grandiosity was the compensation for their vulnerability and bitterness.

Years later, when people were exhausted by the war and national tendencies had proven to be as short-sighted and dangerous as totalitarian anachronistic ideologies, Vinko Brešan made this movie, *Marshal Tito's Spirit*, in which he articulates the repressed problem with much humour.

The film takes place on a small island off the Croatian coast. Tourism, which was the main source of income, has vanished there due to the war in former Yugoslavia in the 1990s, and the situation on the island is now a rather depressing one. The mayor, a nationalist and a dealer who has recently made his fortune from the transition to privatization, as is so often the case in countries which are going through such change, owns the only (albeit empty) hotel as well as the Museum of the Revolution, the local bar and so on. In the new Croatia, the elderly men who had fought as partisans in the Second World War and who were considered to be die-hard communists, are now on the defensive. Like members of a secret society, these veterans have to keep their red flags and their busts of Lenin and Tito carefully under wraps.

But then, out of the blue, Marshal Tito's ghost appears at the funeral of one of the partisans, which was being carried out secretly in communist fashion. The story of Tito's appearance spreads quickly and a young local police officer is appointed from the mainland to investigate the mystery. The reaction of many of the islanders is one of shock, as if they had heard news of a vampire wandering around. Strings of garlic are hung up all over the place and many people display crucifixes. The event encourages the old veterans to dust their insignia and regain once more their self-confidence. And yet these dusted uniforms serve only to emphasize the spectral atmosphere. As for the mayor, inspired by the religious tourism that had attracted millions of visitors to a small town in Bosnia after the apparition of the Virgin Mary there, he now decides to introduce 'Socialist Spiritualistic Tourism' to the island, that is to say to use the communist rallies, slogans and parades of the past as a means of capitalizing: what does ideology matter if one can earn money from it? Indeed, the island is soon invaded by veterans and old communists.

But who is this spectre, this ghost? As the young policeman discovers, the ghost is in fact a patient from the nearby mental hospital, a retired historian whose personality has switched to Marshal Tito's. Tito, being the charismatic individual that he was, inevitably inspired a whole variety of stories. One such story was that he was actually the 'double', the impostor, with whom the Russians replaced 'our' Tito; there is even the theory that he did not in fact die. In the film *Marshal Tito's Spirit* veterans revive this old fantasy: 'They lied that he'd died'. In this way, the mental patient finds himself the object of interest from two opposite sides. At one point, when the veterans (who have in the meantime once again taken over the island) discover that he is a patient, they keep him in custody, where they can manipulate him. This also corresponds to the stories concerning Tito's real life; in the final phases of his life, due to his illness and old age, he no longer governed, having become in reality little more than a puppet.

Narcissism of minor differences

A characteristic of totalitarian countries, such as described here, is a mass, almost institutionalized, worship of the country's leaders – a phenomenon which is instilled from nursery school, carried on into primary and secondary school with textbooks praising and glorifying the history of the rising of communist Yugoslavia, and continued into the workplace and in Party organizations. During the turn-over these same phenomena were to be seen: nationalistic leaders merely replaced the old regime pattern, in a complete imitation of the much-hated social model.

The relevance of all this is that director Vinko Brešan and his playwright father Ivo Brešan have come back to these well-known Yugoslav communist rituals (birthday baton, parades, uniforms, etc.) as well as Tito's famous slogans from his speeches and, with much sensitivity, have used them in their sarcastic comedy about a man who suffers from the delusional fantasy of being Tito himself. Both communists and nationalists are involved in a tourist performance, a Yugoslav history which has been carefully reformulated and which works as a collective psychodrama in which all the participants abreact not just their individual pasts, but also the collective, denied one. This abreaction has nothing to do with Tito's death, but rather with a period of time, after his death, in which past communist history was rejected as being a complete failure, as well as with a time when grotesque communist rituals were silently accepted – a period for which, nevertheless, many people feel a great sense of nostalgia.

The psychodrama involves all the citizens of the village and takes place when the mayor comes up with the idea of bringing back to life the village's tourist

Plate 19 Marshal Tito's Spirit (Vinko Brešan 1999)

industry by using insignia and decorations from Tito's time in order to revive past 'communist recollections'. These include anecdotal past occurrences concerning Tito's pioneers, parades, birthday baton, slogans which are divided according to their initial word, starting with 'Long live', 'Down with' or 'Death to'. For example, 'Down with capitalism', 'Long live Tito', 'Death to fascism' and so on.

This whole interplay also works as an abreaction for the audience of the film itself, in particular for those viewers who are from former Yugoslavia. Here, once again, humour proves to be closely connected with the unconscious. Since the film is based on the mechanism of projection, and it also works as an interaction between the unconscious of the director and that of the public, *Marshal Tito's Spirit* induces emotional reactions in the audience which are revived by repeated routines in a grotesque confrontation of the past with the present. The play splits the self not only between the author and his characters, but also between the actors and the spectator. The spectator's place is in the dark, not under floodlights, reproducing a confessional scene. In the projection room this has been mediated by a director. It is not just the villagers in some organized spontaneous totalitarian play who go through a sort of psycho-catharsis, being actors acting the part of actors while exteriorizing their own (political) drama and freeing their inner selves, transferring them onto external reality by watching the performance, but also the public who goes through its catharsis. The spectators can relive their conflicts by reminding themselves of former situations and even identifying with the characters in the film, reaching a state of relaxation and sometimes even the solution to their problems.

The unconscious factors inherent in the jokes and comical situations are binding moments for the audience. This film, with its humorous and comic dimensions, gives the viewers a chance to feel superior about their past, contrasting with the weakness of their former and present acceptances of the grotesque situations which are now being mocked. Issues that were once taboo are now discussed openly. In this way, the film serves as some kind of cathartic psychotherapy which enables the public to remember and free itself from the unpleasant effect of the traumatic events it objectifies. As it functions through the use of humour, psychodrama in fact becomes *psycho-comedy*.

A jest's prosperity lies in the ear of those who hear it

A joke is an opening from which the truth bursts out. Humour helps deal with difficult issues; revival of the past by dusted scenery, which is anachronistic and out of place and time, produces comical effects.

As Freud has reminded us, 'every joke calls for a public of its own and laughing at the same jokes is evidence of far-reaching psychical conformity' (1905, p. 151). The essential condition for the recognition of the joke is tacit social understanding and correspondence between the structure of a joke and the social framework. Or, as Freud would say: the third person

> must be able as a matter of habit to erect in himself the same inhibition which the first person's joke has overcome, so that, as soon as he hears the joke, the readiness for his inhibition will compulsively or automatically awaken. This readiness for inhibition, which I must regard as a real expenditure, analogous to mobilization in military affairs, will at the same moment be recognized as superfluous or too late, and so be discharged *in statu nascendi* by laughter.
>
> (Freud 1905, p. 151)

Many of the dialogues in *Marshal Tito's Spirit* are not translatable in a way that foreigners could appreciate because the humour in them is connected with particularities of language and consists of an interweaving of the historical and political context of Yugoslavia's past with current everyday life. One such example is Tito's famous slogan, which many adults today know having learned it from their history textbooks in the Fifties or the Sixties and even the Seventies, 'The window must fall down', which in Croatian is '*Prozor mora pasti*'. This command of Tito's originates from the Second World War, in reference to a battle for a little place Prozor ('window' in English) in Bosnia. In the film, this slogan is used to help a mentally ill patient, immersed in the fantasy that he is Tito, to free himself from custody by taking out the window. The translation 'this is the window of freedom' removes the historical reference but retains the humour created by the literal depiction of the metaphor. Humour is also achieved by similarity and incongruity. The young detective couple who arrive on the island look like popular detectives from the television series of the *X-files* and their names are Croatian versions of the American ones. Another example is that Tito's psychiatrist, that is his former so-called anti-psychiatrist, resembles Karl Marx. Drollery is attained by exaggeration: at the moment when the nationalists come across Lenin's bust, they want to call in the police. For them, the hidden collection of sickle and hammer, Lenin's bust and other such objects, are as horrifying as the devil's insignia.

Politics too has been turned into comical nonsense: caricatures of cultural commonplaces, grotesque exaggeration, parody or, quite simply, travesty. A joke is, Freud writes,

> the most social of all the mental functions that aim to yield pleasure. It often calls for three persons and its completion requires the participation of someone else in the mental process it starts. The condition of intelligibility is, therefore, binding on it; it may only make use of possible distortion in the unconscious through condensation and displacement up to the point at which it can be set straight by the third person's understanding.
>
> (Freud 1905, p. 179)

As he points out, 'a joke is developed play' (ibid.).

'Tito rules', or idealization

The words of an old veteran – 'They lied that he'd died' – confront us with something that has not yet been properly buried. *Marshal Tito's Spirit* reminds us of the former trained respect with which Tito is hailed, and in the film it functions even in the situations when it has already been revealed that the person in question is a mental patient. This can be seen when the policeman's assistant arrests 'Tito' and at the same time apologizes for doing that, or when the village fool salutes as soon as he sees someone whom he thinks might be Tito. The reality of the situation was that the 'misuse' of Tito's person was protected by the law. In 1977 the Yugoslav Parliament passed a bill ('The law concerning the use of the name and likeness of the President of the Republic Josip Broz Tito' sanctioning the use of his picture) which, as it were, remained but suppressed as the 'visual unconscious' (Pejić 1999, p. 247). In this way demonstrators used to be able to protect themselves by wearing Tito's photographs as a shield, knowing that no police officer would dare attack it or remove it. A new bill issued in

1984, four years after Tito's death, announced the compulsory presence of his portrait, stating that his picture 'must be' present in every public room of post-Tito Yugoslavia. Although a photograph of the deceased is a dominant iconic symbol used in mourning, this law was a mere political imposition. Tito, as a sacrosanct political figure, was politically idealized in such a way that all over former Yugoslavia were monuments of him or dedicated to him, while museums were being opened everywhere: his place of birth, his summer houses, and so on. Embalmed history has tried to stop, for a while, the inevitable process of democratization.

By mocking idealization and presenting it in a comical context – even when it is done in a simplified and banal version as is sometimes the case in this film – one is given the chance to distance oneself from it. In *Marshal Tito's Spirit* humour serves to detach oneself from previous over-idealization, or from unreasonable idealization which later produces such feelings of shame. Also of interest is that the film has a double plot, combining a general story with the particular story of a mental patient who believes that he is Tito. Unaware of what is going on around him, his personality, as was Tito's, is (once again) protected. This time, however, he is safeguarded as a mental patient. In an unfortunate way he is also a comical figure, like Don Quixote de la Mancha who, as Freud notes, 'possesses no humour himself but who with his seriousness offers us a pleasure which could be called humorous', because he has been influenced so strongly by his history books, just as the fantasies from Don Quixote's 'books of chivalry have gone to his head' (1905, p. 232). This also has an interesting cultural aspect: the history of mental illness shows that nowadays we rarely encounter old-fashioned big figures like Napoleons or Kings or Tsars among mental patients, and that type of megalomania is now anachronistic. Today mentally ill patients are more likely to be affected by a multiple personality disorder, which opens up questions regarding the dynamics of the transformation of mental illnesses and their diagnosis.

In *Marshal Tito's Spirit* the role of the analyst has been assigned to the young policeman and the whole quest is somewhat like a psychoanalytic process. The policeman penetrates the mystery and discovers the identity of the ghost; he then must re-establish 'normality' and 'reality'. Like a psychoanalyst, he maintains neutrality but at the same time he is also interested in the decoding of meaning. However, the moral of the film, which could also be understood as its maxim, is pronounced by the psychiatrist: 'Psychotic patients are the loudspeakers of social madness.' In this film, this is social truth.

The return of the repressed

However, as Simon Critchley (2001) says, jokes could be read as symptoms of social repression and their study corresponds to a return of the repressed. When we mock authority, *we reveal its contingency, we realize that what we have considered as strong and established is nothing much, and that the emperor is in fact naked.* True humour works not just as a critique; it also has a therapeutic function, especially if it is communicated through the direct medium of film.

By identifying problematic situations and indicating ways of resolving them, humour can function as a form of social critique, which is why repressive authorities have always censored comic plays or parodies. When *Marshal Tito's Spirit* had its Croatian premiere in 1999, just before the parliamentary elections, the editors banned the broadcasting of the commercial for the film on Croatian television. This was because of its evocation of associations with contemporary Croatia, which offended the Croatian constitution that officially prohibits censorship. Yet in spite of this, *Marshal Tito's Spirit* was a great success in Croatian cinemas. One of the reasons is, undoubtedly, to do with the humour in the film which articulates the past and present ideologies in such a relaxed way. At the same time, the film, as a powerful rhetorical instrument, becomes itself part of some kind of ideology. The film not only abreacts through humour the totalitarianism of Tito's time, but also makes the public aware of the nationalist ideology which shares all the components of the former autocracy. The joke could be understood to be a 'communion' for the community which shares the same ideology. The final scene of the film is a visual representation of the act of

Plate 20 Marshal Tito's Spirit (Vinko Brešan 1999)

211

freeing oneself from the past: we see 'Tito' on a boat, leaving the island, going out to sea, into the world of legend.

It is interesting to note that in Serbia too (now known as the Federal Republic of Yugoslavia) a film has been produced on the issue of the cathartic moment in which Tito comes back. It is a comedy-documentary by Želimir Žilnik called *Tito Among the Serbs for the Second Time* (1993). Here, Tito comes back after his death to hear people's opinions on all that has taken place since his death. An actor impersonates President Tito walking through the streets of Belgrade where people speak to him spontaneously, as though he really had come back to life. Some praise him and his era, while others accuse him for the way that his followers have been governing the country. Their need to voice their problems arising from the way of life they were forced into completely obscures the fact that they are, in fact, talking to an actor. In their mind, their father is back, this figure whom they both fear and adore, and who has always taken care of the country, providing Yugoslavia with a good reputation. The camera has taken the place of the Other.

In both cases, the film has fulfilled the role of mourning. Something that could be understood as subversion through mockery is in fact the process of mourning itself, and while history has been turned into comedy, the present has become the mockery of history.

References

Critchley, S. (2001) 'A sense of humour', unpublished manuscript. (A part of the text has been translated for the Croatian cultural magazine *Zarez*, summer 2001.) (In the meantime Critchley's book has been published: Critchley, S. (2002) *On Humour*, London: Routledge).

Freud, S. (1905) 'Jokes and their relation to the unconscious', in *Standard Edition 8*. London: Hogarth Press, 1960.

Pejić, B. (1999) 'On iconicity and mourning: after Tito – Tito!', in G. Ecker (ed.) *Trauer tragen – Trauer zeigen*. Munich: Wilhelm Fink Verlag.

DOCUMENTARY DIRECTORS AND THEIR PROTAGONISTS: A TRANSFERENTIAL / COUNTER-TRANSFERENTIAL RELATIONSHIP?

Timna Rosenheimer's *Fortuna* (2000) and Michal Aviad's *Ever Shot Anyone?* (1995)

Emanuel Berman, Timna Rosenheimer and Michal Aviad

Emanuel Berman (EB) As you probably know, the most common involvement of psychoanalysis with cinema, and maybe of much of cinema studies in general, is with feature films, that is to say, with fictional films. There has been a lot of research done on the way roles are created, figures are created, the make-believe world that is established by the directors and the actors, and this of course will continue to interest all of us.

My thinking in proposing this particular workshop was that we may be neglecting to pay attention – attention that is also very well deserved – to the documentary film. Though I would agree with Michael Apted, who said yesterday that the difference is not always so absolute (see Chapter 12), documentaries, unlike feature films, are not about fictional figures invented by the scriptwriter or by the director, but rather they are about flesh-and-blood individuals. Therefore, the relationship that the director creates with these individuals is a three-dimensional, lively one.

As psychoanalysts, we are quite invested in studying three-dimensional relationships – our prime example, of course, being the analytic relationship or the therapeutic relationship, to which we apply concepts such as transference and countertransference, therapeutic alliance, resistance and so forth. My idea was that we can try and see if this kind of expertise, this kind of sensitivity, is applicable also to a very different relationship – though we might find common elements – and that is the relationship between documentary filmmakers and the participants in their films.

My first workshop member is Timna Rosenheimer, who is a 'Jean-of-all-trades', if I can say that! She is a very prolific and creative person who has done a lot in her life. She studied law at the London School of Economics, she has a master's degree in cultural studies from Goldsmiths College and now her activity lies mostly in three different areas. One is that she is still very interested in the visual arts and serves as the artistic editor of an anthology series of poetry. In addition she writes for newspapers and has recently published her first book: *Home – Spaces, Objects, People* (2001). It is a book of photographs and brief texts about the homes that various Israelis have all around the country, people of different styles and different classes, different ethnic backgrounds and so on; it was a bestseller. And she is also an aspiring film director. So far she has one film to her credit, a film which has done very well, and this is the film *Fortuna* (2000) which won numerous awards and was shown on Israeli television. It is this film which Timna Rosenheimer will be discussing here today.

Timna Rosenheimer (TR) First of all I wanted to say what a kick we filmmakers are getting from this festival where we are surrounded by psychoanalysts – it is certainly different to what we are used to!

I worked on *Fortuna* for two years, and I will start with a brief outline of this film. *Fortuna* is a story of six sisters who go away on holiday, once a year, every year: they leave their homes, their children, their grandchildren and husbands and work, and go away together. Every year, on this holiday, they re-experience the fun of sharing a room together, and giggling, and just being on their own, and having a reconstruction of their childhood. We meet them in *Fortuna* as they go on one of these holidays and through the film, slowly, the childhood traumas which shape their later life come into place. The shadow of their mother, Fortuna, hovers over every one of these sisters, and the big question is why their mother acted in the way she did and how that shaped their later lives. It is a film about great bonding, about sisterhood, about pain and abuse, and also about wisdom and humour and a lot of warmth.

For some years I used to have my legs waxed at Shoshi's place. Shoshi is one of the sisters in the film, and that is how I got familiar with this documentary story. It was there, in this beehive of women where no men came in – and no men really exist in this film at all and very little in their lives too – that I started hearing Shoshi's stories about her childhood and I admired her for the way she was coping with her life. She is a very hard-working woman, she works as a cleaning lady, she waxes women's legs, she helps with little children. So I felt that I came to this story with a great admiration for her. She started telling me the stories of her childhood and slowly I realized that there was a real film to be made here. She told me about her sisters and her mother, who was not yet in an old-age home when I met her, though later she went there; so I wanted to meet the rest of the sisters and that is how it really started.

When Emanuel Berman asked me to talk about the relationship between myself and the subjects of my film I started realizing that making this film had been, for me, a very complicated task. First because I came from a completely different background to that of the sisters and I chose therefore to minimize my presence in the film. I felt that the stage should be theirs and definitely not mine, and that I am just there to tell their story, and it was important for me to give them all the respect and all the love and admiration that I had for them. I think nothing happens without a reason, and I am sure that I immersed myself in this closely knit world of women, these warm, volatile, strong, emotional women, because I myself grew up without a mother and I was mostly surrounded by men. It was only after I started working on the film that I realized that that was probably one of the reasons that I was so intrigued and drawn into this story.

The complexity of this film was not from the cinematic point of view; it was because of the subject which was so charged and emotional. It was me, on the

Plate 21 Fortuna (Timna Rosenheimer 2000)

one hand, and six sisters on the other, and it was not an easy task building the trust, I think that integrity was a very important condition here.

At the very beginning I met all the sisters, and they were *all* going to be in the film, but, as shooting approached, the two older sisters became reluctant to take part, trying to persuade the others to forget about the whole idea of the film and just get out of it. The two older sisters were terrified about being part of the film, they felt that some very bad things would happen to them, they felt that their mother was haunting them. One of them broke her arm just before we started shooting, and then she decided that that was it, there was no chance that she would be part of it. I felt that she was a key figure and, at some point I thought, maybe we would not be able to make the film at all. Then, to my surprise, the remaining sisters decided to go ahead with it; they had this very strong urge in them to bring this story into the open.

So, we went out onto this annual holiday, with four sisters, and not six. This was such a pity because I felt that the older sister who did not come really had a lot of stories to tell and was a key figure. It was really, in effect, a situation where the older sister was mothering the rest of them. Anyway, she did not come and that was a problem and there was also a lot of discussion about whether we talk about the fact of the older sisters not coming.

On the third day of filming there was a big drama because one of the sisters said that she thought that what she had taken to be a fire detector was, in fact, a hidden camera that we had put in the room! So there was a lot of drama around that and we stopped the filming, and we had to talk about what they felt, and it was very complicated for them, and very emotional for them to go through this story. And yet there was a great urge in them to come up and talk about it, and I was very surprised to see how open they were, and how frank they were with the camera.

Another thing that happened was the whole issue of whether or not we could show the mother in the film, because the mother, even if she was not shown during the film – and she is only shown at the end – was always present there in the film. The older sisters did not want her to be present in the film, but the younger ones went ahead and they decided that they did want her present, so we had a lot of problems around that too.

There was a big question about different stories, whether we should show them or not. One example was that the sisters did not want a particular story (about an Arab witchcraft belief of using an animal as a sacrifice to save an ill person) to be mentioned. The story that Dina (one of the sisters) tells, explains how their mother, who had a younger sister whom she loved very much and who was ill, offered one of her daughters as a scapegoat to save this sister. It was a very charged story and the question was whether to leave that story in or not. I invited the sisters to come and see *Fortuna* before we closed it up and eventually they decided to go ahead and keep that story. So they did see the film in the cutting room and they were happy with it, and I feel therefore that, in a way, even if there were difficulties, ultimately they were happy with it and that was the main thing.

I left out some details and some stories because I did not want to abuse the sisters' will to bring their story into the open. Showing the elderly mother in a wheelchair in the old people's home was a delicate issue, but that brings into focus one of the conflicts of documentary filmmaking, which is that on the one hand you are dealing with real people, real stories, real lives and a lot of emotions, and on the other hand you want to make the best possible film that you can.

I hope that is what I have done.

Showing of several clips from *Fortuna*

We meet the sisters on the beach and in their big hotel room, having a lot of fun together and expressing their intense closeness and solidarity. We also hear them sharing horrible stories about the abuse they suffered from their mother throughout their childhood and adolescence. And, in the final scene of the movie, we see one of them visiting and feeding the old, feeble and confused mother, who clings to her as an infant, and begs her not to go away.

EB   Our second member of the workshop is film director Michal Aviad. She also has a rich academic and artistic background. She did her undergraduate studies in Tel Aviv University in comparative literature and philosophy and then obtained an MA degree in film in San Francisco. Michal Aviad is now on the faculty of the Department of Film Studies at Tel Aviv University. She has been a director of documentaries for fifteen years now, and has become one of the most established and well-known Israeli documentary directors. Many of Michal Aviad's films deal specifically with women and I think that her feminist interests were expressed in them, for example *Acting Our Age* (1987), which dealt with American women, *The Women Next Door* (1992), on the roles of Palestinian and Israeli women in the national conflict in the Middle East, *Jenny and Jenny* (1997), which dealt with two teenage girls in a very moving way, and now her most recent film, *Ramleh* (2001), about the lives of four women in marginalized communities in one of the poorest towns of Israel. The film that we finally chose to discuss here is Michal Aviad's only film that, in fact, focuses almost exclusively on men. This film, *Ever Shot Anyone?* (1995), was made six years ago and was also successful, shown on television and so on, and like many of her films has been shown all over the world.

Michal Aviad (MA)   My film *Ever Shot Anyone?* is about myself, the film-maker, and my encounter with a reserve unit of Israeli soldiers during their thirty days' annual reserve duty on the Golan Heights. The film starts with me explaining (over home-video shots showing my home and family) that my 5-year-old son is only interested in playing with weapons and war. He is not

217

into that any more, he is now 13 and a half, thank god! But he was then and I was very worried. I felt, I say in the film, that I needed to learn more about male culture and especially about military male culture in Israel.

And so I began my research phase. Once I had made a decision to join a reserve unit, I chose the Golan Heights. It is hard to believe it right now, but at the time, in 1995, the occupied territories were quiet and it seemed that the occupation was about to end. I was looking for a place that would be dangerous, where something could happen. I wanted to choose a harsh location, and it seemed that the winter in the Golan Heights, far away from home, would be hard on the soldiers, who have families and work and day-to-day anxieties. I had a fantasy that they would feel homesick and I would be able to corner them one-by-one during their guarding duties and talk to them about love and about children and about dreams. I met with all the units that were going to do reserve duties on the Golan Heights that winter and I chose a specific unit that seemed representative of men in Israel, in terms of their coming from different classes, having different ethnic backgrounds, and so on. Many of the soldiers were my age, about to turn 40, and I hoped that this fact would bring us closer. I met the men for research only once or twice before the time of the filming. They all seemed enthusiastic about being part of the film. They told me they had been doing reserve duty together for twenty years and that a film could be a nice 'souvenir' of the days of being together.

When I make films I always ask myself what is the motivation of the people I film to take part in my films. Their motivation seemed fine to me and it did not occur to me that what they really wanted was a 'monument' to themselves and their unit, rather than just a 'souvenir'.

Right after we reached the camp, the timid, humble group that I had met in civilian clothes during the research phase, now turned into a very closed, and sometimes offensive, group. I wanted to talk to them about issues that concerned me, about feelings and thoughts and turning 40, but they brushed me off. It was not my first film and I thought that by now I knew how to gain the participants' trust. However, in this case, all my attempts were in vain! They wanted me to film them while they were shooting and running, but I could not get myself to feel interested in that. I found myself asking the wrong questions. Even my crew (which was all male) did not get what I was doing and wondered how I could make a film with my stupid way of directing. The men in my crew were doing reserve duty themselves and they too wanted the film to be about war games and shooting.

Showing of the first clip from *Ever Shot Anyone?*

The soldiers ask Aviad how come her husband allows her to leave their home and children and be absent for days. They claim that for them that would be a good reason for divorce.

Aviad joins a night military patrol, without quite understanding who is fighting against whom. She escapes to the unit's kitchen where she has a chat with the cook.

The next morning she confronts the soldiers with the question: 'Have you ever shot anyone?' Some of them have.

MA My feeling of being weak and unwanted and alone grew over the time that I spent with the soldiers. They kept telling me that, being so far away from women, they wished my behaviour would be more 'womanly'. They told me stories about the legendary women soldiers they remembered from their many years of reserve duty, women who knew how to soothe them, with their soft voices and sweet faces. They made fun of me walking with them, my boots covered in mud like theirs. They thought I was strange: a woman with make-up who could climb tanks as well as they could. I had a terrible longing to have women around me. I remember occasionally going to the women's toilets in a base that was a few miles away from the filming location and feeling excited to see the 'Women' sign on the lavatory door.

Slowly, slowly, I figured out to what extent I was a threat and how hard the soldiers had to work in order to hide from me the disagreements and tensions among themselves. It took me a long time to realize that *I was shooting them*, and that, through this, I had lots of power over these men who, in fact, were supposed to be stronger because they had guns. Only when they used their cameras *to shoot me* could they become my equals. Actually, the miracle of them becoming,

Plate 22 Ever Shot Anyone? (Michal Aviad 1995)

with their cameras, my equals, allowed me to portray them precisely the way I wanted to. As time passed, I started to like them and felt in a terrible conflict between my mission to portray the unpleasant aspects of Israel and male culture, and at the same time not wanting to offend them personally. After this film I made the decision only to make films about people whom I love!

When I looked at the film material that the soldiers had shot, I realized that what they were hiding from me had been fully exposed by their own shooting. Paradoxically, it was this that enabled me to portray them as three-dimensional human beings, as I had originally wanted to.

Only at the very end I realized that, from the moment I arrived in that base to the moment I left, I never even unzipped my overcoat!

Showing of the second clip from *Ever Shot Anyone?*

The soldiers prepare a farewell party at the end of the reserve duty. They prepare a film about Aviad and her crew as part of the party. They film themselves answering Aviad's questions. They make fun of her questions and everyone at the party roars with laughter, but when they answer those questions in their film some real issues are uncovered.

EB I will make a few brief comments to open the discussion. First of all, it is really by chance, as we did not contemplate the content of our two documentaries beforehand, but one could say that one film is about sisterhood, the other film is about brotherhood, and by the fact that both directors are women this already shows us some basic element of the difference between the two films. If I borrow and expand Heinrich Racker's (1968, pp. 134–136) well-known categories, one film, *Ever Shot Anyone?*, is mostly based on *complementary identification*, on the attention to the other, on the fascination of the one who is different; while the other film, *Fortuna*, is based on *concordant identification*, on a direct identification of the director with the characters being filmed. I will, however, hasten to add elements to this statement, because what I said is true if we look at gender as a major issue – and it certainly is a major issue in life and in both films – but of course if we look at other dimensions we can also see that, for example, Timna Rosenheimer is making a film about people from a very different social and ethnic background to her own, so in this respect her protagonists are 'other' for her, and so on.

Documentary films are almost universally on topics that are chosen by their directors, and the point of entry is a certain attraction by the director to the topic/figure. This attraction is sometimes related to deep identification and I think that, especially in *Fortuna*, this element of identification is quite prominent. Timna Rosenheimer mentioned the early death of her own mother and she also dedicated the film to her memory. It is clear that she chose to make her first film about the issue of motherhood and loss, though she chose a very different kind of loss – not a physical loss but a loss of the motherly quality in the living mother, which is a somewhat different issue but may resonate with themes of growing up without motherly attention, a lack which the sisters in the film surely experienced. The attraction to the topic may also be more out of a certain fascination for it, in the sense that Michal Aviad's interest – which she described to us and can be seen in *Ever Shot Anyone?*, particularly in the beginning of the film which happens far away from the Golan Heights – is the interest of a woman in malehood, in manliness, in the malehood of her own son or of her father. As can be seen in the film, the question 'Ever shot anyone?', for example, originated in the maleness of her partner, and the maleness of half the world around her is a central element in the attraction that led her to make the film.

The other question, as in any relationship, is 'What is the motivation of the other side, that of the protagonist?' There can be all kinds of motivations, but I think that maybe here there is a commonality between the two films: one of the basic motivations is the need to be heard, a need to be seen, a wish for mirroring, a wish for a sympathetic eye, for an admiring eye, for an interested eye, for an empathic eye/ear, of course combined. This may be one of the elements in which protagonists of documentary films are a bit, only a bit of course, like analytic or psychotherapy patients who come to a place where there will be a lot of attention to their story, hopefully in an empathic, sympathetic, interested, respectful way, and some wish for the other, the director or the therapist, to be the spokesperson, to be the one who will help crystallize one's story, will help one understand and see things. I think that there are some similarities between the two processes, although again the question of what kind of issue will emerge may be conflictual. I think that people who go into treatment are also anxious (and maybe they are right about it, at times) that the mirroring that they will receive will not be what they expected; for instance the interpretations might point to pathology or to aspects that were ego-alien before, that they did not acknowledge in themselves. Clearly, for example, when the soldiers in *Ever Shot Anyone?* say that they want this kind of 'souvenir', this 'monument' as Michal Aviad put it, they wish for some kind of glorification. They gradually sense from Michal Aviad's presence and from her questions that she may come with a critical eye, with a more sceptical view. In this light, the 'counter-film', to which I will return, becomes one way of handling the anxiety which the situation arouses, for the soldiers could see that Michal Aviad's agenda was somewhat different to their own. Even though initially they agreed and they collaborated, they also became growingly anxious. All this, of course, develops side by side with their wish to be held, to be seen, to be portrayed, and for their story to be summarized.

There are, in general, many anxieties for us as individuals, whether as analytic patients or as protagonists in the documentary, and perhaps the extreme form of anxiety is a fantasy of damage, the fantasy of something destructive, exploitative that will take over one's life story and change it, distort it, bring back something frightening, something ugly. Even when there is a lot of pain to be expressed, this is sometimes counterbalanced by such fears, both in treatment and in film-making. This can be seen as forming a continuum where, at one end, we have exhibitionistic needs (not always pathological!) and variations thereof and, at the other end, a fear of humiliating exposure.

To give brief examples from both films: in *Fortuna* we have the two older sisters, who refuse to participate and clearly see this film as something that may be humiliating, may be traumatic in itself, may re-traumatize them, may give them a bad name; and, at the other extreme, we have one of the sisters who is herself quite openly exhibitionistic, who worked for years as a nude model for artists, and was scolded for this by her sisters. She is very eager for this film to be made and with a strong determination to show everything, because it is her and she does not want to hide any part of her. Part of her way of accepting herself after her traumatic childhood is to say that every aspect of her body – and (as we can understand) every aspect of her personality, of her soul – is beautiful: 'I have nothing to hide'.

In *Ever Shot Anyone?* we can see very strong exhibitionistic scenes, including the toilet scene, or another scene where the director is almost dragged into the soldiers' shower to take pictures there, in contrast to many points where the protagonists become nervous, ask her not to ask about something, not to show something. There is the scene with a soldier who goes home to his wife who is undergoing fertility treatment and is very ambivalent about this being shown. And, as we have already discussed, the soldiers are often afraid they will be shown as sadomasochistic, as militaristic, as savage, as uncivilized. . . .

Still, I think that the fascination for being filmed creates a certain dependence. The protagonists depend on the director to show their story, and while some projects may not come to fruition, many films end up being made precisely because of this kind of neediness. At the same time, however, one of the tensions of making documentaries is the constant dependence of the director on the protagonists; in most situations, their collaboration and their willingness are crucial. I can guess how much anxiety directors must have when, after a lot of research and maybe some shooting, the protagonist vetoes the continuation of the film, blocking the whole project and really taking away the opportunity for this creative work from the director.

The final version is, on the whole, that of the director, although frequently we do hear, as Timna Rosenheimer mentioned, that there is an attempt to get some kind of approval from the characters who participated. It is clear that directors are not eager for their protagonists to protest, after the film is made, and to say that they were exploited unknowingly, as in the episode of the 'hidden camera' that was mentioned, which was of course a fantasy, a creation. I also guess that most directors are ethical individuals and do not want, at the end of the film, to feel that they were cynical exploiters; they do want to maintain this kind of alliance or camaraderie and remain with a feeling of doing something positive and benign.

In some cases this 'positive' may take the form of a therapeutic ambition: Timna Rosenheimer's *Fortuna*, or Michal Aviad's *Jenny and Jenny*, are films where one can sense that the director, who cares a lot for the protagonists, has a certain ambition, sometimes expressed in very subtle ways, to help them build their life, overcome their pain, gain strength. There are some moments, like the passage we saw in *Fortuna* when, through the filming, a secret that only one or two of the sisters knew becomes shared knowledge, and there is then a renewed chance of working through this sorcery story (the scapegoat story), which was indeed very frightening. By sharing and discussing this secret, we get some version of group therapy which may be very effective, but of course is also risky, and it is clear here that we are handling very sensitive material.

Lastly, a comment on style and artistic criteria and models of documentaries, and some insights that I came to develop on how some of our major issues as psychoanalysts may be mirrored, again partially, in documentary filmmaking. It is a topic that was also raised in the discussion on Nanni Moretti's *The Son's Room* (2001: see Chapter 3) and that is the issue of different models of the analytic relationship which, in a very simplified way, one could divide into a 'classical model' in which objectivity, a certain emotional neutrality, maybe even remoteness, are a crucial tool – an approach mostly identified with Freud; and what I would call the 'Ferenczi tradition', which is of intense involvement, of not believing in objectivity, which in recent years got the title of 'intersubjective approach', opening up options of self-disclosure, of directly using the analyst's feelings (Berman 1999, 2001).

I am sure that without any intention, as I did not think about it until after we chose the films, these two films express the two different models. *Fortuna* is very much in the classical psychoanalytic tradition because it is mostly focused on people in the present trying to recover their memories and trying to work through the experiences of the past; the role of the director here is very much like that of the classical analyst who tries to promote this process while remaining in the background, without becoming directly involved. Timna Rosenheimer does not appear in the film, her voice can be heard but at a very low volume, sometimes you can barely hear her ask a question, you mostly hear the answer which is at a much higher volume: so the attention, the flashlight is clearly directed on the sisters and Timna hides in a way, or tries to leave the stage open for them and for their own self-expression. There is almost the feeling that, ideally, there would have been no questions, only monologues or dialogues or group discussions among the sisters.

Ever Shot Anyone?, on the other hand, is much more in the intersubjective tradition. It is a film about the encounter of a director and the protagonists as a continuous mutual interaction and with a lot of elements that erase the difference. The major one, which she did not plan but happened and subsequently was to give a lot of power to the film, is the 'counter-film', the film that they make about her, partly as a parody, partly as a compensation. This is the soldiers' chance to get even or give their own point of view, and this brings to my mind Ferenczi's (1988) experiment of 'mutual analysis', and the fascinating paper by Harold Searles (1979), 'The patient as therapist to his analyst'. We can see how the person who is supposedly passive and is going to be shown has the need to actively watch and show, to turn the tables; and the kind of dialogue which emerges is maybe more meaningful than it would have been if it had remained one way. Michal also makes much more explicit in the film her own prejudices, expectations, fears, concerns, reactions. *Ever Shot Anyone?* is a film that shows how complicated the relationship was, in such a way that when we started to plan this workshop Michal Aviad said, 'Well, I have absolutely nothing to add because it is all already said'. Maybe that was a bit extreme, but certainly the issue of what the interaction and its impact are represents a major vehicle of the film itself and of the way it describes the reality that it both shows and creates. In *Ever Shot Anyone?* I think that the element of the film as an artefact, as a provocation, as changing what is observed, is much more strongly portrayed, although I think that from what Timna Rosenheimer told us about *Fortuna* we can clearly understand that her film too not only showed something that was already there, but also created a new dynamic, a new process. My suspicion is that most documentaries do.

The audience

A1 I wanted to ask you both, Timna Rosenheimer and Michal Aviad, how you yourselves were changed by the experience of making these documentaries?

TR Any strong experience you go through changes you, and working on *Fortuna* for two years was a very strong experience for me. It made me think about the reasons why I made this film. I also think that it changed a lot for the sisters. I know from them that the family started talking about all these things that they had never spoken about before, because between them they knew exactly what they went through, so you see also in the film that there is a lot of giggling going on, a lot of humour, they tell the most terrible stories and then there is a lot of laughing and they kind of half take it seriously but they are very much aware of what they go through; they have basic common sense, they say sentences that people after many years of therapy do not get to, which I thought was pretty amazing.

MA I think that in *Ever Shot Anyone?* the one who was really changed was me. I think that for them it was a fun thing, they were very, very happy with the film at the end. Strangely enough, they never believed that I would include their filming, they thought that it was a real challenge for me and, for sure, I was not going to include it; but then I did and so we all became friends and ended up with them really liking the film. They made sure I would not make them look ridiculous any more than they made me look ridiculous, and that is how I solved it! But in general I think that each of my films shapes a period in my life. Making a film, at least for me personally, has to do with a lot of pain and a lot of suffering, resulting from the struggle to create something. Usually, when that period ends, I really do not understand why I went through it and why it was so hard. I swear never to do it again and then I start on another film! When I look at my older films, for example at *Ever Shot Anyone?*, I try to be really in touch with the passion I had when I made that film and it is really hard on me emotionally as I can no longer remember that passion. But when I am in a film, in the making of the film, I am there; that is what I am doing and I am not aware at all in what way it is going to change me. All those issues I am oblivious to. Somehow, it happens and there is the way it evolves and at the end I know that a period has ended in my life and another child was born.

A2 I was very struck by the fact that both films dealt with people who are more or less in middle age. There were certain tensions that were resolved in very different ways, and I would like to hear what the directors have to say about that. I felt that while in *Fortuna* the tension was put off-screen with the two sisters who decided not to participate in the film, in *Ever Shot Anyone?* the tension is very much that you, Michal Aviad, approach these soldiers with your own approach about your own son, and perhaps inevitably with your maternal anxieties about what he will have to do when he is older. I think that the challenge that you present to these middle-aged men is that, although they might already have their own children, they are still caught up in the obligation to fight. Perhaps what you are asking them to do is to divest themselves of their fighting exterior in a way that is very contradictory to the task that they have being on the Golan Heights. I was interested in these tensions, how in one film they seemed to be off-camera and in the other film they seem to be on.

MA About the middle-aged people, it is true that for me it was a point of identification. I really thought that I would get more intimate with these men because, like me, they were middle-aged and because we had common history; but it really did not work, it did not work at all. The gender difference and the mission difference – me being the director and them the participants – created a gap that was so vast that the fact that we were all middle-aged made no difference. It did not help, we did not work on that level.

TR How do you deal with tension? Well, I think that directors and participants undoubtedly need to talk about tension. However, I did not think that the tension was relevant to this particular film, so that is something that was left outside of it. Nevertheless we did talk about how the participants felt about it all and, as I explained earlier, there were situations which might have meant that there would not be a film. But in the end there was!

A3 This is a question for Timna Rosenheimer. I had a very strong reaction to seeing the mother at the end of *Fortuna* and I really hated her by that point. I have seen this kind of situation in my life, and also in other people's lives, where you say that people in such a state are too old and sick to be confronted. It was a very provocative ending to have the mother so frail, and yet during the whole film I was thinking what a terrible mother she was and I was feeling quite angry about her.

TR It was a problem whether to expose the mother or not. I felt that you could not really finish this film without showing her, especially given the way in which the sisters went through so much and yet they still take care of her and cook for her and feed her and come to visit her. I was not trying to be judgemental about her – there is a scene in which a surrogate sister comes and says what a wonderful mother she was to her through the years. I was trying to show an ambivalent figure rather than just a one-sided one, even if she was a terrible mother to them. I am very happy with the fact that I did put that scene in, and personally I think that it was one of the strongest scenes in the film.

A4 It is clear that the process of making a documentary can be seen in some way as the director putting her subject matter on the couch. However, the major difference is that the director of a documentary is making a product that is for an audience and so it is not in a room and there is no contract drawn up where there is secrecy or privacy. Nor is there any training. Do you see that as being a dangerous situation for the people watching and for those participating?

MA First of all about the fact that we filmmakers are not trained to work with people. There are many occupations in which people work with human beings and they are not trained in a psychoanalytic way. The way I see it, there are in fact many differences between making films and being an analyst, and very few similarities. If we take the similarities to be those highlighted by Emanuel Berman, the main difference then is the ethical difference.

The other is that if I, myself, when I make my films, already know for sure that this film is a way to cure me then I won't make that film, I will go to a therapist! What I mean is that it would be very hard for me to feel that I am using other human beings in order to really resolve an issue within myself, an issue which can be resolved in other ways. I really hope that my films, and that films in general, are more complex than that.

That is, as far as I am concerned, as the director. As far as the participants are concerned, it is a big responsibility in terms of their mental health that one takes upon oneself as director. For my first film, eleven years ago, the premiere was held in San Francisco and one of the participants of the film, who was 70 years old at the time, said that the premiere of this film, attended by more than twelve hundred people, was the happiest day in her life, that she felt that she was a queen for the day. The following day she had a heart attack. Fortunately she survived it, but it is a huge responsibility that one takes upon oneself and I try as much as I can to include the participants in the responsibility, really getting them down to earth and saying what I believe, explaining that there is no glory in it, there is no fame, there is not going to be a major change in their lives. Other things, like love and death and children, are major changes; being in a film is not going to be, and they really have to take it as it is, with the motivation that they come to the film with.

I try to work with them exposing as much as possible their motivation. Their motivation can be an ideological one, they want to bring a political point out, or it can be other kinds of interests, and usually I try not to make films when the motivation is to exploit other people. All these ethical issues are complex and often very concerning to documentary filmmakers. Documentary filmmakers are concerned with the fact that by exposing these people they might do them harm, or they might harm other people, or they might be exploiting them for their own glory – though documentary filmmakers don't have so much glory, so let's put it all in proportion! These issues are vital and need to be discussed and be dealt with, and the integrity of the filmmaker is the fact that decides matters, in that there is no other protection, besides the law. You have to try to really listen to yourself as a filmmaker, and make sure that you remember that human beings are always more important than films. If you remember that, then most things will go right.

A5 That same question about the dangers that was just addressed to the filmmakers could be addressed to a psychologist or analyst as well. That is to say, what are the dangers of someone without any analytic or therapeutic training putting participants on the couch and exposing their stories to the public? And what happens if an analyst becomes a documentary-maker, is that dangerous?

EB It happens to be a topic I am very interested in. In a nutshell, I think that psychoanalysis can be a dangerous profession: we can do harm and sometimes we do, usually unintentionally and inadvertently. To specifically connect to this question of public exposure, I must add that psychoanalysts also publish case studies, and this is a topic that came up a lot in the *International Journal of Psycho-Analysis* and in other publications in recent years. I am very glad that it is coming up now, because I have no doubt that some of the case studies do damage patients. I won't go too far into it, but I know personally of people who feel this way about case studies of themselves that were published by their analysts, with their agreement – at the time they had felt it was fine, and were even proud

– and now part of the feeling is like in *The Picture of Dorian Gray* where the picture painted, that public pronouncement about them, becomes something immobilizing. It has turned into an object that ossifies the patients and stops their lively dynamic development, and this is a very ambivalent situation.

Returning to film directors, I of course agree they are not governed by, and do not have to obey, any ethical rules of psychoanalysts or psychotherapists. But the question of human attentiveness to possible damage does, I think, divide various directors. Let me give one plain example from *Shoah* (Lanzmann 1985) – a film that is so successful that I do not think I will do any damage by criticizing it. *Shoah* was, of course, very powerful and socially had a lot of beneficial impact, but when I saw it I definitely had some moments of great discomfort about the way the director treated his interviewees, because it was clear to me that he wanted to get their story, no matter what. In some cases, for example in the barber-shop scene, it was clear to me that this poor barber was going to be re-traumatized by the way he was being interrogated and put under pressure. He keeps saying, 'Enough, I don't want to speak about it', and Lanzmann insists, 'Yes, tell me more, tell me more how it was'. Whereas the film, as a powerful work of art, benefited from this, the human dimension of taking into account what discussing trauma can do to traumatized people was sacrificed in the process, and I felt sad about it.

A6   I think that when you, Michal Aviad, talk about the changes in you and the changes in your protagonists, you seem to be indicating that they ended up happy with the film while you were left really quite traumatized by the experience, and changed in who knows how many ways. But what comes out of the clips is that, in fact, the men also changed. Here we have a group of tough men being exposed for what they are, that is what most men are – if not all men – a bunch of *schmucks*, threatened by a woman who might castrate them! There is a wonderful scene in which they are all sitting around trying to be aggressive to you, and yet they become humanized.

As for the pseudo-documentary that they made, I thought that it was quite good that they were able to do that, it meant that they worked through something, that they could take some distance from themselves. So of course they were happy at the end, not only with the result, but with the fact that they had accepted a certain vulnerability. On the other hand you found it quite difficult to accept, at least that is what you convey. The difference is that their job is to kill, and for you as a mother going there to make a documentary about these people whose task is to kill, it was unbearable; all the more so, as you are worried about your son going into the army, and so on. In this way there was something you could not like in your subject.

A7   As regards the counter-film, it did not evoke Ferenczi for me, as suggested by Emanuel Berman. Rather, it seemed to me that it could equally point to something that is imminent within any analysis, which is the patient's counter-film, the construction of the analyst, in a way, as something that is 'filmed' all the time. It seemed to me that there is not just the issue of motivation, which is the theme that is being emphasized here, but there is also another theme, and here we can link it with *Shoah*, even if in fact it is very different: and that is the constant erasure of meaning. The point that you were trying to get to is: What does this mean to them? Can the meaning be faced? Can it be represented? The film and the counter-film are an achievement for the soldiers, for they show an ability to represent it at all; the alternative would be the complete denial of any meaning. In a way you, Michal Aviad, get the soldiers to show this fact at the point when they say, 'It has no meaning, it is just a job, it evokes nothing for me', and as the film goes on, it is clear that you retrieve meaning for them.

I was reminded of the anecdotes of traumatized, shell-shocked soldiers who, during the First World War, were treated in psychiatric hospitals at the time when psychoanalysis was still in its early days. There is a strange, macabre film in the Wellcome Archives which shows that part of the treatment that some of these men underwent in these hospitals was to make a documentary film about the Western Front from which they had just returned. Moreover this film has an eerie feeling about it because you know that, at the moment when they were regarded as cured, they would be sent back to the Western Front.

MA   What we did not talk about is that in the Israeli context, making a film about soldiers is a heroic gesture. I come from a political place in which, in my work and in my life, I see the Israeli as occupiers. To begin with, then, there was a big gap between the way most Israelis, the soldiers and my crew saw the soldiers, and the way I saw them, and that background was certainly of some significance.

I try to minimize the change that the participants go through simply in order to minimize the importance of making the film to anyone but the filmmaker. That is to say that, in my experience, for the people who participated in my films, undoubtedly, it was just another experience in their lives. For me, on the other hand, because I choose to do so (and I have no idea why I do – I think that it is totally masochistic!), I live these damn films for years until they are made. So yes, these soldiers went through a change but when they went back to their homes and to their worries and to their children, they remained the same human beings. In that sense I felt it had not made a huge difference to them. The same is certainly not true for the participants in Timna Rosenheimer's film.

EB   Another question that can come up is whether watching such films changes the viewers in any way.

TR [*interrupting*]   I think you are overestimating the power of films!

MA [*interrupting*]   That is our mission!

EB   All changes are partial, slow, minimal. I am not talking about major transformations, which unfortunately rarely occur in therapy and rarely occur as the result of art.

TR [*interrupting*]   On this happy note . . .

EB   That is not my final word! I do believe that both treatment and art do influence people and change them, in subtle, minute ways.

TR [*interrupting*]   Absolutely!

MA [*interrupting*]   Hear, hear!

EB   Let me end with one specific comment. These two films also have a sociological dimension and in this way they sensitize, especially an Israeli audience but also any other audience, to the more negative, problematic sides, the conflictual sides of major social beliefs, whether it is immigration, military service or defence of one's country. The family that Timna Rosenheimer described in *Fortuna* was an immigrant family, a very poor family; and while individual pathology played a role, one could guess that their lives would have been different had they lived in a more affluent milieu, or had they stayed in their country of origin, without all the challenges of modernism and radical social changes that immigration brings about. As psychoanalysts we are interested in those more conflictual sides of social processes, of cultural influences, of transformed identity which political propaganda presents as something smooth and simple; there are goals, there is ideology, and so on. But, as analysts, we know that human stories are always more complicated, more conflict ridden. Patients come to us with the scars of those supposed successes of social mobility, or of immigration, or of military victories; they all turn out to be responsible for various forms of trauma. Good documentaries show us how complex individual and social life is, and it is knowing this that immunizes one from being naïve, from being too easily influenced by propaganda, from having a flattened view of life. In my view this is an important change.

References

Berman, E. (1999) 'Sandor Ferenczi today: reviving the broken dialectic', *American Journal of Psychoanalysis*, 59: 303–313.
Berman, E. (2001) 'Psychoanalysis and life', *Psychoanalytic Quarterly*, 70: 35–65.
Ferenczi, S. (1988) *Clinical Diary*. Ed. J. Dupont. Cambridge, MA: Harvard University Press.

Racker, H. (1968) *Transference and Countertransference*. New York: International Universities Press.

Searles, H. (1979) 'The patient as therapist to his analyst', in *Countertransference and Related Subjects*. New York: International Universities Press.

FILMING PSYCHOANALYSIS: FEATURE OR DOCUMENTARY?

Two contributions

Hugh Brody and Michael Brearley

The filmmaker (Hugh Brody)

Let us begin with asking a quite simple-looking question: is it possible to make a documentary film about psychoanalysis? Michael Brearley and I were keen to address this if only because, over the past two years, we have been part of a group that has set itself the task of making just such a film. So the issues that are raised in this inquiry have been very real for us – and if some of these issues have been resolved in theory, they certainly have not been resolved in practice: we have the idea for the film, but not the financial backing.

Aware of the relevance of the actual practice of filmmaking to our panel, my contribution has three sections. I begin with an introduction to my film *Nineteen Nineteen* (1985); we then show the first 15 minutes of the film; this leads to some reflections on some of the questions about film and psychoanalysis that I think working on both *Nineteen Nineteen* and our recent project has raised.

To begin with an introduction to *Nineteen Nineteen* is to begin by saying as little as possible. Talking before a screening – even of a 15-minute clip – always strikes me as some kind of assassination attempt upon film. The images and first pieces of sound and dialogue should flow into darkness: of the cinema itself, of course, but also into the viewer's open anticipation, a lack of knowledge. Film is best as a journey that begins we know not where, and that gives us the excitement as well as the puzzle of working out what is going on and where it is all heading. The director's explanations, descriptions of contexts and background belong after the film has been seen, not before.

232

The minimal facts, then, about *Nineteen Nineteen*: it was first conceived as an idea by Michael Ignatieff in 1982. Ignatieff and I co-wrote the screenplay in 1982–1983. It was shot, in London and Vienna, in 1984, and went into general release in 1985, opening in London at the Curzon Mayfair. The project was first supported by Channel Four, but was then picked up and financed by the British Film Institute.

The first 15 minutes of *Nineteen Nineteen*

The credits for the film fade in and out over still, period photographs of the entrance to 19 Berggasse, where Freud had his consulting room, the halls and stairway leading up to the famous door, the name-plate on the door itself.

The names of the main actors appear over these grainy, black and white images: Paul Scofield, Maria Schell, Frank Finlay, Diana Quick, Clare Higgins and Colin Firth.

The camera moves over and through more period photographs. We see – and move through – the door, up the stairs, into the consulting room, towards the couch. We see the fabrics, carpets and objects of the room, the things a patient would have seen again and again. We close in on the collection of objects from antiquity, representations of ancient stories and myths, that are both real and dream-like. Movement across black-and-white images evokes the process of memory, the roaming into somewhere both familiar and strange. Music, composed for the film by Brian Gascoigne, adds to the sense of strangeness – distant bell-like sounds, fractured percussion and abstract shifting tones punctuate the camera moves.

Then a face appears on a TV screen. An elderly woman (Sophie Rubin, played by Maria Schell) is recalling, in a documentary film, having been a patient of Freud's. And we see the same woman watching herself. Puffing on a cigarette, she observes sourly that she looks awful.

An elderly man (Alexander Sherbatov, played by Paul Scofield) appears on the TV.

He also is recalling his analysis with Freud. He seems very unsure, somehow haunted or hunted by his memories. Sophie watches, fascinated. The unseen interviewer asks Alexander if he was cured. 'Cured?' Alexander replies, avoiding the idea, 'I read everything of his. . . . He was a great man'. And he goes on, trying to remember, 'What did he say? Something about converting misery into everyday unhappiness?'

Sophie makes a decision. She will go to Vienna, to find this man. They are the two survivors of the most famous of all couches; they must share their memories of Freud, of analysis, of being alive. Perhaps Sophie sees in the face and hears in the voice of this man on her TV something of her own sadness, something unresolved. Which may be to do with Freud and analysis; or may be to do with history; or just everyday unhappiness? She and Alexander are two people, alone at the end of the twentieth century, and caught on a TV programme. Cut off in that frame from the real and vast landscapes of their actual lives and the era they have lived through.

So Sophie Rubin goes to find Alexander Sherbatov in his lair in a courtyard in Vienna. On her way from the airport to the city centre, triggered by glimpses of streets and

233

facades of Vienna, Sophie is reminded of one of her sessions with Freud, when she was a young woman of 19, lying on the couch at 19 Berggasse. She has had a dream – an old man appears in a lake, where she has been swimming. In the dream, she is very happy, perfectly well. Freud sees this figure as himself, and he interprets the dream as a lie, an attempt to dream the analysis away. Sophie recalls – and we glimpse – the tension, a sense of a struggle, between the young woman and the old man. But we do not see the man – here, as in the rest of the film, Freud is just off camera, a tiny distance beyond the edge of frame, a presence so close but remembered as a voice, not as an image.

Sophie arrives in central Vienna. She finds the courtyard, the door to Alexander's apartment, he comes to the door, he is uneasy. She reminds him who she is – they were on television together. With rather grand gestures, he shows her in. The apartment is Viennese, and therefore – coincidentally? – rather like Freud's consulting room. In one corner is a couch. The fabrics, colours, textures evoke that other place. Alexander, in his discomfort, asks 'Why have you come? What do you want from me?' Sophie tells him she has come 'to remember'.

Alexander may wish to resist this intrusion, but he does remember. And we see his memories as flashbacks – though (as Maria Schell observed during rehearsals) perhaps there is no such thing as a flashback, since all takes place in the same film-time, in the same moments of the same mind, memory and mind being at all times exact contemporaries.

Plate 23 Nineteen Nineteen (Hugh Brody 1985)
Source: bfi Collections

The young Alexander (Colin Firth) *is on the couch, pale, tense and dressed in warm clothes. He tells Freud a joke:* Two children are playing in the mud, making a model of a church. They are asked if they are going to make a model of a priest too. They say that they do not have enough shit to make a priest. *Freud chuckles off camera. Then the young Alexander recalls having to . . . (he is shy, and Freud gives him the words: 'You were taking a bowel movement'). And his sister saw him, and laughed at him*

Sophie summons Alexander from his daydream, his memory. And Alexander shows Sophie the photographs crowded on his mantelpiece. His pony, his monkey. And his father, with his hunting dogs, that leaped all over him, terrifying him.

Alexander remembers a memory he had from far back, before the analysis, that he might have brought to the couch. A glowing, beautiful young woman walks with three magnificent Borzois on a lead, pressing towards him; her wide, sensual mouth is bright with ironic laughter. The young Alexander has been fencing — he tears off his mask in fury — at the laughter, at the full, laughing face. Now he is on the couch, and he begins to speak to Freud: 'I've been thinking about my sister'.

I was not comfortable at having to stop the film there. The first 15 minutes of *Nineteen Nineteen* leave you immersed and perhaps puzzled. A glimpse of a story is such a small clue to what the story amounts to! Just as a single analytic session would hardly tell you who a patient is, what the relationship is between analyst and patient, still less what problems and explanations were emerging. But the clip perhaps did evoke the kind of journey that we embark on in *Nineteen Nineteen*, and at least suggests the starting point of the film: Freud and his patients. And the clip of its opening sequences indicates the different levels of memory with which the film builds its story. To see this 15-minute clip, though, does remind me of what making a film of that kind is like, and evokes for me the first, and perhaps most important thing, that I want to say about the nature of the link between psychoanalysis and film.

As I think back to the first stages of making a film, I always find — and perhaps this is true of all art — that after all is done and finished, it is very hard to remember where the project began. The early ideas and discussions and even draft scenarios become part of deeply buried archaeology. Writing a screenplay, and rewriting it many times; then building a shooting script; then all the shooting; and at last the long edit — each stage has its own kind of intensity, and its own way of transforming the film. The filmmakers get very deeply buried in a series of quite different kind of creative experience; and each stage to some extent depends on at least partial amnesia about what went before. So it is quite difficult to remember where *Nineteen Nineteen* began. I do know that it started out as a documentary project and I can remember Michael Ignatieff's original idea. And I can have a go at setting out some of the main steps along the way. Some of these may well be steps towards the wider questions that I want to raise.

The starting point for Michael and myself was the idea of making a series of four documentaries about men who constituted themselves experts on female

235

sexuality. We thought we should start with Freud. This, like the other parts of the series, was conceived as a mixture of straightforward documentary and dramatic reconstruction. We would make films about ideas in which there would be documentary footage, a narrator, interviews with practitioners and, where appropriate, dramatic reconstruction of some of the real people and events at the centre of each episode.

At the early stages of this project, we thought that when it came to Freud we should re-create scenes from one of his less-known case-histories, 'The psychogenesis of homosexuality in a woman'. This was an analysis that took place in 1919 and which Freud wrote up in 1920. Obviously this is a case where Freud deals with sexuality, and the fact that it is a woman patient means that his focus must have been on female sexuality. But the 'Psychogenesis' case-history is intriguing because of all that Freud *does not* tell us. It is brief, even cryptic, lacking in detailed description of the analysis, limited in analytical conclusions, though rich in suggestive hints. More striking, these hints include allusions to an argument, and, in due course, a confrontation, between Freud and his patient. There are glimpses of the protagonists and a sense of an analysis that breaks down, perhaps quite dramatically. The case is also remarkable for its ending: Freud suggests that his patient should find a woman analyst.

So we began to explore the 'Psychogenesis' case-history for the material with which to build a documentary about Freud. As we worked, however, we found ourselves more and more imagining the events that are *not* in Freud's account; and we began to write dialogue between Freud and his patient. Then we began to construct the memories that the patient would have brought to Freud. We also began to construct what history – through the experiences of both Freud and the young woman patient in Vienna and Europe of 1919 – would have brought to the analysis.

As the work moved forward, therefore, we found ourselves developing three levels of imagination, three levels of script-writing. And as soon as you start writing this kind of imagined script, you leave documentary behind. We had crossed the divide between two genres. There are ways in which fiction enters documentary, and issues of verisimilitude and 'reality' influence feature film making. Yet, once you begin to create a script, you have left the documentary arena. Feature films are made, first of all, by writers; documentaries are, or should be, made by a film-crew following events as they unfold in the real world.

The script we began to write relied on all three levels I have referred to – the patient on the couch, the memories (or the dreams) the patient brings to Freud, and the events of public history. Yet we found ourselves longing for a fourth level: the retrospect. This led us to introduce into our screenplay scenes with the patient forty or fifty years later, as an elderly woman, remembering her analysis. Level four became recollection from the present. This meant that the history level was much expanded: now we could bring pivotal events into the story from most of the twentieth century. So we now had the idea for a film with four clear, separate levels. This may appear to be complicated, but as fiction not as facts – the screenplay that we were writing had moved far from documentary.

Then, having got this far, we decided that we needed to have two characters, not one. So we went to another case-history, that of the famous Wolf Man. Using the evidence of Freud's account of that case, we imagined what the Wolf Man's sessions on the couch would have been like, drew on the relevant historical episodes (taking us from Vienna to pre-revolutionary and then revolutionary Russia), and created scenes in which the elderly man recalls his analysis, critical events in his life and the times through which he had lived. For the fourth level – the long retrospect from the present – we were helped by the fact that the Wolf Man did, in reality, talk about his analysis as an old man.

Once we had the two characters and the movement of each of them in and out of the events of the worlds they had lived in, their two stories could intertwine – as memory of that same couch, as an engagement with the shared events of their times, and as the day they spent together in Vienna.

So we had a story with two characters remembering analysis, on the couch; we had the couch itself, with the young characters in their analysis; we had the memories the young characters brought to Freud; and we had history itself. It was by writing the four levels we wrote the film. Also, the interplay of levels meant that we were writing a film that was not *about* psychoanalysis but to some extent was *in* psychoanalysis. An immersion rather than an abstraction, and an exploration of elements that inevitably comprise the weave of any extensive analysis. One time, or one kind of explanation, defined and seemed to explain events – only to be dislodged, or complicated, by another time and another kind of explanation.

Thus building the story of *Nineteen Nineteen*, like the process of analysis, depended on letting different elements and levels play out together. As we wrote, as in analytical sessions, we began to get a sense of a web that is both a layer of different considerations and, at the same time, a single, extraordinary pattern: both every kind of story, and one single narrative. In this layering, facts and fantasies, present reality and old memory, the personal circumstances and public history, are inseparable. This attempt to immerse those who watched the film in the complexity of its levels, in the tangle of stories, in the imagined as much as the actual, meant that it became a completely non-pedagogical undertaking. We did not seek to show the nature of Freudian thought, or the 'truth' about two of his cases. Everything is a matter of interpretation – within the film, for its two protagonists; in relation to the film, for its audiences.

So, is *Nineteen Nineteen* a film with a documentary level? It begins with a real person, Freud, and two cases that Freud describes, with a view to showing the reality of aspects of two real people's lives and the nature of his analytical technique. We relied on historical facts: about Freud (for example, that in 1919 he could not afford to heat his consulting room, so his patients would sometimes lie on the couch shivering with cold) and about Vienna and Russia. The 1917 revolution figures in Alexander's story; the Nazi invasion of Austria is important to both Alexander and Sophie's lives. Also, as we worked on the film, we drew on archive material to portray history, first to reduce the costs of dramatic reconstruction, and later in the realization that archive footage, with its grain and abstraction, could be used to evoke the past but also to tackle the problem of seeing the past, and hence of memory. Yet *Nineteen Nineteen* is not a documentary if only because it is, above all, a work of fiction: imagination created the story and much about the two central characters. The one person who is not imagined, and who would be recognizable to audiences, is Freud, whom we do not allow into frame. Also, the *project* is not documentary: there is no reality test that the film must be subjected to in order for it to be deemed a success or failure – as is the case with documentary. It stands or falls on its imagination, not its accuracy.

Of course, Michael Ignatieff and I would both hope that the way our film represents analysis, and the nature of memory in human life or indeed the way history can impinge on the personal (and vice versa), has validity. In this sense we always hoped that the film would offer insight, would deal in truth. But this is the insight and truth of art rather than social science. As we worked on *Nineteen Nineteen* we abandoned the documentary form precisely because we found that it did not meet and accommodate the kinds of questions we were asking or the stories that we were telling. The four levels of story in the film led us in a particular direction, towards *l'imaginaire*.

I think that this leads to separate, much wider questions. Is it possible, at all, to make a documentary about psychoanalysis without having all the four levels in the project? I think not. The patient, or ex-patient, must think back to the process, and must recall the memories or dreams that were brought as memory into the process. The patient must also locate life in relation to public, historical events, as well as private, personal ones. And the making of a film about psychoanalysis would become its own story: those interviewed would have to reflect on what it is like to be making the film – an innocent fly-on-the-wall camera would be both naïve and a missed opportunity.

But can you make documentary employing all four levels? Or is there something intrinsic to the interplay of these four elements that makes a documentary film about psychoanalysis extremely problematic? On the face of it, I do not see why documentary should not work at any number of levels. Interviewees can have memories, reflect on their memories and on their lives, can relate themselves to the world, while also thinking aloud, on camera, about how the making of the film is affecting them. And the filmmaker can insert archival footage to illustrate, or in counterpoint.

It may be that multilayered and self-reflecting work is complicated and would be hard to sustain within any single compelling narrative. Yet it could have drama, as well as intense interest, because it did make real use of different layers of human reality and inner life. A documentary that tells the story, or parts of the story, of Freud's life and work is possible, as is a documentary that explores his case-histories. But a documentary that reveals and explores analysis itself is not easy to construct. Difficulty in construction, however, is, and should be, inherent in much filmmaking. Meanwhile, there is the core problem of how a documentary filmmaker can show the central business of psychoanalysis – real live scenes on the couch. No fly-on-the-wall could be hidden; its presence would have many kinds of implications and would no doubt transform the event itself. So can there ever be a documentary camera within the treatment, inside the process?

I am very attracted to the idea of a documentary film about psychoanalysis. There is something about film*making* that is very like psychoanalysis itself. This analogy is contested, I realize, but in at least one crucial way the analogy can be made, and can be helpful: the filmmaker, in order to work, has to be lost in a very confined and confining place. You may well start with an idea, an image, a theme, and then become lost in it. At these early stages, there are no limits to where you go, what you think, how you dream, what you might follow and find. Then, as you tie down the ideas, you have to yield up to producers, financiers, cinematographers, actors, editors – the freedom of imagination and boundless internal process goes away from you. You end up in a small space, with a row of shots or a collection of tapes – the rushes – and you have to turn this already limited set of material into something far smaller still: an intelligible and compelling film, perhaps no more than fifty minutes! And yet, if it has been done well and has gone well, this loss of control in the creative process is just what delivers the wonder of film. One of the central experiences of filmmaking, unlike other arts, is this loss of control; but the loss, if you are lucky or those involved are all skilful enough, turns out to be gain. Selection of the key moments from an infinity of possible moments is the route to coherence and, if you are a little wise and very fortunate, to some insights and glimpses of truth.

This swing from every fantasy to limiting realities, with both resistance and eventual (though only possible) gains, is shared by feature filmmaking and psychoanalysis. Documentary filmmaking, because it does not rely on script, is not generated by a scenario that exists before you start shooting. It never takes place without limits, in pure fantasy. In documentaries you depend on whom you might meet, what they might say, how one discovery leads to another. So there is a degree of lostness in documentary filmmaking that is much greater than in the case of feature filmmaking. You have to yield up everything to the process. There are facts, a 'real' story, events and people to be disclosed. One of the jobs is to get at the truth despite the many obstacles in the way. There are fantasies, and they may be of immense importance, but a core assumption of the work is that the job will be done only in so far as fantasy and reality are separated; and reality, however unwelcome, prevails. Which is where documentary film work and psychoanalysis might well meet.

239

Getting this kind of documentary – a multilayered and self-reflecting film about psychoanalysis – from idea to production is not easy. We do not live in times when commissioning editors are quick to say 'yes' to a good idea, and trust that the unpredictable journey to follow will deliver a good enough TV programme. Documentaries about ideas may be alright if they are presented and led, or if they reveal some hidden and shocking truth – with a clear glimpse of the so-called smoking gun. A film that is about, and to some extent inside, psychoanalysis does not sound like good television. My hunch, however, is that it could be. The layers of its form can achieve compelling story-telling, all the better for being unpredictable, rich, elusive and – therefore – all the more real.

The psychoanalyst (Michael Brearley)

Privacy

Psychoanalysis is an intimate relationship.[1] Two people meet regularly in a quiet room. As a rule, one lies on the couch. They discuss whatever comes up, attempting to take seriously the most powerful current feelings of the patient. The intimacy is not enacted but monitored and used for understanding. Complete privacy is intrinsic to the process.

Curiosity

Privacy means exclusion. Such a scenario inevitably arouses curiosity. What are they up to? I remember my 6-year-old son asking me why I wouldn't change places with him: I could go to his school while he would lie down on my analyst's couch. No one is immune to the temptation to peep through the keyhole; no one lacks Oedipal wishes.

Filmmakers and the portrayal of secrets

Such a prospect is also, naturally, alluring to filmmakers, whose art, like the psychoanalyst's, is a sublimation of voyeurism and listening in. Krzysztof Kieslowski offered an affectionate image of this in *Three Colours Red* (1994), while the perverse use of a camera in Michael Powell's powerful *Peeping Tom* (1960) offers an altogether more cruel analogy to the finding out of secrets by filmmakers (and psychoanalysts).

Finding and showing secrets is a sort of second nature to the director. And ever since Pabst's great film *Secrets of a Soul* (1926) – made rather against the wishes of Freud, but with the help and advice of his psychoanalytic colleagues,

Abraham and Sachs – film directors have attempted, in feature film and on television, to portray the dramas of psychoanalysis.

Secrets of a Soul may well have been based on an actual case. But the film was a dramatization rather than a documentary. I will argue here that, in the case of psychoanalysis, one thing that differentiates dramas from documentaries is that actual sessions cannot be portrayed directly without distorting, damaging and degrading the analytic process itself. This leaves us with a problem if we want to make a documentary that is not merely a studio discussion or a presentation of talking heads.

Frustration

And this is frustrating. A well-made, fly-on-the-wall documentary on psycho-analysis would undoubtedly win acclaim for the filmmaker and demystify psychoanalysis, while informing and entertaining the public. And it might seem that such a film would be the most direct means of letting the public know about our work and ideas at a time when they are in competition with so many other psychotherapeutic approaches.

Dead-ends

In my experience, negotiations between interested filmmakers and psychoanalysts tend to come up against a wall on this issue. The former are wedded to the idea of filming, no doubt often with respect and care, sessions as they occur, which is precisely what in the end, we reluctantly conclude, we can't with integrity allow.

Arguments

The directors/producers are not insensitive to the analyst's problems, but tend to believe, deep down, that our qualms reveal a kind of reticence about exposure with which they are familiar in other fields. They assume that it is no different here. They believe that once they have established their credentials of trust-worthiness, our quaint, archaic over-caution will fall away. They suspect that we share with other establishments a fear of open access to what we do. Perhaps, like the fraudster who opposes the intrusions of the Inland Revenue, we have something to hide. Are we not all in favour of open government, at least until we become the government ourselves?

My view is the opposite: that this is a situation in which those who demand to look, to get right inside, are the ones on the side of perversion of the truth.

Such a stance goes against a prevalent contemporary view, according to which nothing should be kept private.

Here I can only give my arguments in a schematic form.

First, more than any other process, analysis both requires a measure of co-operation and trust – so that the patient may become able and willing to say whatever comes to mind – and is also an ongoing examination of the conscious and unconscious reasons for lack of trust. Any (mechanical or personal) third-party presence would be an intrusion into that delicate process. A comparable example might be the confessional, though I am not suggesting that the two processes are in other respects similar. The filming of sessions would turn psychoanalysis into something entirely different. It would be on a par with the popular series of radio interviews by psychiatrist Antony Clare entitled *In the Psychiatrist's Chair* – good journalism, even sometimes some revelations – but not an occasion for the patient's freedom to express whatever he or she thinks and feels in a setting of confidentiality.

Second, the issue of intrusion is a fundamental one in any analysis. We are bound to find fantasies of others getting into the sessions from outside, and wishes in the patient to get into the analyst's life or mind. The presence of another in the session would make it inevitable that these fantasies would be sidestepped or acted out. If the analyst were to allow it, he or she would be colluding in such an acting-out, whatever the meaning for the patient who has sought it – whether exhibitionism, appeasement, triumph, the creation of a dilemma for the analyst, or whatever.

Third, the presence of a camera in sessions, however discreet, would inter-fere with the analyst's attempt to achieve a proper state of 'evenly suspended attention'. Analysts, like the patients, are vulnerable – though for different reasons. They would certainly be vulnerable to their own tendencies to appeal to a neutral audience, or to fear of rebuke from peers and seniors, and this would interfere.

Fourth, so far my reasons have been that giving permission to film would be anti-therapeutic and unethical. Such a film would also fail to give what is wanted. The hoped-for transparency could in fact be an illusion, as these conversations and silences have their own dense history and unique code. Much is taken for granted between the participants, rather as in intimate conversations between people who know each other well. Moreover there would also be falsification. The psychoanalyst Wilfred Bion (1962) speaks of the idea of *mechanical recordings* being introduced into sessions. He writes:

These have the truth that pertains to a photograph, but the making of such a record, despite a superficial accuracy of result, has forced the falsification further back – that is into the session itself. The photograph of the fountain of truth may be well enough, but it is of the fountain after it has been muddied by the photographer and his apparatus; in any case the problem of interpreting the photograph remains. The falsification by the recording is the greater because it gives verisimilitude to what has already been falsified.

(Bion 1962)

I agree.

Fifth, nor would I accept various watered-down scenarios, like filming a consultation (with regard to which the same arguments apply), or doing pretend-consultations or trial sessions. These would simply be inauthentic. Analysis is not play-acting. It is a living relationship, often dealing with explosive and sensitive material, which needs to be nurtured. Our objections to the presence of a camera or other recording device in a session are, then, ethical, therapeutic and epistemological.

Outcome

The outcome is that potential filmmakers tend to feel that, without this inordinately desirable peep into the exciting intimacy of the consulting room, the whole idea of the film loses its fillip and appeal. The warning story of Teiresias, blinded for having seen too much, does not carry much weight when placed in the balance against the delicious prospect of being the breaker of this taboo. The obstacles feel to them insurmountable. They suspect, perhaps correctly, that they will not be able to sell any less explicit scenario to those who might commission such a film in the present atmosphere of ratings wars, and populist pressures. And the enthusiasm drifts away. Except with one filmmaker. I met Hugh Brody when, in March 1999, he attended a showing of *Nineteen Nineteen*, as part of the 'Film and Psychoanalysis' series chaired by Andrea Sabbadini and Peter Evans. Hugh has been, as you have heard, intrigued by the challenge, and has grasped the nettle. For the past two years or more, he has been working with two colleagues, Andrea Sabbadini and Paul Williams, and myself, on a different idea for a documentary on psychoanalysis.[2]

Obstacles to assets

In our brainstorming debates over the two years, we have voiced all sorts of possibilities, but we keep returning to one guiding idea: that we want to make a creative documentary film whose central issue is the fact that we can't make the film we instinctively wanted to make. We are attempting, that is, to deal with our obstacle by embracing it, by embodying it in the filmmaking process itself. We thus follow in the footsteps of psychoanalysis itself; Oedipal feelings, like the transference and countertransference, began by being perceived as obstacles, but are now part and parcel of every treatment. These *interruptions*, as Freud at first

243

called the irruption of transference, have had to be accepted as intrinsic. Thus, our approach is to orient the film round the deep psychological situation that refusal of access echoes and repeats: the Oedipal situation.

Oedipus complex

Ever since the late 1890s, we have followed Freud in the idea that as children we all experience an Oedipus complex. That is, we have all had to come to terms with the fact of the sexual and emotional relation that gave us our existence, and the fact that our mother has desires for someone other than ourselves. We have to deal with these blows to our omnipotence and our narcissism by mourning their loss, and valuing what we do have – which in satisfactory childhoods is also a special relationship with each parent or parent-figure. We develop sexual and emotional desires to have one parent to ourselves; we have usually unconscious desires to eliminate (kill), and take the place of, the other. Our childhood exclusion from our parents in their closest emotional and physical intercourse has been, and often continues in symbolic form to be, a source of often intense frustration for us all. I mean not only physical exclusion (though most people would feel it best for the child to be protected from the incomprehensible, alarming and arousing position of witness to 'love-making'), but also emotional exclusion. For the child is simply unable to understand the nature of adult sexuality. So the idea of his parents' sexual life leads to unconscious fantasies of many kinds, such as that what is going on is violent or defecatory. The child has to learn that the parents can do something that he or she cannot yet do, that there is an unavoidable difference between the generations, as well as between the sexes. The complex of feelings – including the various ways in which we attempt to resolve them – structures our minds in permanent, though not unchangeable, patterns.

The prospective film

To return to the idea of our film, Hugh Brody is willing to try to find ways of turning this pillar of psychoanalytic theory to advantage by not only retaining the privacy of the analytic encounter, but also making it a focus in the film. The film could be structured and enriched by the fact that both director and viewer must bear with and modify the pain of being in the position of outsiders, experiencing the feelings of that position imaginatively and thoughtfully, rather than evading it by means of smuggling the voyeuristic camera into the parental bed of the privacy of the session. The pleasure principle gives way to the reality principle. The plan is that Hugh will weave into the documentary the theme of exclusion and the reasons for it, whether for a small child painfully becoming

244

aware of his or her 'special' relationship, or for the director and viewer of this film. Such a film would be, like psychoanalysis itself, self-questioning and self-reflective.

We think that our letting go of the Oedipal desire is not a matter to be, in the end, regretted; it is, rather, to be celebrated. Let me give a brief example of what I am getting at from another art form. Architect Daniel Liebeskind makes the physical centre of his Holocaust Museum in Berlin an empty and inaccessible space, a space of absence. Thus, in moving around the museum visitors experience a central fact of the Jewish experience – absence, loss, emptiness, a terrible gap at the centre. These felt or unfelt experiences also represent the impact of the Holocaust on survivors and descendants. And since the memorial is in the heart of Berlin, it also represents the hole at the heart of the members of the non-Jewish majority, whose parents, grandparents and great-grandparents were involved in perpetrating or turning a blind eye to the Holocaust. The building conveys, finally, something universal; an experience of feelings of loss or exclusion, as well as a vision of an outcome of our murderous impulses when unbridled.

What we have in mind, then, is a film which will make its point about exclusion by means of its structure and its content.

Notes

1 This is an altered and abbreviated version of an article published in 2000 in *Journal of Psychoanalytical Psychotherapy*, 14(2): 163–174.
2 Regrettably, it now appears most unlikely that the film will ever actually be made. This is basically due to our failure to find funding.

Reference

Bion, W. R. (1962) *Learning from Experience*. London: Heinemann.

FILMS INDEX

Index

Note: Page numbers in **bold** refer to plates; 'n' after a page number signifies an endnote.

249